ONLY THE HALF OF IT

ALBERT TONKS

ONLY THE HALF OF IT

ALBERT TONKS

Published by Magic Flute Publishing Ltd. 2023

ISBN 978-1-915166-12-8

Magic Flute Publishing Limited

231 Swanwick Lane

Southampton SO31 7GT

www.magicflutepublishing.com

A catalogue description of this book is available from the British Library

MAGIC FLUTE
PUBLISHING

Contents

Foreword by Author
Foreword by Bertie Tonks

Acknowledgements

Photographs are on page 33, between pages 171 - 185, between pages 220 - 226, and on page 262.

This book is dedicated

To Aileen and Albert Tonks - My Mum and Dad
I miss you both so much xxx

Foreword by Author

I am not professing that my life has been an unusual one, nor that the situations that I have faced are any more than a lot of people have had to face. Most of the time, the situations that we encounter are not of our own doing. Indeed my experiences are nothing compared to what some great people have had to deal with. This account of my life covers the time up to forty two years of age. I wish to show people that they are not alone when they think that they are safe in their little bubbles and then the unexpected comes along and disrupts their way of life. I do not say this in a pessimistic manner, merely to say that these things happen in life and we all have to just get on and deal with them. Admittedly, some people are unable to cope with certain situations and are adversely affected for the rest of their lives. I was lucky enough to get through my experiences without having to fall back upon professional help, but others are not so fortunate. Money problems, marital problems, problems at work - these are all things that the average person will encounter in their lifetime. My story is a recollection of my times like this and how I was lucky enough to get through them. I have a loving family and I am close to all of my children who I adore. They will actually chuckle when they read my words.

I appreciate that what is contained in this book are my own memories, recollections of the key points in my life that for some reason have stayed in my head when so many others have long since been forgotten. I was actually laughing as I write this foreword, because those that know me, will be all too familiar with the Tonks tendency to flower up a story just a little bit in order to capture people's attention. My inspiration for writing this book came from Bertie, my eldest son. His reasons for inspiring me are written in his own words on page viii.

This whole story is not my *Life Story*, as it would take too long and would probably bore the pants off the reader. I have stopped when I became 42 years of age. That was when I started to live a completely new chapter in my life and it was also a new chapter in the lives of my children, which have been shaped by all of my experiences and life's decisions that I have personally made, or those that were thrown unexpectedly at me. I am sure that this is the same for all families.

There is a belief in something called "Sliding Doors". I have made bad decisions in my life but on the whole, I will blow my own trumpet and say that the majority of them have been pretty solid. When I sit down seriously and think that had I not made certain decisions in my life, I may not have had my kids, grandchildren, I would not have met Wendy, I would not now be retired and enjoying everything and everyone around me. Life is Great!

They say that there is a book in everyone of us. We are all different. This is the story that I have created in my life.

Foreword by Bertie Tonks

As a 50 year-old man with an incredible wife and two lovely children I find myself increasingly reflecting on my life's experience. Whether I'm walking to the local shops or riding around on a skateboard I obsessively observe those around me, wondering who they are, what sort of life they have lived and whether what I see in front of me in any way goes to tell their full story. I remember riding around on a skateboard in the summer of 2020 during the country lock down when a young boy came up to me and asked me my age and he was stunned to hear that I am still skateboarding. 'I wish my Dad skateboarded and was into cool stuff too,' the boy replied. I explained that his Dad had probably done so many cool things in his life too, that they boy was probably just not aware of them and that perhaps he should go home and ask him more about what he was passionate about etc. Then it hit me like a brick, why don't I do the same with my Dad. I know a variety of little stories about my Dad, but there is a whole world to explore in terms of his life experiences: the good, the bad and the ugly, the most poignant moments in his life and what lead to the creation of the man, the Dad, the brother, the husband and the friend that exists today.

I wanted to see if my Dad would be willing to go on a journey to relive the key moments in his life and let me take a walk in his shoes to see the world through his eyes. My goal here is to create a body of work that enables all those that know and love my Dad to get a personal insight into his life, exploring stories that many would not have heard about and to create a lasting record of the key moments from one of the greatest men to have ever walked this planet – my Dad!

Chapter One

1952

1952 was actually quite a memorable year. Winston Churchill was the Conservative Prime Minister. Britain still had troops fighting in Korea. Alan Turing, the famous Enigma Code Breaker was convicted of Gross Indecency after admitting to being a homosexual. Agatha Christie's play *The Mousetrap* started its run at the Ambassador Theatre, London. Around 4,000 people were killed in London during a Great Smog which lasted around 5 days. The foggy conditions also caused Traffic Chaos. King George VI died on the 6th February, resulting in Princess Elizabeth becoming the new Queen. It was also the year that the first ever UK Official Charts were published by the *New Musical Express*. This chart is as published below:-

1 Here In My Heart	Al Martino
2 You Belong To Me	Jo Stafford
3 Somewhere Along The Way	Nat King Cole
4 The Isle Of Innisfree	Bing Crosby
5 Feet Up (Pat Him On The Po-Po)	Guy Mitchell
6 Half As Much	Rosemary Clooney
7 High Noon (Do Not Forsake Me)	Frankie Laine
7 Forget Me Not	Vera Lynn
8 Sugarbush	Doris Day And Frankie Laine
8 Blue Tango	Ray Martin
9 The Homing Waltz	Vera Lynn
10 Auf Wiederseh'n Sweetheart	Vera Lynn
11 Cowpuncher's Cantata	Max Bygraves
11 Because You're Mine	Mario Lanza
12 Walkin' My Baby Back Home	Johnnie Ray

I think that my favourite song would have to be the number 5

1

spot by Guy Mitchell. And then of course I came along and was born on the 29th February 1952. How lucky was I to be born on a Leap Year? But before we get ahead of ourselves, let me take you back to the beginning.

My Dad's name was Albert George Thomas Tonks and he was born on 8th February 1929 in Gloucester. Born to a family who worked and lived on the waterway (His father is registered on his birth certificate as having the occupation of "Waterman") and who by today's modern definition would be classed as water gypsies. He was named Albert after his Dad, which in turn spurred a longer tradition of passing on the Albert name down the line as we will get to later on. In those days as he was growing up, he never really went to school properly as we know it now. Water people, or Bargees as folk who lived & worked on the canals & waterways were called, had always been allocated schools close to the Rivers and Canals by The Education Authority who had to keep so many places free for them. It was quite usual for my Dad to go into school one day in the morning for say 9am and may be two hours later his Mum or his Auntie Ethel would come in and say they had to collect him because they were moving on to a different location. They would travel from Gloucester on the boat up to Birmingham, Worcester or wherever to collect whatever load they had been contracted to collect and transport. My Dad's schooling was very erratic and certainly not really very steady. Aunty Ethel was my Grandad's sister and she was married to my Uncle Jim. My Dad's Uncle Jim was Dad's favourite Uncle and with his Aunty Ethel, were the couple who my Dad used to live with a lot of the time with on the waterways. Interestingly I think they were the first people to take charge of a motorised canal boat on the River Severn as opposed to the horse drawn barges, certainly in Gloucester anyway.

My mother's name was Aileen and her maiden name was Gordon-Daly. She was born on 4th May 1929 in Elphin in County Roscommon, Southern Ireland. She ended up with a double barrelled name because she was born out of wedlock and so when she was born she carried her Mum's name, Gordon, and then also took on my Grandad's name, Daly, when my Nan and Grandad married. I don't know much about my Mum's background because trying to find out anything about the Irish is notoriously difficult. All I know is that my Mother left Ireland when she joined the Women's Auxiliary Air Force (WAAF) when she was 17 years of age and was transferred to Gloucester. I haven't ascertained how long she stayed in the WAAF. All I know is that at some stage she became a "Clippy" on the busses in Gloucester and as far as I could determine this is when she met my Dad. "A Clippy" is what a ticket collector used to be called on the buses.

Until his dying days my Dad would tell me how beautiful my Mum was and that she also had a great singing voice and used to sing regularly when they were out and about in the local pubs. I have to say that as long as I knew my Mum, she always liked a drink and a sing song.

When he was 17 years old my Dad decided to join the Royal Navy. He was posted to Devonport Dockyard in Devon and was on a ship throughout the Christmas period. In the dockyard, there are some steps leading down to the River Tamar called Flagstaff Steps. Dad told me how he remembered sitting at the top of the steps staring across along the coast to Cornwall and crying his eyes out because he couldn't get back home to Gloucester to be with his family. The distance wasn't that great, but you have to remember that they never had the transport that we have today, motorways didn't exist and he certainly couldn't afford a car. It was so close and yet so far away. He felt really miserable and lonely. I have had similar feelings during my lifetime and so I can relate to how he must have been feeling. Later in my life, I also would be working in the Devonport Naval Base and would stand by the same steps thinking about my Dad. I was even lucky enough to take him and my mum to the exact spot that he remembered years later.

One day, Dad decided that he was going to volunteer for the Submarine Service. He had heard that the food on submarines, especially the breakfasts, were far superior to that on board skimmers (Surface ships), so thinking of his stomach he stepped up. Submariners were also paid something like an extra shilling per day (5p in today's money) which was a lot of money over a working week.

When my Dad joined the Royal Navy he already had a girlfriend called Shirley, he even had Shirley's name tattooed on his arm and they got engaged to be married. Unfortunately, he then also started dating my Mum and so eventually called off the engagement to Shirley before marrying my Mum. Dad, of course, had to have Shirley's name blacked out across his arm, but we always knew it was there and obviously I always found it quite amusing. Mum & Dad got married when they were both 19 years of age on 18th of December 1948 in St Peters Catholic Church in Gloucester.

My mother was a Roman Catholic and my Dad would have had to convert to Catholicism in order to get married. In those days, the Catholics were very strict because if you missed church on a Sunday, the priest would come around knocking on your door asking you why you didn't go to church. He would then give you a right old rollicking no matter what excuses you might have had. My Mum always told the story of when the priest, Canon Roche, came around to her one day because she hadn't been to church and they had a really big fall out over it because there was obviously no excuse for not going to church as far as the Catholic Priest was concerned. So this is when she fell out with the church and she never really went back to it from that point on.

My eldest sister Dawn was born on the 20th November 1949 in Gloucester. Because Dad did not have a Service Married Quarter at this point, Mum and Dawn went to live in Ireland with my Mum's family in Elphin in Ireland. Eventually, they moved back to Gloucester to live with Dad's parents in Coney Hill in Gloucester. At this time, Dad was stationed on HM Submarine Artemis which meant his home base was Gosport, in Hampshire. He then transferred to HM Submarine Alliance which was, and still is, based in HMS Dolphin at Gosport, in Hampshire. Mum and Dawn joined him and they moved to Portsmouth, just across the water from Gosport. Not long after they had moved to Portsmouth I was born on 29th of February 1952. I was christened Albert Cyril James Tonks; Albert after my Dad and Grandad; the name Cyril after my Uncle Cyril, who was one of my Dad's brothers, and in 1952 he was in Korea with the Army, serving as a cook in The Royal Gloucesters Regiment, and everyone was concerned for his safety at the time. The name James came from Aunt Ethel's husband, my Dad's favourite Uncle.

Dad was stationed at HMS Dolphin in Gosport which is the Royal Navy Submarine Base in the south of the UK and was also the submarine training facility. Dad was actually working as a stoker mechanic on the submarine called HMS Alliance when I was born, a fact recorded on my birth certificate. HMS Alliance is now to this day the centrepiece of the Maritime Naval Museum in Gosport, Hampshire. If you go down to the museum today, you will see the submarine raised on a plinth and the subject of the main outside display. The submarine doesn't look like it did when my Dad was on it though; I recall going to visit it with him many years ago and he said that whilst the inside was pretty similar to in his days, the outside had changed significantly. Apparently the conning tower had been raised over the years which had somehow allowed it to stay submerged over a longer period of time. It was still a diesel powered boat though and the crew must have really ponged after a tour of active duty.

I was actually born not too many miles away from where the Alliance is now situated at St Mary's Hospital in Portsmouth and we lived at 48 Carisbrooke Road, Milton a suburb of Portsmouth. A house literally just around the corner from Portsmouth Football ground. My Mum and Dad used to say that on a Saturday afternoon they would look outside the window and could see all the crowds queuing to get in to watch the match. We never had the whole house to ourselves though, we rented a couple of rooms. There were two other families in a similar position to us who rented other rooms in the house. The kitchen and bathrooms were communal and so I suspect that this may have caused a few problems at times.

My Dad eventually left the Royal Navy to spend more time with his family, and having moved back to Gloucester, he resumed working on the waterways with his father on a regular route from Gloucester Docks along the canal and River Severn up to Avonmouth. Sometimes the destination changed to Swansea, Port Talbot, Worcester or Birmingham but this still involved a regular amount of time being separated from his family as the trips would take a full week or so. But on the 9th February 1955, I was blessed with my sister Aileen being born. It used to be quite funny as my sister Aileen could never understand when she was very young how her birthday was only one day after Dad's, she used to think that Dad must be only one day older than her! My young brother, Terry, was born on the 12th November 1958 whilst we were living in Avening

Road and was born in my Mum and Dad's bed. I really remember the occasion when he was born. We knew that Terry was due imminently to make an appearance and then the midwife came down stairs and told us that we could now go and see our new brother. It was such a happy time.

My Grandad, Albert, (the first), had worked on the waterways for most of his life and was well known locally for being one of the youngest skippers on the water. I remember hearing my Grandad was a real bastard to my Nan. Whenever he went home, he demanded his dinner and if his dinner wasn't ready (even though Nan wouldn't know exactly when he was coming home) shit used to hit the fan. The crew used to get paid once they had completed a trip and like all watermen at the time, their first point of call was often to the pub! They wouldn't just go home even though they would have been away for days at a time. Let's bear in mind there were no mobile phones, no communication or easy ways to contact each other so they never actually knew when they were coming home or anything like that. Working class people did not have phones in their homes at the time.

My guess is that my Dad must have started to settle in to a similar life style but unfortunately for him, he had married the wrong woman. There was no way that my Mum would allow herself to be treated in this manner. My Mum eventually gave Dad an ultimatum and said, "You have to choose me or the water" and Dad chose my Mum. This is when he left the waterways and found regular work ashore.

When I was a real babe in arms I was quite ill. One of my own first memories was when I was around one or two years old, barely able to walk, and at the Gloucester Royal Infirmary as I had been admitted with double pneumonia; I distinctly remember leaving hospital and everyone saying to me, "Wave to the rest of the children". My chest and lungs were really quite weak and on doctor's advice, my Mum and Dad used to literally stand opposite each other and throw me from one to the other just to try and decongest my lungs. I don't think Gloucester was a particularly healthy place to live back in those days, as it was thick with smog and smoke, pretty much like London at the time.

At some point we moved from Coney Hill to Avening Road in Tuffley, Gloucester. There was a coal merchant who used to deliver our coal and he was soon to 'diversify' as we call it these days. Mum and Dad had paid the coal man to help us move, we used his horse and cart to move all our furniture and belongings including the beds and settee etc through Gloucester to our new home in Tuffley. As proud as punch, my Mum plonked her bum on the sofa with cigarette in hand as it was being pulled along. That's definitely a Dellboy moment and one I have never forgotten. There was no such thing as a man and a van in those days so you did whatever it took to get the job done.

A lot of my memories of growing up were in Avening Road, that's when I had a best mate called Eddie Foote. His mother's name is Hertha Foote and she has helped me with some memories to write this book. I swear to God that I am not making these names up. They are real and lovely people.

I think Edward and his family must have been a bit better off than us and I remember him having a pair of roller skates. Because my Mum and Dad could not afford to buy me any skates, Eddie used to lend me one of his and we used to have one skate each. Because he was right footed I would wear the left one whilst he rode the right, unless he was being really kind to me, but anyway, we never skated on two skates. On another occasion I made a go-cart with Eddie and we were so proud of ourselves. It started with some old pram wheels and we got some bits of wood, tied them to the wheels and then we were off; it was so much fun and was typical of what kind of stuff that kids at that time got up to.

We lived at 60 Avening Road and Eddie lived at 68 so they were only four doors away but it seemed a long way when we were young. In the summer, myself and some of the other kids would regularly go around to his back garden in our swimming trunks. Eddie's Dad, Brian, would get us to stand against the shed where he would aim his garden hose at us for ages - or what felt like ages. We used to think it was great fun, just cold water too! It was simple innocent fun but we really enjoyed ourselves and felt nothing could beat it - as a child I felt life could not be better.

I very recently re-connected with Eddie Foote and I recalled the time Eddie and I embarked on a big adventure, which by all accounts his Mum still remembers very well to this day. She kindly shared her account of this story which goes as follows:

"The boys were both two or three years old. I gave them both a wagon wheel to keep them busy whilst I went out to get some bread from the bread man who was doing a delivery in his van. When I came back, the boys were gone! I went straight down to Albert's house and asked Aileen (his Mum) if she'd seen the boys. She said no and we quickly looked around for them, but still no joy and I said oh my goodness, they have gone on the run and the front door was clearly open. I spoke with my husband Brian and we wondered if they had snuck in the bread van door without anyone knowing and therefore probably driving around Gloucester at this point. Brian looked after my daughter, the neighbours were all out looking and I headed to the Police station to file a missing persons report. The boys were so young, we were extremely worried and anything could have happened to them.

Nobody had lunch that day as all the neighbours joined in the search and were all so kind as we were deeply upset and worried. Later that afternoon, a black car was seen driving down our road and someone shouted, 'the boys are in the car.' Edward came out of the car holding a Daily Mirror Newspaper with a train/locomotive engine on the front page. We found out that these people found them playing out in a garden in Gloucester in Stroud Road. The person asked them if they were hungry, which they were, but were not able to state where they lived. Fortunately the people contacted the Police who were already on the lookout, who then collected them and brought them home. They were such naughty boys and myself and Aileen both said we would tell them off when we saw them, but we were so emotional, we just gave them both huge hugs.

A few weeks later we went for a family trip along the canal in town and Eddie said, oh this is where we were before and we were watching the water. I nearly froze on the spot as I then realised just how dangerous this could have been, with them hanging around so close to the water at such an age."

Chapter Two

Stinking Willy and The Pea Pot

The house we lived in at Avening Road had old metal windows in it, obviously no double glazing or anything like that, so in the winter all the ice was on the inside of the windows! There was an old open coal-fuelled fire in the front room, but certainly no central heating or hot water at that point in time.

Our coal was stored indoors in a bunker under the stairs, opposite the pantry. The coal man used to walk around the house to the back door where he would come traipsing through the house and empty the coal under the stairs. So you can imagine the dirt and dust that this used to create inside the house. We couldn't light the fire very often either because we couldn't always afford the money for coal. I used to have to climb in the coal bunker and try to get all the slack and dust together with my hands and then put it through a riddle to capture any decent sized bits of coal. We found that by adding a small amount of water to the dust, we were able to make a small ball of coal which we were able to burn quite efficiently.

The pantry consisted of a cupboard containing thick slabbed shelves which tended to stay cool all year round and so this is where most of the food was kept. There were definitely no such things as fridges or freezers, Mum never even had a washing machine for years, although I think she had a twin tub years later, but that was when they were probably slightly more wealthy.

I remember all of us kids, me, Dawn and probably Aileen at the time, trying to warm and dry our clothes on the airer which was positioned in front of the open fire to try and make sure our clothes were dry and warm before we left for school. On the other hand, first thing in the mornings when my Dad was at home, he used to make us go into the bathroom, which was downstairs, and run the cold tap. We were then made to take our tops off and splash cold water over the back of our necks and into our eyes to wake us up, even when it was icy cold inside and out. I guess this was how he washed when he was travelling on the Rivers and Canals.

I think I was about four years of age when I started school at

Finlay Road in Gloucester. I was quite excited about starting school and I loved going in to play with all the other kids. From what I recall I used to walk to school with other kids although I'm sure my Mum would have also taken me at times. At this age however, I did develop a bit of an inferiority complex because of part of the school routine. That particular routine involved all the kids having to have a quiet period after lunch. Camp beds were supplied by the school for the children to lay their heads down for a mid-day sleep. I was still a bed wetter at this point so for me this was somewhat of a disaster waiting to happen. We slept in the school uniforms that we were sent to school in and more often than not I used to wake up from sleep soaking wet, having had an accident in my sleep. If I was lucky the school would have some spare clothing for me to change into but it depended on what they had available, so it was a fairly regularly occurrence for me to have to walk home in wet clothes. The worst thing, when I think back, was that they used to have my camp bed up against the wall outside the school to try and dry it off in nicer weather and everyone knew it was mine.

I'm really interested in why we remember certain things above all else. For example my bed at home at the time had springs but not pocket springs like we have today, almost every spring was individually placed in the mattress and it was super uncomfortable; you could feel each and every one of them as you moved in the bed. The bed was so old that it actually used to dip in the middle, almost making it look like a hammock.

I didn't stop wetting the bed until about 10 years of age and I just remember waking up in the morning soaking and moving across the bed to find a dry spot so I could have a lay in, even though it was full of piss. Horrible and stinky - boy was my bed stinky! We used to have a little alcove in my bedroom where we put all the dirty washing and I'm afraid to say that because the toilet was downstairs near the back door, quite often instead of going downstairs to the toilet I would just pee all over the clothes and just push other clothes on top so no one would notice. This was particularly so in the depths of the winter when the house itself was freezing cold. None of us possessed pyjamas let alone dressing gowns. In fact we never had sufficient bed clothing and we used to use Dad's big great coat or Mum's fake fur coat to put over us in bed to keep us warm. It was quite horrible really.

Whilst living in Avening Road Mum and Dad were great friends with Eileen and Norman Hayward who lived next door to us. They also used to have kids. Norman and Eileen used to go out with my Mum and Dad and leave us with no baby sitters, in fact I think Dawn was often on duty for this and she was only two years older than me. I bet Dawn was only seven or eight herself when we were first left on our own.

Because they would not arrive back home until after pub closed, which used to be 10.30pm, Norman and Eileen's children used to stay over and sleep in our house. Well, we all used to sleep in the same bed. One of their children was a girl named Sandra who was about the same age as me and before too long we discovered that it was quite exciting if one of us lay on top of the other. We used to alternate lying on top of each but neither of us knew why we enjoyed this so much! I don't remember, but I can only hope that on these nights that I did not wet the bed and I hope that I never see her again!!

Even though my Dad and Grandad were what you would describe as men's men, I felt I always grew up in a loving environment. We always had a great, great time and I don't think Dawn, Aileen or Terry would say any different. I mean, we were happy; we never had anything but we never knew we didn't have anything. Although eventually I was aware of it; as even at school when there used to be holiday or educational trips which, as the years progressed and the world became smaller, places abroad like France or Germany would be somewhere the school would arrange to go on a school trip. You know, I never even used to go home and tell my Mum and Dad if there were any school trips arranged as there was no point, I knew we couldn't afford it and so it was never going to happen.

I can tell you about one story when both Dawn and I were both at the same school, Finlay Road, Infants & Junior School. I was only six or seven and in the infants while Dawn was in the junior and perhaps 9 or 10 years old. Dawn had been learning how to knit as one of her subjects, the idea was that you would knit something and then your parents would pay for the wool afterwards. So anyway, Dawn knitted this pullover that resembled a coat of many colours from *Joseph and* the *Technicolour Dreamcoat*. Well, you can imagine what this pullover looked like. Guess who had to wear the bloody thing to school one day because I never had anything else to wear! It got worse though! The day I had to wear it into school one of the teachers pulled me aside and said, "Where did you get that pullover from?" Now I knew, because I'd heard a conversation between Mum and Dawn before I went to school, that Dawn wasn't going into school that day because we couldn't afford to pay for the wool used to make the pullover. So although I was still sent to school in this really ludicrous garment, which obviously didn't fit as it was all over the bloody place and there was definitely only one of these in existence. When the school teacher pulled me aside and asked if this was the pullover my sister had made and we hadn't paid for? I quickly said, "Oh, no, no, no, my sister made this one separately at home and that she had knitted a different one whilst at school."

When I arrived home from school in the evening, Mum and Dawn pounced on me in the certainty that I had just dropped everyone in it. I then explained that I had told the school that Dawn had knitted one at home to practice which was what I was wearing and also another one at school in her class. I became an instant hero. I had gotten my Mum and my sister out of a very embarrassing situation. I just wish someone had thought about my embarrassment having to wear the monstrosity!! I think I might have had to even wear it a couple of times before the school finally made me give it to them, why though as it would have only gone in the bin as it wasn't really good for much else to be honest. I rather liked going to school. Apart some of the embarrassing moments that I had to endure, there were parts of it that I really liked. One of these was playtime during the infants and junior schools. We still had free milk in small bottles. It was widely believed that children were lacking calcium in their bodies and that it was up to the Education System to ensure that this was remedied. We used to have milk monitors and it was up to the monitor to pass around the milk to each of their class mates. Sometimes there were spare bottles of milk up for grabs and I always tried to make sure that I claimed one of them. They were not always so tasty, especially in the summer if the crate of milk had been left in the heat of the sunshine. Never the less, I was always there to claim a spare bottle.

Another form of authority for the kids was when we reached

junior school and were taught how to write with an ink pen. This is when each desk had an ink well fitted into it and the children were supplied with a pen and a nib that had to be continually dipped into the ink, along with a piece of blotting paper. If you had been good during the week you would be chosen to have the responsibility as being the ink monitor. Your job was then each day during that week to ensure that all of the desks ink wells were topped up without spilling it all over the desk. In the initial stages of learning this new art, I can tell you that there were plenty of children who returned home in the evenings with ink on all parts of their bodies and clothing.

These ink wells and the blotting paper were also put to good use in our geography class at one time. I do not think that I did this little trick, but who knows, somebody did. This someone discovered that if you dipped the blotting paper in the ink well, and then used a elastic band as a catapult, it was very useful to aim at the map of the world and catapult the blotting paper at the map. The blotting paper would then stick to said map. We also used to use our rulers to flick the blotting paper at the map. This is how we tried to teach ourselves geography. Someone would call a country out and then whoever was using the blotting paper system, would aim at the map and try to get it to stick on the country nominated. I can't remember what stopped this form of entertainment for us.

It was also customary to have to read a passage from any particular book that the school had approved. Each pupil would stand up and read a a few lines of a given book and then sit down whilst another chosen pupil was elected to do the same. I loved reading anyway and so this was not a problem for me. The book that I mostly remember was *Coral Island*. The book was written by a Scottish author called R.M. Ballantyne and is a work of fiction. The story tells the adventure of three boys marooned on a South Pacific Island being the only survivors of a shipwreck. I was thoroughly engrossed and couldn't wait to hear the next chapter.

Morning assembly was also prominent in schools at that time. This would include morning prayers and the singing of one or two hymns. The words of the hymns that we would sing were displayed on the stage for all to see. We would then also be given any information for that day which might affect the school such as if the heating wasn't working, shortage of staff, sometimes the serious illness or accident that one of the pupils may have had. Unfortunately these reasons were sometimes used. I remember one day being told that a girl who lived near me had had an accident with a pair of scissors and had subsequently lost one of her eyes. Her name was Patsy Turk. I wonder whatever happened to her in her life?

There was a day in October 1962 that I particularly remember walking by myself down Avening Road on the way to school. It was the day when we knew that the world might end. I would have been ten years old at the time. The USA and Russia were in a fierce dispute over where they were placing their nuclear missiles. Russia had been deploying theirs to Cuba and America were adamant that this was not going to happen. In the end the Russians backed down and the end of the world was postponed. Even though we never had any type of social media in those days, I was still fully aware of what was going on in the world. I was thinking to myself that if the world was going to end, I hoped that I could run back home to be with my Mum and Dad before it happened.

1962 was also a memorable year for another reason and would affect my thoughts on the way to school. I was ten years old and still in short trousers. I would have to wait at least another year before I became grown up enough to wear long trousers. But on Boxing Day of this year it started to snow. At that time of year of course that was wonderful, except that it did not stop snowing for almost three months. There were reported snow drifts of up to 20 feet deep in places and many parts of the UK were cut off from one another. This did not mean that we had three months off school though and I remember ploughing through the snow to get there. This freak weather became known as the Big Freeze of 1963. Roll on Long Trousers!!

My last catastrophic occasion that I distinctly remember at around the same time during my school years occurred on November 22nd 1963, the same year as the Big Freeze. I can clearly remember being at home watching the black and white television when it was announced that the President of the United States of America had been assassinated. John F Kennedy was travelling in a car with his wife, Jackie, when he was shot in the head by a sniper. The footage on the news was quite graphic and showed the moment that this had taken place along with scenes of Jackie sitting in the car covered in blood. Just as well we only had black and white TV. I remember being very sad because he was a young man for a President and he seemed to be so well liked and admired by lots of people.

Another big television event that I clearly remember watching during those years was on 30th January 1965. Again this was shown on the television worldwide I should think. This was the State Funeral of Sir Winston Churchill who had been the Prime Minister when I was born. Having been instrumental in helping to get this country through the second world war, this honour was awarded to him. As a matter of fact this is the last State Funeral that this Country has ever had up to the time of writing this book.

We used to all listen to the radio every Sunday afternoon. There were programs like *Two Way Family Favourites*, which was brilliant because it joined people in military forces together from different parts of the world to their families in this country. They could actually sometimes speak to each other or pass messages on and then play a tune and all the rest of it. That was then followed by something called *The Navy Lark* and then the *Clitheroe Kid*, a grown man who was vertically challenged. We all used to love Sunday afternoons as we would all listen to the radio together.

In 1953, when I was only one years of age, the Queen's coronation became a central event. A lot of people started buying televisions. A few years later we eventually got one ourselves as we were able to rent it from a company called 'The Link'. The telly had a built in meter on the back and you would have to put in the equivalent of two shillings (10p) in the back and this would give you something like an hours-worth of viewing. If you ran out of money for the meter, you couldn't watch telly anymore. Many times I remember us being in the middle of a programme or movie and we ran out of money and never be able to see the end of the programme that we were watching. Of course there was only a black and white option in the early days.

This was a big thing as not everyone had a telly and we would watch everything we could including the long list of credits go up the screen. There was pretty much only the BBC at the time and of course it was on a little black and white screen. Mum used to deliberately mix the words up as she read credits. I think that there is even a name for this type of talking these days, but my Mum invented it. She had us kids in fits of laughter and we loved it when she did this, for example there was somebody called Richard Green who used to play Robin Hood and she would read Richard Green, as Gichard Reen. She was doing this one day, having us in stitches as kids and she came to Friar Tuck and she read it as Triar Fuck. We were only really young and knew it was a swear word. The whole house was in hysterics. That is one of the small family memories we would talk about forever and the story would never get tired.

We would often watch a film on a Sunday afternoon and would put blankets up against the windows to try and make it look dark like a cinema. If we were particularly lucky we would have a glass of vanilla ice cream and would pour crème soda over the top of it and eat it with a spoon, that was always so exciting, we absolutely loved it as it felt like we'd gone to heaven. We had a leather settee that we sat on at the time and it was covered in the blankets because the springs had all gone and there was dips in it.

Most Sundays my Mum would treat my Dad to a cream cake from the bakery. Just my Dad for some reason and I suspect it was because we couldn't afford a cake for everybody. She used to keep this cake in the pantry, which was literally opposite the coal bunker located under the stairs. We didn't have a fridge, the pantry kept things quite cool. One day she went to get this cake for Dad and there was nothing there. The cupboard was bare as they say. Needless to say, we were all interrogated, particularly Dawn and Aileen. "Where's it gone?" my Mum kept shouting. The worst thing ever was to see the utter disappointment on my Dad's face as someone robbed him from his weekend ritual. Each one of us kids denied it and it turned out to be one of the most upsetting moments in our family history. To this day 60 years or so later, we kids still discuss it and argue who took it and as the culprit never did own up. It wasn't me, honestly!

We had a great list of sayings that my Mum had made up over the years. Mum would often pull out some really obscure old Irish sayings. She was the queen of the one liners and they would seemingly come from nowhere as she had such a dry sense of humour. She once asked me to pour her a drink of whatever she was drinking. She looked at the glass and then at me. I obviously hadn't filled it to the brim and she looked at the glass, then at me and said, "May the Lord spare your spit in case you die of the thirst".

She used to say I was always quite a happy child and her favourite quote for me used to be, "You would laugh if your arse was on fire." On another occasion, Dad had had a nice hot bath after which he wore a towel over his waist and one over his shoulders and come and sit down to watch the telly and dry off. Mum looked at him and said, "Oh for god sake Albert, go and put some clothes on or people will think I married you for your money." She was bloody brilliant.

Saturday morning pictures was always a big thing for me as a young kid as well. We were allowed to go to town at a very early age to watch the Saturday morning pictures. Whatever film we used to watch used to always be cut off just as it was getting exciting and we would be told, "To be continued Next Week". Again I bet we would have only been about 8 years of age but we used to catch a number three bus and go into Gloucester Town to the pictures on our own. What I do remember was that when the pictures finished, *God Save The Queen* would be played and everyone was expected to stand to attention until it had finished. You were not allowed to walk around the picture house whilst it was being played, the ushers would soon put you right. And the last thing we wanted to be banned from the picture house because we loved it so much.

I'll go on to my poor brother Terry now and that poor boy was tortured properly by us as a kid, especially by myself and Eddie Foote. In those days you wouldn't dream of running around to your Mum if you've had an argument with someone. As part of my research for this book I spoke to Terry and he recalls when he was about eight years old. He had arranged to have a fight with his best mate, a lad called Jimmy Best. I sort of barely remember it. But Terry's recollection of it is absolutely brilliant.

The fight had been arranged and they both intended to beat seven barrels of shit out of each other. (8 Years of age! Yeh!) Anyway Eddie and I decided we were going to train Terry up, so we made this punch bag and told Terry to take his top off as he practised his boxing skills. The day of the fight came and we all agreed where they would both be meeting up. Eddie and I were determined not to get involved as it was between them both. We got some Vaseline from somewhere and Eddie and I took off Terry's top and we smothered him head to foot in this Vaseline so that anything this boy had to throw at Terry, would just slide off. We must have used a whole tub of this stuff, putting it on his body, arms, face including all in his hair and eyebrows too. When they both arrived for the fight, Jimmy looked at Terry, screamed and ran all the way home because he looked so strange in this Vaseline. Terry still loves this story too as it was hilarious.

Oh, another thing that Eddie Foote and I did to Terry on a really hot summer day was when we filled the water pistol with methylated spirits that we found in the shed. Terry was really hot and sweaty and asked if he could have a drink of water from the pistol. Eddie was like, 'oh yes sure,' before proceeding to squirt the gun full of spirit into Terry's mouth. Terry was nearly sick from that one and was choking for ages as I remember. Let's be honest, it was actually bloody dangerous but we just didn't think like this at that age as it was all just a bit of fun.

One last amusing game that Eddie and me played with Terry was "William Tell". For those of you who are not aware of this folk legend, he was made to shoot an apple off his son's head with a crossbow for the freedom of his family. It used to be a TV programme and it gave me and Eddie a great idea. Obviously we never had a cross bow but we could easily get hold of an apple and a set of darts!!! We stood Terry against the side of Dad's shed with an apple on his head. We then proceeded to throw darts at Terry to see if we could hit the apple. We were only practising. When one of the darts imbedded itself in some part of Terry's body, I forget where now, but we weren't very good at darts in those days, we decided that this game was best shelved until we had become more competent.

Another childhood game which everyone used to play in the day, was "Split The Kipper". This was a brilliant game and required two players to face each other about two feet apart. We would stand with our feet together. One player would have acquired a penknife or if not, one of our mum's carving knives from the kitchen (as long as she didn't find out). The player with the knife had to throw it as close to the foot of his opponent as possible so that the blade stuck in the ground. The opponent was required to open their legs as far as the knife had landed, provided that it stuck in the ground. That player would then retrieve the knife and throw it as close to the foot of his opponent. The idea was to see who could be made to open their feet the widest without falling over. It was great fun and encouraged us kids to use knife skills. Much better than sitting on our backsides playing X-box or something like that.

Our food in these days always consisted of a big Sunday roast with beef or lamb. You never had chicken, as you only really had that at Christmas time, probably the exact opposite to what it is today. Mum's cooking was, in our minds, always the best; she made it just the way we liked it or was it just that we didn't know any better? Her cooking was always slightly burnt and her roast potatoes were always very crispy which is exactly how I still like them. I remember one Sunday when she was checking on the meat, she had to slam the oven door shut because the whole thing was on fire, fat spitting and smoke everywhere.

One day Dawn and I had come home for lunch and Mum had cooked us an Irish stew which normally was the one dish that even my mother couldn't spoil. On this occasion I recall Dawn saying, "I can't eat this Mum it's too fatty." My mother became very annoyed and angry at her for rejecting this lovely dish that she had slaved to make. She was so angry that she slapped Dawn all around the house and gave her a real good hiding. As I couldn't eat it either I got pretty much the same treatment then off we were sent, back to school for the rest of the afternoon with nothing else to eat. When we came back home at around 3-4pm my mother was so apologetic, because by that time the stew had cooled down and there must have been two inches of congealed fat floating top of the now cold stew. As I remember, Mum had thought that she had cooked a beef stew when in fact it turned out to be a Lamb stew. needless to say that she had not drained any fat from it whilst it had been cooking. It was awful and that put me off stew for a very long time.

At one point in time Mum would be out working during the day time and this would be when she started to give me and Dawn "lunch money". Dawn and I used to go up the local shop and get a couple of jam doughnuts each and a tin of tomato soup to share between us. One time, we never ate lunch all week so we could save our money and then on the Friday we both bunked off school and went to the pictures; we went to see *Rasputin the Mad Monk*, great picture!!

We were always lead to believe in things like Father Christmas and the Tooth Fairy, I really used to love all of it. I distinctly remember being young and looking up at the sky, especially in Avening Road and waiting to see if I could see Santa travelling through over the roof tops. Very much like kids do these days. I don't think we ever got lots of presents though, in fact the main present I remember getting was a *Dan Dare* space station which was well overhyped for what it really was. It was cheap plastic, with two non-electronic microphone shaped objects and you would stretch a piece of string from one to the other, with one person listening and the other talking into the microphone, I absolutely loved that present.

Aileen was lucky at one time to get every little girls dream, her first tea set. Before wrapping it in Christmas paper Mum and Dad hid it all under their bed to wait for us to be out of the way in order for them to wrap it all up. Unfortunately a problem arose because in those days it was common for people to keep a pee pot under the bed, in case you needed to go for a wee in the middle of the night. One evening my Dad had been out and had a right skin-full and in his drunken state, pulled out the tea set and peed all over it thinking that it was the pee pot. It was a famous story within the family for years as my Mum was fuming and funnily I can't remember Aileen ever making us any tea in it.

Talking about my Mum and Dad's bed reminds me of another great game us kids used to have. It was brilliant fun and we used to call it Stinking Willie. I have never heard of anyone else having ever played this game and so can only imagine that this was a game that had been invented and played purely by ourselves. It was a double bed and one of us kids would take turns jumping up and down on the bed while the others would have to smack hell out of you with a pillow and try and knock you off the bed. It was called stinking willy because as you were jumping up and down we all used to sing, "Stinking Willy's gone to town, gone to town, my fair lady" (sung to the tune of "London Bridge is Falling Down"). None of us to this day knows how or why we had ever invented this game in the first place.

Chapter Three

Electricity and Religion

I had the best childhood ever, as when we were growing up we never realised that we didn't have very much money and so were happy and content with what we did have. In hindsight, we were very poor but fortunate and happy in so many ways and we certainly always felt loved. It's funny how people change over time, because my mother was the more affectionate person out of our parents really until Dad got a bit older and he became a lot more affectionate and cuddly. I guess that my mother's influence paid off in the end.

In the early years when Dad was away working a lot, I have memories of sitting with Mum and Dawn waiting for him to come home, we were always so excited at the prospect of seeing him. I'm not even sure how we knew he was coming home but I think Mum could judge it on whatever location they had been sent to in the first place.

There was one time when my Mum had received an electric bill of £20 for the quarter while he was away, and she was almost suicidal before his return as it was so expensive. We definitely didn't have £20 to spend on bills! She didn't want to tell my Dad how much the bill was for fear of him hitting the roof. I can't imagine why it was so expensive, and can not remember the outcome of that conversation between them. This is just indicative of how, even at such young ages, we were all fully aware of our financial circumstances.

We still didn't have hot water at this point! None of the people living around us did either. In fact, when the local council tried to modernise Avening Road by putting hot water cisterns into all the houses, my Dad refused to have one. Perhaps this was after having received such a high electric bill previously. He caused quite a fuss, but in the end the council insisted and with a few strongly worded conversations he accepted his fate.

The hot water system consisted of brass tanks which were plumbed in above the bath. Nobody had even invented the jacket insulations that you sometimes see these days. By today's standards, they certainly had health and safety issues. Even when we got one we never really took baths as they took too long to fill with water, and of course we were all afraid of how much it would cost. We must have been quite stinky really as kids. I do know that because of the fuss that my Dad caused, we were the last house in Avening Road to get hot water.

My mother told me later on in my life that she was always fascinated with me because I always really excelled in English. It came naturally to me, unlike topics such as maths that I had to work hard at. I used to sit on the back doorstep reading the Bible which as you know has many unpronounceable words. I had my own Bible and used to love reading the different stories from it. Unbeknown to me, Mum used to just look at me when I was sat there reading aloud to myself. I still enjoy reading today, but not the Bible.

I used to attend church regularly when I was growing up. Because my Mum had fallen out with Catholicism I attended the local Baptist Church. The church was, and still is, on Finlay Road which was just a short walk up the road from me. The local Catholic Church would have been a much further walk and so St John the Baptist Church became my chosen church.

It never entered my head at the time about any differences in religious teachings. As far as I was concerned, church was church, God was God etc etc. During Bible lessons we used to play a game called "Swords". This consisted of the leader to say something like, "John, Chapter 3, verse 16", and then we all had to look this up in our bible and the first one to find that spot in the bible would put their hands up. We would then be asked to read aloud that particular verse. I used to love playing that game as the winner would always be awarded with a paper book marker. I won that book marker on several occasions.

My religion used to change from one to the other depending on what was on offer at that particular church. My Mum never seriously encouraged me or my siblings to go to church, it was all our own decision. I don't remember any religious conversations back home and there were certainly never opinions as to what the best religion would be for us to follow. My siblings and I were all given free rein on our own religious thoughts.

I always wanted to join the Cubs, but in order to do that in those days, you had to be a member of the Baptist Church, so that's exactly what I did to get in and I really loved my time with the Cubs. I loved my garters on my socks and my woggle around my cravat. I don't know how long I kept this up for but suspect it wasn't too long. I never did graduate to join The Scouts.

When I was about 8 or 9, I was introduced to a girl called Maureen O'Toole and really fell in love with her, but she was a practising Catholic. So I had to change religion again and became a Catholic and started going to Catholic Church to meet this girl.

One day my Mum and Dad said to me that I could invite Maureen around for tea. I was thrilled but asked my Mum and Dad if they could call me by another name as I didn't like being called Albert, due to it not being a very fashionable name. Mum asked me what I wanted to be called and so I said Bret, as it was the name of a Cowboy that used to appear on television at the time.

You can imagine how the family responded to this when Maureen turned up for tea, everything was BRET, BRET, BRET as they were looking to embarrass me at every opportunity. I never did know what happened to her or whether I actually got to see her again at all after that evening.

Another fond memory of mine from Avening Road was hearing the Salvation Army Band coming along the street on a Sunday morning. Sometimes if I was still in bed I could hear the band as it marched around the other streets close by to me. I would then get so excited to see them that I would quickly get dressed and rush out in order to stand by the side of the road and wave at them as they passed by. The sound of the beating drums, the triangles and the trombones were exhilarating. I supposed that this was nearest thing that we ever got to for Live Entertainment in those days.

To this day I am not a church goer, but I do envy those who have "found religion". It must be such a comfort for getting through the many traumas that life throws at you. My wife Wendy, is a good practising catholic girl and so I get her to mention me in her prayers. I guess that I am still waiting for "my calling", but being the cynic that I am, I don't hold out much hope in the near future.

Chapter Four

Sticky Drips and Rough Seas

Our day-to-day living always relied upon living on 'tick', an old fashioned version of the phrase I.O.U. or credit. We had a shop called Sparrows on the Finlay Road that used to provide tick for our family, so us kids were regularly sent to the shop and asked the shop assistant to stick the items onto our family bill. Whilst I didn't always like going shopping for my Mum and Dad, every once in a while, we could get something ourselves for going and I used to love these cakes that locally were called "sticky drips". They had thick treacle at the bottom, were full of raisins and were always fresh and warm. The true name for these beauties is "Lardy cakes", but I can tell you that today's cakes are nothing like the "Sticky Drips" that we used to buy from Sparrows. The toffee on the bottom of the cake was thick and sometimes slightly burned. I have recently seen talk on Facebook from old timers like me reminiscing about these cakes. I don't know if they still exist in Gloucester but I certainly haven't seen them for many a year.

We would never dare put anything on the bill that we hadn't been told to get as we knew we would always be found out.

Mum once sent me to out to buy two Swiss Rolls from Sparrows. The Swiss Rolls used to cost a shilling each (5p in today's money). I somehow got confused with my mission having heard my Mum telling me to get 2 x Shilling Swiss Rolls as a treat for after tea. Tea was always the Evening Meal in our house. (I was much older before I got to call tea - dinner). Anyway, Sparrows did not have any Swiss Rolls, but they did have bread rolls which were a penny each. I was delighted and rather pleased with myself that I managed to get 24 bread rolls for the price of of 2 x Shilling rolls. Needless to say I was sent straight back to the shop to return them.

The bread rolls in those days were not vacuum packed or anything like that. In fact they were all just placed loosely in a couple of paper bags. With Health and Safety as it is, I suspect that I would not have been able to return them back to a shop today.

I always remember my Dad having a Lambretta scooter with

registration VAD 3. When ever he wasn't using it, I would sit on the saddle and pretend to ride it. I can't find that registration on the GOV.UK. site now and so I expect it would have been scrapped a long time ago.

There's a great story of the time when my Mum and Dad had decided to have an afternoon out by themselves and had gone to visit a pub at a place called Wainlodes Hill near Gloucester. It was, and still is to this day, a really popular destination for people in the area because it had a kind of beachy vibe going on, with the nice little pub nearby. We went there regularly over the years, but this one particular day Mum and Dad headed out on their own.

Leading down to the pub is a really steep road. After having had their fill of whatever nectar they had purchased from the pub, they set off to ascend the hill. Obviously my Dad in the front and Mum riding pillion on the back. As they headed up the hill, the bike was struggling with lack of power and so Dad had to shift into lower gears. It was a bit touch and go for a while. Then, the bike caught momentum and started to speed up the hill with little effort. It wasn't until Dad got to the top that he realised Mum was no longer sat behind him . She had fallen off halfway up the hill. Being a gentleman he then waited for her to walk to the top to join him to reunite herself with him. I can only imagine the conversation that took place once they were reunited once more. I always loved hearing that story.

During the time of growing up in Avening Road we had a cat called *Tiddles*, which I don't think was named after me and my bedwetting activity. Unfortunately *Tiddles* got run over right outside of our house, quite some doing given there were hardly any vehicles on the road in those days. I can only assume it had already used up all its other lives beforehand. I was really upset and my Mum kept me off school.

I think I was more sentimental at that time than any of my other brother or sisters. Perhaps I just learnt that you could act that way to get extra time off school, which always seemed to work for me. So on my day off school due to *Tiddles* demise, I joined Mum on the bus into Gloucester. We were going to collect Mum's wages from the Royal Infirmary as she worked there as a nurse. No bank transfers or such in those days. If you wanted your wages you had to go and collect them from your employer. Mum asked me if we should we go to see Auntie Ethel as she lived just around the corner from the hospital. Well Aunt Ethel's husband, Uncle Jim, was my Dad's favourite uncle and as I have already described, my Dad spent a fair amount of time growing up with them in their Narrow Boat when they were Bargees. Of course I agreed to the visit. Much more exciting than going to school.

When we got to Aunt Ethel's house, she said, "Oh I'm just about to cook some faggots and peas, do you want some?" I said yes, but for some reason, my Mum declined. As we were walking home, Mum asked if I enjoyed the faggots and peas? She then went on to explain that Aunt Ethel had a cat and Mum had noticed her pick the cat's saucer up off the floor and without washing it, served my faggots and peas straight onto it. Mum didn't want to offend my aunt Ethel so decided not to say anything and just let me eat off the bloody cat's saucer. Needless to say that when my Mum related this to me, she found it to be highly amusing. I guess that was her Irish sense of humour.

I've mentioned my Grandad a few times but as it turned out there is a lot that has already been written about him and his time on the waterways. Just type in to your search engine "Severn Tanker Disaster 1939". He was only 29 years of age when he was a 'skipper' of an oil tanker which was involved with two other boats in a horrendous accident.

As I was growing up I spent a lot of time travelling with my Grandad on the boats up and down the river. The rivers in those days were bustling with activity as the waterways were Industrial and used for workers to transport goods rather than leisure travel as we see today. He is also recorded as having to serve a small amount of time in jail for his actions during the The Great Strike in 1926. He worked with the John Harker company until he was given notice in January 1972.

I would always be given jobs to do when travelling on the boat with my Grandad, like painting the deck red, or shining the brass around the boat, such as the boat's bell. The boat always looked spick and span. Grandad kept a dry boat so there was never any booze allowed on board, even though the workers were all actually quite heavy drinkers when they were ashore.

I have memories of going under the Severn bridge, the very first one, as it was being built, you know, when it was just a shell. There was one particular trip where my Dad had got a pass from my Mum to come with us. We had gone through the locks at Sharpness to Port Talbot. As we had left Port Talbot, there was quite an infamous dangerous area of waterway. This was made worse on this particular day because the water was exceptionally rough with high waves. My Grandad called us all up to the wheel-house along with the crew and made everyone put on lifejackets. By this time we were hitting waves which would make the boat shudder and then wash right over the top of the wheelhouse where we all were. My Grandad was braced up against the great big wheel which was used to steer the boat. It was so impressive to see him spin that wheel and it would rotate so fast that you could not make out the spindles in it. He would then stop the wheel spinning by just catching it in his hand with a hard slapping sound. As a young lad I thought it was exciting and had a brilliant time. People afterwards told us that they were really concerned because we actually disappeared several times below the waves and they couldn't see us at all. On the other hand, I always felt extremely safe as I had my Grandad and my Dad with me.

In late 1962 a phenomenal occurred that would change people slightly all over the world. I was ten years old, going on eleven when a new rock group appeared on the scene. That group was *The Beatles* which consisted of, Paul McCartney, John Lennon, Ringo Starr and George Harrison. As a young person growing up in this era, we could not have been more lucky. Their singing, style of clothes and general persona were completely new and refreshing coming to the music scene. Their first hit single was *Love Me Do* and it went straight to number one in the charts.

Apart from the music, their hair and clothes also caused a stir and changed the way young people behaved. They wore suits without collars and these became known as Beatle Suits. Their hair was longer than we were used to seeing on other artists and they also wore shoes with cuban heels. Apart from the hair, I wanted to emulate everything about them. When they conducted interviews on the television they were cheeky and funny. They were a big influence on the youngsters growing up around that time. They became successful all around the world from about 1964 when they performed in the USA and other large countries. When I think about it, the 60's was the decade that shaped my life.

When The Beatles broke up around 1970, all of the individual members of the group managed to pursue their own careers in music. Sadly today, in 2022 there are only two out of the four still alive. John Lennon was murdered in 1980 and George Harrison died of lung cancer in 2001.

Chapter Five

The Trouser Incident

While us kids were still at quite an early age Mum and Dad used to leave us alone when they would go out on an evening to go to a pub. I imagine that this was not an unusual thing for parents to do back then. I can't remember if they used to get a neighbour to look in to us now and again or not. We certainly never had baby sitters who stayed with us the time that they were out. Dawn was often put in charge as she was the eldest, which I never did really like as it was a licence for her to tell me what to do. On one particular occasion when I was about eight and Dawn my sister was about ten, Dawn had been her usually bossy-self and I remember getting so annoyed with her. I don't know where it came from, but I picked up a hammer belonging to my Dad, and I aimed it between her eyes, throwing it with all my might. It missed Dawn and unfortunately went straight through the front room window and smashed it. I was so lucky that it didn't hit its target. Or more to the point, Dawn was very lucky!!

Immediately following this incident, Mum and Dad arrived back home but I never remember getting a rollicking over it for some reason. What I do remember though is my Dad having to fix this window. Dad was never a DIY enthusiast. He got two pieces of hardboard, one outside the window and one inside and screwed them together. We lived in the house for months like that with wood instead of glass on this window. Mind you I think Dawn began to stop bossing me around so much then. She still had my younger brother and sister to play "Mother" with though. Aileen would have been around five and Terry would have been around two years of age.

On another occasion with Dawn, she was doing the bossy boots thing again. She was winding me up and eventually I got so fed up I just started laying into her. Dawn became really so frightened that she pretended to faint on the floor. She was there lying on the floor in front of me, not moving an eyelid (Did I mention that she also had aspirations to be an actress?). I was doing all the usual tricks like throwing water over her, pinching her underarms and the usual sort of First Aid training that I imagined, but she still didn't move. I resorted to shouting that our Auntie Phyllis was coming, at which point she shot up and it transpired nothing was wrong with her at all. I can't remember whether Aunty Phil was coming to us or not!! Anyway I got her to give in and move which in my books is a Victory to me!!

Dad always said he had one regret in life and that was that he never told his Dad that he loved him whilst he was alive. His Dad never told him either, let alone put their arms around each other and hug. They just weren't tactile in any way, shape, or form. You see, more than just a Dad, my Grandad was also my Dad's hero and he worshiped the ground he walked on. Even when my Dad eventually passed away at the age of 77, this was still something he sadly regretted and had played on his mind all his life. I don't know what it was like with his Mum, my Nan, as we never really talked about it, but she died quite young at the age of about 56 through Cancer.

I'm pleased to say that the relationship with my siblings and I, was completely different to that. We did cuddle and we did kiss and would often say that we loved each other, freely showing emotion and affection. The only thing that comforted my Dad in this regard was recognition that our relationship together was so different to what he had experienced with his father, and we all knew that we could always put our arm around each other for a hug when we needed one.

My Dad became so sentimental that later on during Christmas time, when Johnny Mathis would sing *When a Child is Born*, he would burst into tears. Mind you he used to "tear up" for all manner of reasons.

When I was around 11, I think I saw myself as a bit of a comedian. I think I used to try and make people laugh because I could see it as a way to get people to like me. I always wanted to be liked, be in with the in crowd and so forth. Some people say I would come across as really confident but it was probably the other way around and this was my mask.

I am afraid that the Tonks' sense of humour is quite renowned. This is because we all find ourselves to be very funny. A Tonks will tell a joke and before we have even finished the punch line, would end up in hysterics. And the more we laughed, the harder we would laugh at ourselves laughing. Sometimes we will even be the only ones laughing - which made us laugh even more.

One of my "really funny moments" happened one day during lunch break. By this time I was having school dinners and I have to put my hand up and say that I really loved them. On this particular day I had finished my dinner and my pudding and was walking out of the dining room. A friend of mine was still eating his dinner. I thought that it would be tremendously funny to pour pepper over his pudding whilst he was eating it. Picking up a pepper pot, I threw the pepper over his plate and started to laugh uncontrollably. It was really funny seeing him sneezing on to his plate. Unfortunately I have never been too clever at getting away with my misdemeanours and so was the case this time. A teacher had seen me and instantly began to reprimand me in front of the whole dining room. I was then sent to wait outside the headmaster's office to receive any further punishment that he might wish to dish out. The headmaster was a Mr Booth who was not afraid to use the cane, and so I thought that that would be my punishment. After entering his office he informed me how wasteful it was to spoil good food etc. etc. He then awarded a Black Mark against the House that I was in. This also meant that on Friday afternoon at the Friday assembly, all of those pupils who had been awarded a black mark were called up to stand on the stage in front of the whole school. Each one of us would then have our "crime" read out to the whole school. Also, they would call out which House was top for that week and because I had lost my house a point or two, my house came last with the inscription that this was all due to the efforts of Albert Tonks being a rascal. Happy days. What a start to the weekend.

When I went to first year senior school, I was still in short trousers. Of course I wasn't the only one, but by this time some parents had decided that their little darlings were beginning to grow up. It wasn't till the second year, when I was 12 or 13 that I was allowed to wear long trousers. I didn't know anything about fashion at that point, it helps that we didn't have the social media that we do today so fashion wasn't a high priority. Just as well it wasn't as we couldn't afford it.

I remember very clearly my first pair of long trousers. My Mum had taken me out to buy them in Gloucester City. I can't tell you how grown up and proud I was to be wearing them. They were my pride and joy and I believe that they had cost my Mum a fair amount of money. I was now (almost) a grown up.

True to Tonks form, when I got to school I joined in all of the fun of the playground. One of these was called 'The Whip.' A long line of us would hold hands and run straight along the playground. The end kid would then stop abruptly and make everyone turn into a bent line. If you were in the front of the line, this had very little effect on you. If you were on the very end of the line, you would end up running at around 100 mph. On this particular day, of all days, muggins was "tail end Charlie". I was travelling so fast that my little legs couldn't keep up the speed of the whip. Inevitably, I ended up being thrown with great force along the concrete flooring of the playground

Whilst I was slightly injured, nothing could have hurt me more than seeing a gaping hole in the knee of my brand new long trousers. I was devastated and it played on my mind all day long during lessons. I conceived a plan that when I arrived home after school, I would find a needle and thread and sew the hole up myself. And so this is what I did. I couldn't bring myself to tell my Mum about about the incident, mainly because I knew that she could not afford to buy me a new pair of trousers. I got away with my deception for many weeks as I remember until one day my Mum noticed my sewing technique. Having explained what happened and giving the reasons why I had not said anything, I was expecting the world to explode. But my Mum wasn't like that. Being the Irish girl she was, the first reaction was to laugh her head off. She forgave me without punishment and I assume at some point I must have acquired a new pair of trousers.

On March 27th 1963 I had just turned 11 years old, and whilst at school, we heard a report of a local plane crash. We were in lessons at the time. There were some reports that a plane had crashed but had just missed our school. My friend's Mum, Hertha Foote, has supplied me with her audio account of this and states that she was probably one of the last people to have seen the pilots alive as it came to crash.

"There had been two test pilots at the controls. They had gotten into difficulty and were trying to land on a school playing field. They were gliding in to find a landing spot but they never made it and quite literally landed on top of a house. There were three people in the house at the time but apparently none were injured as they were all downstairs, but sadly the pilots both died."

The crew had been engaged in a local training flight. Shortly after take-off from runway 22 at Gloucester-Staverton Airport, while climbing to a height of 600-700 feet, the airplane stalled and crashed on the roof of a house located on Tuffley Avenue. The aircraft was destroyed.

Avening Road was a huge part of my growing up days. We used to play marbles, hopscotch, five jacks, climbing trees and all that sort of thing. There was a lady (Mrs Russell) who used to live on the road opposite who would give us money to go to the local Northfield Hotel to get her some supplies. We were all under 11 and she would give us empty flagons of cider and we would have to ask the landlord to sell us cigarettes and fill up the flagon with beer that we would take home and deliver back to her. This was a great way to earn a bit of pocket money but certainly something you wouldn't be allowed to do today at that age.

Photograph of the crashed plane on 27 March 1963

Chapter Six

Sports and Disappointments

Like all kids, I was interested in all kinds of sports. I didn't follow any particular football team, not until it came to the 1966 World Cup. And then I followed that strangely enough, right from the beginning all the way through to the end, which is the only time I've ever done that. Perhaps I should do it again, to give us a chance and share my luck.

I had a printout from one of the newspapers showing all of the rounds to be played up to the Final. Of course I had to fill in the teams names into the appropriate sections as the competition progressed. And so when it came to entering England in to that spot where the final was against West Germany, I can say that I have never been so excited about football to this day. And so when we eventually won the World Cup it was a great excitement to me. Strangely I have never followed and supported any particular football team. Maybe that is because I have moved around the country during my lifetime. But I do enjoy watching a good, clean and entertaining game.

I used to enjoy Judo and Football. My mate Edward (Eddie) and me used to go to the Glevum club in Gloucester every Sunday Morning for Judo lessons. I don't like to hark on about how un-wealthy we were, but I never did own a Judo suit. Even though I went regularly, I always fought in whatever clothing that I was wearing for the day. I didn't even expect to get a suit. It never even crossed my mind to ask my Mum and Dad to pay out for a suit for me because I knew that they would not be able to afford it.

My biggest disappointment with Judo was the day that I had to fight another lad who was smaller than me. We were roughly the same age and obviously we were more or less matched to fight each other. However, he was definitely smaller. A few of the students who did have Judo suits had to place their belts together to form a circle. The idea then was for two students to enter the ring and fight each other with Judo techniques that we had been taught. With all of the other students watching, we began to circle each other to await the appropriate moment to get a good hold or grip on each other. Being the bigger of the two students, I was fairly confident at this time. The next thing I remember was that I was flying through the air with such a suddenness, that I left a trail of snot where I had been standing just a few seconds ago. My opponent had whipped his hip under me and performed a hip throw as quick as you like. My only consolation was that I did perform a really good Judo fall and making a really loud slap as I landed on the canvas and thereby losing the match.

We had so much freedom when we were kids. Don't get me wrong, as I do not advocate that the kids of today should have the same amount of freedom. I don't know if we are more aware of what COULD go wrong these days; there have been so many changes over time that have changed the whole perspective on how much freedom children should be allowed in modern times.

There is an old song that we kids used to sing regularly. I have no idea where it came from but I have recently been reminded of it. It goes like this:-

> We are the Gloucester boys
> We are the Gloucester Boys
> We know our manners
> We spend our tanners
> We are respected wherever we may go
> And when we're walking down the Bristol Road
> All the windows opened wide
> You could hear the women shout
> Put those bloody Woodbines out
> Cause we are the Gloucester Boys

We used to go missing from the house for hours on end and get up to all sorts of situations in the name of fun. One of our favourite trips out on our own would be to climb to the top of Robinswood Hill and walk along what we called *The Camel's Hump*. This was just the top of the hill with undulations which became known as the *Camel's Hump*. On the way up or down we would stop off at the reservoirs. These were great fun. There was very little water in the reservoir but the concrete sides were great for sitting on some stray bit of metal or wood and then sliding down the sides of the reservoirs and then climbing up to do it all again. This area was also great for catching frogs, tadpoles, newts and so on.

Not far from the reservoir were the "Bluebell Woods". I recall one time when we were climbing the hill. There was a natural stream that used to run down the hill and through the "Bluebell Woods". The water was freezing cold and was really lovely to drink. Of course at the top of the stream there would be cows in the field who would take their drink at the top end of the hill. It was a wonder that we never caught some horrible virus or disease.

We would often arrive home with bits of skin having been scraped from some part of our bodies. We were usually too far away from home to go running to Mum for her to put a plaster on us, and besides which, that would interrupt our playtime. By this time we would be any age between 6 and 11 years of age.

One incident that happened to me and still lives with me to this day, was when I was about ten years of age. Again, I was still at Finlay Road School. I used to walk across the school field to get home. One day I heard this almighty crash and thought, what the hell is that. Right outside the school was a bus stop. I was on the other side of the fence and I walked across to see what the noise was all about. At this time, school kids, some with their parents, had been waiting for their bus to take them home from school. When I looked, I could see a boy I knew, pinned up against a lamppost by this car and he was clearly dead. I don't know why I knew this at the time, but to me it was obvious. There was a woman by the side of the car, her skirt up and her stockings all laddered and who was also looking as if her life had expired, she looked terrible. There was also a lad lying underneath the car and the car caught fire. There were loads of people trying to help out at the scene and some even trying to move the car and I think whoever was under the car probably died as well.

I don't know why, but I've never said anything to anyone when I got home. I just carried on as normal until my Mum said to me that I was looking a bit pale and my eyes a bit funny. I then opened up and said to her that I had just seen an accident and that I saw some people I thought had just been killed. My mother started to really look after me at that point as she was obviously aware of the impact it can have on seeing something like this. As soon as she showed me sympathy, I started crying. As I loved that kind of attention. It transpired that the bloody idiot driver of the car had been drink driving at the time and the penalties for drink driving at the time were not as severe as they are these days. There is no doubt that once you have seen something as horrific like this, the memories stay with you forever. Perhaps that is a good thing. With today's Drink Driving Laws, I do not need to be shown any gruesome photos to deter me from driving while under the influence of alcohol.

My first experience with death of a family member came to me in June 1964. My Nan (My Dad's Mum) had been ill for some time with lung cancer. I was 12 years of age at the time. I remember her being in a great deal of pain. When she passed away, my mother told me and my sister Dawn that it was traditional for the eldest granddaughter and grandson to kiss the departed before the burial. I had never heard of that tradition before and certainly not since. So Dawn and myself duly went and visited my Nan when she was laying at rest in her own bedroom. It was not a pleasant thing to do. However, my Mum being the Irish girl that she was always instilled in us that, "It isn't the dead that you had to be careful of, but the living". My mum was very mystical and had great beliefs in the after life, especially ghosts and the like.

I think that at this point it would be good to try and understand the characters of my childhood. My Mum and Dad were pivotal to everything I was and everything I am. I know that my siblings would agree with me that we had the best of childhoods that left us with many fond and happy memories. Even years later when we are all too busy with our own lives to see each other often, I know that the deep rooted love for each other will always be there.

When I went to senior school, which was the Central Technical School for Boys, the only game they played was rugby. They didn't play football. They chose me to be a Hooker because I was damn quick on my feet. I was also quite light, small and thin, so they used to be able swing me into the pack and I would then scrabble about in the scrum to get the ball. I have to admit that they did play cricket in the summer and I quite enjoyed being the bowler as I was quite good at throwing a ball.

I used to love playing a game of rugby. We were taught how to make a tackle by wrapping your arms around your opponents feet when they were running with the ball, without getting a kick in the mouth. I remember one particular day when I was chasing an opponent who had the ball. I didn't get the chance to dive for his feet. He turned his body around and pushed the flat of his hand into my face. I was still running forward at this time. The momentum of me running forward and my face being pushed backwards kind of stopped me in my tracks. It never put me off Rugby, but I sure as hell was learning fast.

Dad never really took a lot of interest in any sport or activity that I took up. There are only a couple of occasions that I remember him sharing my enthusiasm for any of them. My biggest and fondest memory was when I was at Finlay School and a trip had been arranged to go to Wembley to see a boys International game. It was an England versus Germany match and I do not remember the score. Our school trip started with all of us getting a train from Gloucester railway station to Paddington (I believe) in London. It was so exciting going with my dad as I suppose he must have been a volunteer adult to accompany the school party. The train stopped just outside of the station and I remember someone asking if we could now get off the train. My dad had explained that we were not yet properly in the station and that everyone should remain seated for the time being. I felt really important because it was my Dad telling everyone else what to do.

That was my first experience of attending a big event. Wembley looked so big and the grass was immaculate. Nobody could attend and not get caught up in the emotion of the day. I absolutely loved it and it is a memory that has stayed with me all these years.

Not all attendances by my Dad were quite so successful though. On the only occasion ever that I remember him coming to see me play a sport was when I was in a cricket team. A match had been arranged against a team from another part of Gloucester. I was chosen to be part of our team. Either that or they let me play just to make up the numbers. I don't know. It came to my turn to go out to bat. I had put on all of my pads, practised my arm swings with the bat and tried to look the part. I looked into my Dad's eyes as I started the long walk towards the stumps and could see that he was quite excited and proud of me right at that moment. I set myself up and measured my stance in agreement with the umpire, and then waited for the first ball to be put my way. The bowler started his run and my heart started to thump. Never mind, I was sure that once I settled down after a few balls I would feel more confident. The bowler let go of the ball which then headed towards me. From the corner of my eye I could see the spectators around the area I knew that my Dad would be standing. The ball hit the ground just in front of me where I had my bat raised ready to give it some welly and hopefully knock it for six.

Unfortunately I missed the ball which continued to travel past me and took out my middle stump. I was out for a duck. I was devastated that I had let my Dad down. He was never one to wrap things up in cotton wool. He told me what a plonker I was and then went on to remind me that he had taken time out of his whole life to watch me humiliate myself. He never did come to watch any of my other sports that I participated in.

The whole of my family used to settle down on a Saturday afternoon to watch the Professional Wrestling on the television. The wrestling was shown on the television at four o'clock every Saturday afternoon. Kent Walton used to be the commentator and when the programme started he would announce "good afternoon grappling fans, welcome to another afternoons wrestling". There used to be such big names as Steve Logan, Mick McManus, Big Daddy, Giant Haystacks, Billy Two Rivers and Johnny Quango. We would all be shouting at the telly for one of them to do real injury to the other. This was an exciting part of the weekend before we all had to stay really quiet whilst Mum listened to the football results and then checked to see if she had won the pools or not. There were so many plans being made for what we were all going to do if we had ever won. Which of course, we never did.

I found out that there was a fan club for a wrestler who was quite well-known in his day, so I joined this fan club and I used to receive lots of information about wrestling as well as photographs of all the wrestlers. I used to go with my Mum and Dad regularly to Gloucester

Baths to watch the wrestling and really loved it. A couple of times, my fan club wrestler came to Gloucester baths and we got to know him. He used to take me right in the back to the dressing room to meet the wrestlers and I used to get all their autographs and get to say hello to them all.

During these days my Dad was in the Territorial Army, and I was 11 years of age. He went to Norfolk with the Territorial Army because you have to do a week or two weeks camping as a requirement to staying in the TA's. So me, Mum and my brother and sisters went away to London to stay with my Auntie Tess. Well, the wrestler's address was also in central London and we had arranged to meet him at a pub called the *Sherlock Holmes*, which is still on the corner of Craven Street, the Strand today.

During that evening, I became a bit concerned because I noticed he was holding my Mum's hand a lot and I started to get a little bit upset. I was beginning to feel a bit protective not just of my Mum, but mainly for my Dad. Anyway, we came to the end of the evening and Mum said to me, "Do you want to stay with him overnight and we'll pick you up in the morning because we know he is your hero?" By this time, I was little bit uncertain, but I thought you know, everybody's making an effort and I didn't want to spoil the evening so, I said, okay, and everyone else went off to Aunt Tess's.

After my Mum and Aunt Tess left us, we went back to his address. At this time he had been mentoring a new and up and coming wrestler named Ricky Starr. Ricky was only 19 year old. I had seen him wrestle a couple of times, indeed he had even been on the TV on a Saturday afternoon. When we got into the house, Ricky was asleep on the front room floor. I didn't think too much of it when I was told that we would have to sleep in the same bed and that we should be quiet so that we didn't disturb Ricky. As I said, during the night I had gotten a bit jealous of his behaviour with Mum. Well I needn't have worried in this respect. I was soon to find out that my hero was a *kiddie fiddler* and he set about molesting me.

So I didn't want to shout or scream because I was petrified that Ricky might be of the same trait, so obviously, I was frightened. I was shitting myself and waited until I could hear him snoring. He had obviously had enough to drink while we had been out and about.

As soon as I heard him snoring I got up, grabbed my clothes and I crept out of the house, got dressed outside of the house and started wandering through the streets of London. By this time, it would have been the early hours of the morning and it was still dark outside.

I started to walk and I found myself walking around Trafalgar Square. Obviously at the time I didn't know where I was going or where I was, what I was going to do or anything like that. I was 11 years old and from Gloucester. Eventually two Policeman saw me and came up and asked me what I was doing? I said I've just been assaulted and the next thing I know is that I was in a Police station being interviewed by a Police Medical Examiner.

The police found my Mum from the information I had given them. As soon as my Mum came in to the room I was in, I just broke down in tears. When I was interviewed by the police they asked me why I hadn't shouted out for help, knowing that Ricky was right next to us sleeping on the floor. I explained that I was frightened just in case Ricky was also of the same ilk as his flat mate. So, anyway, he was obviously arrested and went through whatever procedures were carried out. I don't know what happened to him even to this day, and I am not the least interested.

When I look back on this incident, what fascinates me about the whole thing is was the way my Mum and Dad dealt with it. I was so young and also their son. They convinced me that he wasn't very well and that he was really sick and needed help. I actually remember at one stage, beginning to feel sorry for him and so I started to write to him telling them I was the one that was sorry for getting him into trouble. When my Mum and Dad found out what I was doing they said, no, no, no, no, you mustn't do that, he's been really naughty, he shouldn't have done it! But that's always fascinated me, the way they dealt with that situation. All I know about the incident was when we got back to Auntie Tess's, my Uncle Paddy and Uncle Joe went out looking for him as they were both living in London at the time. Wrestler or not, I would not have fancied his chances had they caught him.

Chapter Seven

The Demon Drink

Because our house in Avening Road was so cold in the winter, Mum used have the gas oven on full pelt with the door to the oven left wide open. She would then stand with her back to the oven and hitch her skirt up at the back and stick her bum practically inside. This produced a really satisfying look on her face and used to make us kids laugh.

One of my Mum's favourite routines first thing in the morning was when she would disappear for a good half hour or so in the toilet. God only knows what was going on in there but she would stay for ages. We only had one toilet in Avening Road, which was downstairs with the bathroom. One morning, while she was ensconced in the bathroom, my sister Aileen started to be physically sick and started wobbling all over the place. I think she was only about three years old at the time, and I shouted to Mum through the toilet door that something was wrong with Aileen. Mum rushed out of the bathroom with her knickers still around her ankles asking frantically what had happened.

Well, in those days we used to store paraffin in any containers we could get our hands on, one of which was a pop bottle, like a Tizer bottle. Apparently Aileen had decided to take a few swigs from this bottle, thinking that it was Tizer. Anyway, an ambulance had to be called and she was taken to the Gloucester Royal Infirmary where she had to have her stomach pumped. Looking back at this, when we all reminisce our childhood, we have a laugh but I'm sure it wasn't at the time.

When I was around 11 years old, I had saved up my paper round money to buy my first racing bike. I was so proud as it was just mine and had drop handlebars too so I thought it was awesome. I'm not quite sure why I called it a racing bike as it didn't even have any gears, had just two cogs and even the handlebars didn't have grips as they were just bare metal but man I loved this thing. This one day at senior school I got home and my sister Aileen was in tears, because

42

a young lad of a similar age to me from my school who had a similar bike to me had been knocked off their bike and killed and the police had brought the bike into the school to identify who it belonged to. Aileen thought it was me and she broke her heart bless her.

When I was out riding my bike one day, with my sister Dawn and her then boyfriend, we had cycled up to Prinknash Abbey. This was a five or six mile ride I guess. Obviously Dawn wasn't very old either, so when I say boyfriend!!! We were having a great day out cycling around the roads and lanes. Prinknash Abbey was built by Benedictine Monks and they were still living there farming the land around them. You could go and watch them make pottery which they used to sell in their shop. It is still a nice place to visit today but unfortunately, the Monks have disappeared.

Anyway, I digress. We were cycling around the Lanes when I decided to go ahead and leave the two love birds on their own for a while. They were still cycling behind me but obviously not so quick. I was tearing it around the bends when I happened upon a very gritty bit of road. Like the amateur that I was, I immediately applied my brakes. This sent me spinning sideways with my body now in contact with the road. I had lots of friction burns and grit stuck in my skin. Dawn and her boyfriend eventually rounded the corner to find me flat on my back in severe pain. I couldn't have been too badly hurt though as we then had to cycle back home.

When I look back, my Mum and Dad always had trouble with the way in which they handled their alcoholic beverages. I will give some examples of this. I remember Mum being ill in bed with something once, Dad would have been at work. We were living in Avening Road and so I estimate my age to be between 8 and 10 years of age.

Mum had discovered that one of the local shops served draught sherry. Apple Brandy sherry if I remember right. This required you to present yourself at the shop with an empty bottle - usually a pop bottle with a screw lid - which would then be filled with said sherry. I think that there might also have been a Peach Brandy sherry as well. Anyway, I remember keep being sent up to the shop whilst Mum became merrier and merrier in her bed and in ill health.

The problem with Dad was that he sometimes became aggressive, particularly if he had drunk too much whisky. This aggressiveness didn't materialise as abusive behaviour but he was certainly not as loving as his sober manner. I remember once when Mum and Dad had gone out for a drink leaving us four kids at home (Dawn was probably in charge, but under my supervision and with my consent). As Dawn was the eldest, she would have been no more than 10 years of age. It was Halloween and us kids had hung some apples on string from the front room ceiling. I know what you are thinking about pin holes all over the ceiling, but this didn't matter as the whole ceiling was full of holes from Christmas decorations!!!

Our idea was to have some fun when Mum and Dad came back home with "Apple Bobbing". I remember being so excited about playing some games with Mum and Dad. I think we had put some apples in a bowl of water as well as part of the fun for Apple Bobbing. Mum and Dad duly arrived home, all the worst for wear. Dad then thought it hilarious to go around the hanging apples and punching them down with his fist. Us kids were so disappointed and needless to say, we never played any games.

Dad had just finished with whatever firm he was working for (I think it was Walls Ice Cream Factory) and had gotten a job with British Nylon Spinner (BNS) in Tuffley. He and his old workmates decided to have a celebration with Dad for getting a new Job. Although Dad could drive, he couldn't afford a car.

A friend of his offered to lend Dad his car. Dad filled the car up with his friends and I understand that there were six of them in the car. This would have been in the early 60's and so seat belts weren't an issue at the time. Needless to say that Dad had a skinful even though he was driving. Drink driving was also not an issue in those days, unless you killed someone. As he was driving under a railway bridge along Tredworth Road, he didn't make the corner and ran straight into a bus stop. Nobody was seriously injured although the car and the bus stop were right offs. He ended up with a fine and I remember him having to pay £20 for a new bus stop. Thereafter, that bus stop was always referred to as Dad's Bus stop. He was so lucky that nobody was seriously injured. I can remember my Dad, probably the next day having to go around to his mate to explain that his car was a write off. I don't know how Dad compensated him (he never had any money) and I am pretty sure that they never spoke again.

Another famous incident for us kids whilst growing up and living in Avening Road occurred one Boxing Day. Mum and Dad had again been drinking when they had a fall out about something or other. They came to actual physical blows. I reckon that I would have been around 8 years old at the time. I guess we had plenty of alcohol in the house as it was Christmas time. Anyway, I think the whole neighbourhood must have been aware of their argument and Mum ended up running over the road to her best friend Joan Long. Obviously this incident passed by as well but I do remember us kids trying to intervene on many occasions by running messages between the two of them, trying to make them 'be friends again'.

I don't want this to sound as if we had a miserable childhood because I didn't. Normally my Mum and Dad were the best parents ever, unfortunately, they couldn't take their alcoholic beverage.

Mum had a couple of jobs whilst I was growing up. One of them was when she was employed by the *English Glory* matchstick makers in Gloucester. I don't know how long she did that for, but she was at her happiest when she did a bit of nursing. She did a bit of General Nursing as well as Psychiatric nursing. One of her proudest moments was when she passed one of her medical examinations in 1964. I have the original letter which she must have kept and it is dated 24th July 1964. I was twelve years of age.

The letter states: "Dear Madam, I have pleasure in informing you that you have been successful in passing the Intermediate State Examination held in June 1964". I can literally remember her excitement with opening and reading that letter. For passing the exam, I believe that she was awarded something like £20. This was a lot of money for people like my Mum and Dad. It was with this award that Dad bought our first ever motor car. It was an Austin Standard 8. A good museum piece now. We were all so proud of that car and the fact that "We had a car" even though we lived in Avening Road in Tuffley, Gloucester. I remember Dad taking us all for a trip down to Sharpness which is about 16 miles away. We were in our element and felt that we had really made it. All because Mum had been awarded a few pounds for passing an exam. Dad was driving down these little lanes and everything was absolutely brilliant. I can still smell the leather now.

I have already explained how my Dad's education in school was somewhat intermittent. Despite all this, he was always particularly good at maths for some reason. I guess different people are natural in different things. Anyway that was enough for him to pass his 11 plus and was sent to the Central Technical School for Boys at Derby Road in Gloucester. In those days, the school was split in to two. One side for girls and the other for the boys. Moving on to around 1960/61 my sister Dawn also passed her 11 plus and was sent to the same school as Dad. I think Mum and Dad would have been really proud of her.

Lo and behold, during 1963/64 I also passed my 11 plus and was sent to The Central Technical School for Boys. By this time the boys part of the school had moved to Cotteswold Road. I was not too clever with maths but my English was excellent. All through my senior years, I was always in the top class and always came either first or second, taking it in turns with my friend Chris Ryan.

At senior school, I discovered that if you were a Roman Catholic, you didn't have to attend morning assemblies, which were held every morning. Instead, you could go to the separate classroom, where prefects were supposed to look after you and take you through your own Catholic morning worship. I liked this idea so much that I became a Catholic again. I have to say that most of the time when in the classroom, we never did morning worship, but instead we caught up on our home-work that we should have done the night before. So it was great, and I got used to this routine of not doing my home work at home. Because in the mornings when the rest of the school were at assembly, I would go in and either do my homework OR copy somebody else's.

This actually got me into trouble one day however. I said, I always excelled in English studies but my maths always let me down. One morning I arrived at school, having not completed the homework from the night before. I grabbed hold of a good mate and asked him if I could borrow his own work, and he was happy to oblige. I'd done this a few times before and gotten away with it but unfortunately for me this particular homework was quite a difficult piece and only two people in the whole class got the question correct. That was me and my mate who I copied from.

The teacher stood in front of the class holding up our two separate books and praised us both and was so pleased that at least two students in her class had paid attention to what she had said. That is until as she started to look at the contents of the works. Her voice began to falter as she noticed our work was identical. Not just in the answers but the fact that I had even copied every mistake, including crossings out suddenly gave the game away. I saw the expression on her face change in front of the whole class as it became clear that someone here had been cheating. She asked 'did you copy each-others work?' I can honestly say, there was no hole deep enough for me to hide in.

We were duly both sent to the Headmaster Office where I was lucky not to receive corporal punishment and I think the other lad was let off with a warning.

My favourite pastime during these years was tennis, and I used to play this a lot with my friend Chris Berry. I would cycle to the tennis courts every night after school on the bike that I had bought with the wages from my paper round.

I used to do a general paper round in the mornings before school which consisted of the main daily papers and then I would deliver the Gloucester Citizen after school. This was my first real taste at earning my own money. This was really good money. I think the morning paper round brought me in ten shillings a week and the evening citizen round brought me in seven shillings and sixpence. That was nearly a pound a week which wasn't bad money as far as I was aware at that age. Also from that age, my Mum and Dad used to make me pay a small amount for "Housekeeping". I can't remember how much they took but it obviously wasn't very much. Just a small amount to go towards their fags and a drink maybe!!

By the age of about 12 years of age, we bettered ourselves. Mum and Dad had been offered a new council house at 33 Emerald Close in lower Tuffley. The house was not only brand new but also had hot air central heating, powered by oil, which was a real revelation to us. I can still remember the smell of moving into a new house. Newly decorated and so fresh and clean. When we put the blowers on, the heat was bliss coming out of the walls, it was that horrible hot air system that you wouldn't want these days but back then it was bliss.

47

Mum and Dad said the rent was more expensive but it really did feel like we were going right up market as a family.

The house was on a brand new estate and it included a pub called the *Gladiator*. Dad applied for a part time job as barman there, which he was lucky enough to get. I can only imagine that the money from this part time job would come in really useful for us. We had moved to a new a house, earning extra money and things were going really well. The downside if you can call it that was that it now meant I would have to travel around four miles to get to my school instead of the one that I was used to, but not the end of the world.

We used to go down to the pub on occasions and I remember they sold something called a triple decker sandwich, where you get three pieces of bread with a bit of filling in between each slice. Again, I thought that this was very posh. Like most pubs they occasionally did a lock-in, which worked well for a while until my Mum put her foot down with Dad who might come home a bit later than she was prepared for on occasions. They used to have some almighty arguments about this for a while.

I eventually gave up the paper round and got a Saturday job with Woolworths filling up their fruit and veg shelves. Youngsters had to have attained the age of 14 years before you could do this. I was given a big knife for taking the tops off cauliflowers to make them presentable on the shelves. I really enjoyed this job but I must also have cost the company a fair bit of money in the long run. I used to have to put bunches of bananas on the shelf and I wasn't used to seeing bananas much let alone having access to them. I would quite often fill my belly with as many as I could eat and on most days this was probably more than I was putting on the shelves. The big challenge I had was figuring out various ways of how I could hide the skins from the manager so that no one would catch me out.

I have never given it too much thought until recently as I write these memories down and that is that when we were children we never actually went away on holiday as a family. There was a time when I was ten years of age when we went over to Ireland to the Butlins Holiday in Mosney. My Nan and Grandad (on my paternal side) as well as my Uncle Eric came with us. In fact the occasion of us going "abroad" was such a big deal that I remember loads of our neighbours coming out to their garden gates to wave us off. I remember that we had a taxi to take us to Gloucester railway station. The taxi belonged to Mr Nyland and I believe that his family still run a taxi service from along the Finlay Road by the parade of shops.

The Irish sea performed its usual good self in giving us plenty of waves to ride across. There were people being sea sick all over the place. Obviously we never had a cabin and so I stood out on deck for the majority of the time with my Dad and Grandad, admiring the power of the waves. I was lucky and never did get seasick myself.

But this was the only holiday we ever went on. I do not even remember Mum and Dad taking time off their work so that they could be with us during the school holidays. I don't think that we even ever considered that we might all go away from home together to "have a break from the stress". Just not going to school, or not having to go to work in Mum and Dad's case was enough relief from the stress of every day life.

I know I am an old fart now and I can hear my own children shouting at me for saying all this, but I do get annoyed in the hard times that we are all presently facing since the Covid Epidemic, the Ukraine War, and the Cost of Living Crisis (2022), when people complain that they can not "even afford a proper holiday" or "they desperately need to get away and have a proper break as a family". I wonder why this is? I wonder what is missing out of their normal lives that they are allegedly under so much stress living together that the only way that they can de-stress is to fly away on a foreign holiday costing thousands of pounds. I could go on, but I won't. I just genuinely feel sorry for the generations below me who can not find pleasure in just being together without having to spend a fortune on each other to show how much they love them. Here I go again, I can't help it can I? I will stop now before I get into any more trouble.

Chapter Eight

Getting a Job and Moving On

Dad working in a pub gave my Mum and Dad some brave ideas and they decided that they would like to apply to become pub landlords themselves. They applied to Ind Coope with the proposition. I was in my fourth year of senior school and three months short of my sixteenth birthday when we moved from Gloucester to Donnington in Oxford. Mum and Dad had been allocated the *Donnington Arms* as their first pub. If I remember right, we moved in on my sister Dawn's eighteenth birthday and she started work as a barmaid that same day, 20th November 1967. My Grandad had to lend my Mum and Dad their deposit which they had to pay before they could take over managership of a pub. I think this was in case they ran away with the takings or something.

The move to Oxford marked the end of my schooling. I never had time to sit GCE's or any other exams. The move at this time of my education was destroying but there was no other choices open to me. There was no chance of Mum and Dad paying for me to stay in Gloucester whilst I finished my education. Later on in my life, I was determined that my own children would at least have a choice of their own should it be necessary.

At 16 years old I got myself a job at a Tesco store in Oxford, working in the warehouse. I was happy, I had a full-time job and finally earning real wages and yes, still paying housekeeping. I made a great friend in the warehouse, a guy of Indian descent although in honesty, I never gave his race any thought whatsoever. One day when we were talking he asked me if I could get him a job working at my Mum and Dad's pub, so of course, I would do anything to try and help a mate out. He was a bit older than me so his age would not have been a problem. When I spoke with my Dad he asked what colour he was as I had explained that his name was Ahmad, and I explained he was Indian but that if he met him he probably wouldn't even notice the colour as it is certainly nothing I really picked up on that much. I guess I was naïve, as when he turned up to meet my

Dad, he immediately saw his colour and nicely told him that there were no immediate vacancies but he would definitely bear him in mind in the future.

Anyway, my Dad said to me shortly afterwards, "Whatever were you thinking?" Obviously, my mate must have had a darker coloured skin than I thought he had. Dad explained that because of the area we lived in, if he had hired him to work behind the bar, it would have caused a lot of problems with the local neighbourhood. I know it's not right and I hate to think that my Dad thought in this way and in some respects I have to consider that it was a very different era. There is no doubt that it was certainly my first introduction to racism.

Whilst living in Oxford, I experienced my first taste of driving a car, albeit illegally. My sister Dawn had started courting her now husband Richard. He had been a representative for Canada Dry which were used as mixers in the pub. Anyway, Richard's brother, Terry, must have been staying with us for some reason and he drove a Ford Escort Estate. Whatever he was with us for meant that we had stayed up all night (probably drinking). It had just turned to dawn (daylight that is, not my sister Dawn) when Terry suggested that I might want to try driving his car. I was 16 years of age and jumped at the chance. I remember weaving in and out of cars parked both sides of the road and how we got away without having an accident I do not know.

The *Donnington Arms* in Donnington was a very rough pub. Most of our customers had probably been barred from other pubs. We did see some aggravation but one incident in particular stands out. Dad had a barmaid who was being threatened by her partner. She wasn't a young girl. She was probably in her 50's as far as I can remember. Dawn's boyfriend (Richard) and me were nominated somehow to make sure that she got home safely one night. Dad had a rather vicious dog at the time called Jason (more about that later) and we decided to take him with us. We saw the barmaid into her house and her boyfriend was inside. An argument took place and the man ended up threatening me and Richard with our lives. He told us that he had a shotgun and that me and Richard were dead men walking. I was only 16!!! Anyway we are both still here and alive today to tell the story.

As soon as I was old enough i.e. 16 years of age, I got myself a Honda 50cc motorcycle, I think it probably cost me around £50. My mate who Dad had not accepted to work behind the bar, told me about some kind of jobs that were going in the telephone exchanges, and that the money was good.

I applied for such a job with GEC (General Electricity Company). My Dad took me for the interview and I was accepted, I suppose as a kind of apprentice. The only problem was that the telephone exchange that they wanted me to work in High Wycombe which was around 30 miles from my home in Donnington. This did not phase me as I had my Honda 50cc to get me there and back. I remember that it was mid winter and that I had to scrape the ice off the bike before I could start it. It used to start fairly well most of the time but obviously early starts to get me to High Wycombe for 8 am were the order of the day.

My Dad told me that he would lie in bed on a cold frosty morning and listen to me trying to start the bike in order to travel to work. He said that he always felt sorry for me. I on the other hand found the whole situation very exciting. I can't imagine what I looked like but my crash helmet was a Deerstalker with the floppy ears. To me, I looked the business.

I have to tell you that there are some very steep inclines between Oxford and High Wycombe. This required the poor Honda 50cc to alternate between 2nd and 1st gears to get me up them. Sometimes it was all very embarrassing with cars whizzing by me. Modern push bikes these days could have gone faster than I did.

On one occasion, a work colleague had asked me if I could give him a lift to work. I don't rightly remember where he lived now, but I do recall it meant having to ride up this big hill. He had a motorbike licence and so I was able to let him ride pillion. (That's what he told me anyway). To get up this hill I had to put the bike in first gear while it screamed away with everything passing us. I was still wearing my deer stalker crash helmet as well. We must have looked a proper sight.

After just three months of working with GEC in High Wycombe, I heard of exactly the same job being advertised in Oxford where I lived. Just as an explanation, my job that I was being trained up for was the installations of telephone systems in telephone exchanges. I seemed to have lost contact with my Indian friend by now and I can't remember what happened to him.

Anyway, I was accepted by Plessey and continued with my new career in Oxford. The job involved running lengths of cable from one end of the exchange to another. Wiring and soldering the systems appropriately. Installing whole racks into the exchange which included having to wrench the racks up the sides of the telephone exchange. I quite enjoyed the work and worked with some good people.

Obviously being so young, I was the subject of a few practical jokes, one of which I found to be very embarrassing at the time. My crew were lined up in the telephone exchange canteen and a group of them were looking at photographs and making various comments. Being an inquisitive 16 year old I asked if I could have a look at the photos. Someone gave me a pile and before I could look at them, they were deliberately knocked out of my hands and went sprawling all over the canteen floor. I couldn't understand what the joke was until I bent down to start picking them up and found out that they were all hard core porn. There were many comments as I continued to make sure that I had picked everyone up.

With my first wage packet, I wanted to feel grown up. The only way that I could think this would happen was if I started to smoke. Up until this stage of my life I had never smoked a cigarette. Both my Mum and Dad were smokers. I went into a tobacconists without any idea as to what I wanted. I remember that my Mum and Dad used to smoke *Players No. 6* and I didn't want to be like them. No, instead I saw a packet of cigarettes with the face of a Red Indian complete with feather headdress on. They were called *Passing Cloud* and were oval shaped. They also did not have a filter on them and they were rather expensive, especially compared to *Players No. 6*.

If I said that I started to smoke at that stage I would be greatly exaggerating. I used to suck smoke into my mouth and then immediately blow it out again. None of this inhaling into my lungs for me. I never even realised that I was not smoking and to be honest was beginning to wonder what all the fuss was about.

Plessey sent me on a course to Bootle in Liverpool to their main factory. This was my first time being away from home at 16 years of age and staying in a hotel, not knowing anybody else. God knows what the course was about but I did learn one very important thing that was to last me for many years in my life. I watched the instructor chatting away to us. He constantly had a cigarette in his hand. I was fascinated with him as I observed him put the cigarette in his mouth, produce a cloud of smoke, and then inhale it deeply into his body. I then realised where I was going wrong. From that time until many years later, I learned one of the worst mistakes of my life. I started to smoke in the manner in which my instructor had shown me and before too long I was addicted.

One day we had a visit from my Uncle Norman and his partner, Joan. I need to take a minute to explain that 'Uncle Norman' had once been married to my Mother's sister, Aunty Tess. They had divorced, and so Uncle Norman was not a blood uncle, more of an honorary uncle if you know what I mean. Anyway, Joan brought her daughter with them to meet us. I don't know why or how Norman and my parents had kept in touch. Joan's daughter's name was Pauline and little did I know that one day we would be married and have three sons and one adopted daughter between us. They were only visiting for the day and Norman was taking a great interest in Dad being a publican. Again, fate was to bring us all together again in the not too distant future.

From what I remember of living in Oxford it was pretty boring, and I don't seem to be able to recollect any events of particular interest. My main memory is regarding a dog we used to have. I think Dad had only decided to get the dog to deter any unwelcome customers in the pub. We called the dog Jason. Jason was a lovely German Shepherd with a great temperament not a particularly large dog but had a determined bark and growl on him when provoked. Dad used to let him loose behind the bar just so that he could be viewed by the customers.

Unfortunately for Jason, Dad decided to get Jason trained in obedience. There wasn't any real reason for doing this but Dad thought that it would be beneficial. They found a trainer who boasted having trained animals for TV and films and so he seemed to have all of the credentials to fulfil my Dad's requirements for the dog. The trainer took Jason away for a few weeks to train him. This would never happen today because it is a known fact that if you want to train a dog, you train it with its owner. You certainly wouldn't send your dog away for a couple of weeks on its own to be trained like a circus animal.

When the trainer brought Jason back, the trainer demonstrated how obedient Jason now was. Commands to the dog were transmitted not through verbal commands, but by body gestures with his hands. Sure enough Jason walked to heel, he waited and sat and all that kind of stuff without having to say a word to him. But there was something that had changed with Jason. He didn't seem to have the character any more that we all loved before he was sent away for "Training".

When I look back now I still have a guilt feeling for that lovely dog. He turned from being a lovely family pet to being really aggressive and nervous. It absolutely ruined the poor dog. Lord only knows how that scoundrel of a trainer had trained him without verbal communication. All I know is that I wish that I could have been more knowledgeable at the time because I could have shown the so-called dog trainer how to communicate with non verbal communication. In the end we had to make sure that he couldn't be around anyone that he didn't know as he couldn't be trusted to not take a snap at them.

Living in Oxford was a life changing move for my sister, Dawn. We had moved into the Donnington Arms on Dawn's 18th birthday, or very near that date on the 20th November 1967. Dawn instantly became employed as a barmaid and she was so pleased to be a 'grown up' now. This left me, my other sister and brother on our own upstairs away from the bar when they were all busy in the pub. This wasn't as tranquil as it might sound. We never sold hot meals in the evenings then, only rolls and sandwiches. When a customer came in in the evening and requested some type of food, Mum or Dad would shout up to us kids to make it. This was so infuriating when we were in the middle of watching a television programme that we were interested in. There was no pause or rewind buttons in those days either.

Of course product reps used to come into the pub and try to push their products. One day, a tall slim handsome fella came into the bar when Dawn was serving. I imagine that there must have been some sort of instant attraction between the two of them and so this fella invited Dawn out. He turned out to be called Richard and he was a rep for Canada Dry mixers. Always quick off the mark, Mum and Dad soon had Richard employed behind the bar and then eventually I think they called him a trainee manager which meant that he worked for very little money and also afforded my Mum and Dad to take a fair bit of time off for themselves.

Richard used to perform his party piece when he had had a few drinks. He would put two chairs one behind the other and then he would sit in front and generally get Dawn to sit behind him, holding him around his waist as if they were on a motorbike. He then gave a rendition of a song called "Just For Tricks" which was sung by an artist called Mike Sarne. It was very funny and if you don't know it, it is still available on Prime. The start of the song went like this:-

If there's one thing that I like
Its a burn up on my bike
A burn up with a bird upon my bike
etc.

Of course the two chairs were supposed to represent the bike. Brilliant!

In the future, Dawn and Richard would get married and eventually have a pub of their own in Cheltenham. After which Richard would join the Gloucester Police where he became a sergeant until he retired. They got married in Torquay in 1969 and I am pleased to announce that they are still together to this day and have two children, a boy and a girl, although the children are both well and truly grown up now.

At some point Mum and Dad heard that quite a big public house was going to be vacant in Torquay in the not too distant future. The thought of moving to the seaside and managing a pub in a holiday town really excited the pair of them. I have to say, us kids were pretty jubilant as well. They applied through the brewery (Ind Coope) for a transfer to the pub and were so excited to be accepted for the vacancy of the *Abbey Hotel* in Torquay. On the 11th March 1969, we uprooted from Oxford and all moved to the said premises in Torquay. One of the reasons for us transferring was because the new pub was much busier than the *Donnington*, my parents were entitled to a higher wage. I still have my parents Agreement between Ind Coope and themselves for them to take the transfer. It states that my Dad's wage was going to £15 per week and my Mum would earn £3.12.6d per week. We were going to be rich!! Dawn and Richard were still only just courting at this stage and so they both moved with us.

I loved living in Torquay. I had just turned 17 years of age and still too young to serve behind the bar. I had been lucky enough to transfer my job from Oxford to Newton Abbott with Plessey and so I could continue with my job and training. Before too long I had met up with a work colleague who also lived in Torquay and so I was able to scrounge a lift with him on a daily basis from Torquay to Newton Abbott. The old Honda 50cc got relegated to an old garage which was part of the *Abbey Hotel's* property.

One of the really good things about the pub in Torquay was that it was opposite two theatres and lots of the artists used to come over to us for a drink, especially at the end of the evening when they knew that they could get a lock in. One of these artists was Sue Nicholls who first starred in a poor but infamous TV show called *Crossroads*. She later went on to become one of the long running characters in *Coronation Street*, playing the role of Audrey Roberts. She constantly put money in the Juke Box in the pub and over and over again we heard Marvin Gaye singing 'I Heard it through the Grapevine' which she confessed as being her favourite song.

The short time that I lived full time in Torquay was a wonderful experience. To live on the seaside in such a popular area made me feel as if I was on a permanent holiday. My brother Terry got himself a weekend job on the local ferries. I think the same ferries are running to this day.

Chapter Nine

The Moon Landing and Other Strange Things

Around this time, or not too long after, Norman and Joan ended up in a pub just up the road from us. They had applied to a brewery called Plymouth Breweries. In fact their pub was called *The Plymouth Inn*. It was right across the road from the local police station, and of course was frequented by many of the "Plod". Mum and Dad could never understand why they wanted to be managers of a pub because Norman didn't even drink alcohol. My Dad's motto was that if the customers saw you not drinking your own beer, why should they, or more importantly, what is the matter with it. At this time, I didn't really see much of them. I think Dad used to help them out from time-to-time as they were complete novices.

I had started to get restless feet and decided that my whole life career was not going to be with Plessey and so I was on the hunt for a new career. I had gone up to the local Job Centre and I cannot remember if I had an interview with anyone or if I had just strolled in for a look around. Whatever it was, I came away with an application to join the Merchant Navy. I remember coming home from the job centre and saying to my Mum and Dad, "I am joining the Merchant Navy'. I don't know if I should have been insulted or not but they were both really pleased for me.

My Dad told me how envious he was of me. Although he had been in the Royal Navy, he had not travelled abroad very much. Indeed, once he was in the submarine service he didn't have a clue where he had been. He certainly never got to see much of the world and if he had his time all over again, he would love to have joined the Merchant Navy.

By this time, my sister Dawn and her now fiancee, Richard, had decided to get married. This was after many horrible rows at home with Mum and Dad which had resulted in Dawn and Richard moving out of the house and into a local B&B. They got married in the local church in Torquay on the 28th June 1969. I have to say that the atmosphere at the wedding between Dawn and Richard and my

Mum and Dad was not great, but the wedding took place anyway which was the important thing and the point of the whole day.

Norman and Joan had been invited to the wedding which obviously meant also with Joan's daughter, Pauline. They were sat at the back of the church and we didn't get a chance to speak until after the ceremony. Once the ceremony was finished the usual photo session took place and I then had the chance to speak to Pauline. We hit it off really well and I ended up inviting her out somewhere.

When my Mum and Dad found out that I had invited Pauline out, they were not very pleased. They tried desperately to put me off seeing her, I think mainly because of their dislike of Norman who had been married to my Mum's sister after all. The trouble is, when you are a teenager in particular, the more that you are told NOT to do something, the more and more you become determined that that is what you are definitely going to do. It wasn't only Mum and Dad who were against us seeing each other either. Joan and Norman had sided with my Mum and Dad which meant that there was going to be a bumpy road ahead.

On top of all this, my application to join the Merchant Navy was successful and they had immediately given me a starting date for July 1969. I had only known Pauline for about three weeks by this time and so we were not exactly a serious boyfriend and girlfriend.

On the 20th July 1969 I left Torquay to travel to The Merchant Navy National Sea Training College at Gravesend in Kent. This was also a momentous day famously known for the first Moon Landing. Neil Armstrong and Buzz Aldrin had been the first humans to step out on to the Moon. Armstrong had said that, "This is a small step for man, but a giant leap for mankind". Well I can tell you, this was equally as much a memorable day for me and many other youngsters starting their careers in the Merchant Navy. I had travelled by way of a train. I was very nervous and apprehensive as you would imagine. My Mum had made me a pack up for the journey. I can not remember how long the journey was but I think that I had to go into one of Londons rail stations and then catch the another train to Gravesend. It was a lonely old journey and it left me hours to ponder on what was happening in my life. I had just met a girl who I liked, everybody was against us being together, I had no idea where I might be going in the Navy and I worried about being lonely. My head was spinning and I was wishing that I had taken the easy choice and just gone to the moon. By the time I had reached Gravesend I was probably in a right old state of mind.

Do you remember how I told you how my Dad had cried his eyes out in Devonport Dockyard when he was seventeen years of age because he was missing his family and feeling lonely? Well here was I at the same age doing the same thing.

My Mum and Dad bought me a St. Christopher engraved with the words, "To Albert. From Mum and Dad. 21st July 1969". The 21st was my first day of training and the 20th had really only been our travel and Joining day. I cherished my St. Christopher for many years and it was rarely removed from around my neck. For my Mum and Dad to have bought me something like this, it was really something special. In the future I would regularly look at this and remember my Mum and Dad. My sister Aileen had also bought me a writing wallet to put my pen, paper, stamps etc in when I was away so that I could write. I still have that wallet to this very day. It really brings back memories when I look at it.

I was sat at the Railway station at Gravesend waiting for the coach from the College to come and pick me up. At the same time there was another lad of the same age also sitting on his suitcase waiting for the same coach. We introduced ourselves to each other little knowing that we would still be good friends over 50 years later. His name was, and still is, Mick Shaw. We were both pleased to meet someone in the same boat as each other so to speak.

The coach picked us up and took us to the college. On arrival, we were allocated dormitories and given a brief introduction as to what was expected of us during our 10 week stay. We had 4 weeks doing seamanship which included Life boat drills. We had to pass this element of training before we were allowed to continue with our catering course for another 6 weeks. Mick was allocated the same dormitory as me. There were about 16 students to each dorm.

Not all students were taking the course like me and Mick. Some were there to train as deckhands. A few years later, my brother Terry would follow me to the college and would train to become a deckhand. Deckhands also had to complete a longer course than us catering lads. They had to complete a further four weeks after we had left and gone to sea already. By the end of my course, I was glad that I had not opted to be a deckhand.

Prior to Sea Training taking place here at Gravesend, the training was mainly carried out in Sharpness, sixteen miles from Gloucester, on a training vessel called the *Vindicatrix*. Many a time when I was on a car ride out there with my Dad or when we were in the area when I was on my Grandad's boat, I often used to see the students walking to the pictures or wherever. I always used to think that they were 'Naughty Boys' who were made to join the Navy as a punishment. This was because the students were not allowed ashore unless they were in uniform which consisted of navy coloured trousers, blouson and a beret. Now here I was in the same uniform and with the same disciplinary conditions but in a different location. It is a shame in a way that the *Vindicatrix* was not still operational as I would not have had so far to travel.

The Sea Training School became known as the Peanut Factory. Nobody really knows why it had this nickname as that reason was a long time forgotten. The regime at the Peanut Factory was very strict. We had loud speakers throughout the dorms which gave a reveille first thing in the morning. This call announced that we were expected to gather in the parade ground in our classes and await Mail Call. This is when students would be issued with any mail that had been sent to them. After Mail Call we were expected to return to our dorm where we had to make our beds, having been shown how to make them in hospital style. If I remember we then had to attend the canteen for breakfast after which we returned to the dorms and had to polish the floors and literally dust and clean every crevasse. To this end we were supplied with a tin of orange coloured polish which had to be applied to the floor and then buffed to a very high shine. Once we were at breakfast or our first class of the day, an instructor would inspect the dorms including our cupboards. Officially, food was not allowed to be stored in our dorms or it would be confiscated.

My Mum used to send me food parcels. Each one consisted of biscuits, general goodies and of course a few packets of cigarettes. I was always excited and appreciative to receive these lovely packages from home. Not every lad had such parcels and so I did share a fair amount with my new ship mates. The foodstuffs were very carefully hidden from the dormitory inspection.

One of the strict disciplinary regulations were that we would only be allowed to have a certain amount of cash at any time. This was a necessary rule to make all students equal and worked fairly well. Like me, a lot of the students had learned how to smoke and so cigarettes became quite a luxury. We all became close friends and there were very few arguments, and those that did start were soon quelled.

I never had any problems following the strict regime. It came naturally to me and in fact I really enjoyed the whole experience. I had some consternations in life boat drills because some of the routine involved climbing up the structures to get to the boat in order to launch it. The boat we practiced on was hanging over the River Thames. I never did and still do not like anything to do with heights.

Before we were allowed ashore in the evenings, we had to line up on the parade ground in uniform and be inspected by one of our trainers. Shoes had to be polished, creases in our trousers, berets at the right angle etc. Bearing in mind we had next to no money and we were too young to go into a public house. Because we were so recognisable because of our uniforms, there wasn't that much for us to do. We used to like cruising around Gravesend and having a general meander. It soon became apparent that the local youths were not too keen on us. We were labelled with pinching their girlfriends and whatever. Some on our course were only sixteen and I was now 17 years of age, and with no money. I don't think that we were really much of a threat to anyone.

One evening, a group of our students had been into town and been attacked en masse by a group of locals. Some had been badly beaten and the incident had to be reported to all of the local authorities. However, we were young, hot headed youths who then became hell bent on taking revenge for our 'Band of Brothers'. The college authorities had got wind of our intentions and for a few nights our liberty ashore was curtailed.

Then one evening we were allowed ashore. The word had gone around that we were going to get our own back on the locals and that we should try and take sticks or any other type of weapons that we could get our hands on. I have to say that I don't really remember trying to take anything out with me and I am not sure that anyone else risked getting caught in such a compromising position.

There were probably 40 of us or so lined up on the parade ground ready to be inspected before we went shoreside. When the inspection was over and after strict lecture from a member of staff, off we went having been issued with a warning not to to get into any trouble.

We got as far as a bridge on the way into town when we were jumped upon by a large group of locals who had obviously been waiting for this occasion to arise. Mayhem ensued and a very large gang fight commenced. During the confusion, I managed to get separated from my own group and found myself on a bridge with hostiles grouping on me from both ends of the bridge. Apparently, I gave almost as good as I got but inevitably ended up on the wrong end of a good beating.

My friend Mick Shaw remembers seeing me on the bridge fighting for my life but there was nothing at this time that could help me. I ended up getting a good thrashing and then someone decided to throw me over the bridge. There was a river or canal under the bridge and luckily for me, I landed on the deck of a boat, landing head first. I honestly to this day do not remember anything else about the actual assault. I do remember waking up in a police car with blues and twos screaming away and we were on our way to hospital. I next woke up when medical staff were trying to look at me and give me an injection for something. I shouted at the medics to leave me alone and to go and look after the really ill people. Everything after that was and still is a blank. I had been so lucky that a boat had been under the bridge where it was and that people were on board at the time otherwise I may not have been here to tell the story today.

Mick remembers seeing me get cornered on my own in the middle of the bridge. He also saw a couple of the lads throw me over the side of the bridge in to the river and he then lost sight of me. He was trying to find out where I was and how I was when he was pulled aside to be questioned by the police. He said that they confirmed to him that I was safe and had been taken to hospital.

I woke up the next morning with a tremendous headache. I was still in hospital. However I was able to be discharged and go back to the college. The college vicar had come to collect me and take me back. I actually can't remember which religion he was but it didn't make any difference to me at this time. Religion has always been around me in my life even though I am a sceptical believer.

When I arrived back at the college, all of the students were on the parade ground. As I entered the parade ground a large cheer went up and everyone was clapping me. I felt like a hero. Even though I didn't have a clue as to what had happened. Apparently it turned out that I was the only student that had been hospitalised. In fact, out of both gangs, I was the only one that had been hospitalised.

It transpired that whilst we were heading into the town and were jumped by the other gang, a load of our students ran away from the scene altogether leaving just a handful of us to take the brunt of the locals wrath. This was certainly a good lesson in life about being in a gang and NOT being able to rely on your backups

Shortly after arriving back at the college, a couple of CID officers from Kent came to interview me. They were trying to find out if we had gone ashore with weapons, or if we had deliberately gone out to cause a fracas with the local youths. It is amusing really because I could genuinely reply that, "I couldn't remember" because of my memory loss caused by being thrown off the River Bridge and landing on my head on a boat. I never even had to revert to "No Comment".

Having arrived back at the college, I carried out whatever tasks I was instructed to carry out without too much trouble even though I still had a terrible headache. That evening I had gone to bed in my bunk, I was on a top bunk and gone out like a light. The next morning, I awoke to a member of staff banging a big stick against my bunk and shouting at me that I was late for parade. My head had been resting alongside that side of the bunk and so it did not make my head feel too good.

When I looked around the dormitory, I was the only one there and everyone else had reported to the parade ground. I later found out that practically everyone had tried to wake me up but I was literally comatose. I rushed as quick as I could, head really banging away, and got myself to the parade ground and to my class lineup. Of course the staff could not let this lax behaviour go unpunished and I was put on Jankers for a couple of nights. This involved me being denied shore leave and having to wash pots and pans after evening meal in the galley for about a week. I was gutted and felt that the staff could have had some compassion but that was not forthcoming. Rules were Rules.

My mother was very quick to write to the head of the college to complain that they hadn't looked after their poor little lovely son properly. Obviously I was interviewed by the college staff but I always gave the stock reply which was, "I can't remember." I was getting fed up with being asked the same questions as well.

When we had all first arrived at the college, we were not allowed home for the first few weekends as it was supposed to accustom us to being away from home. When we were, I was straight back to Torquay to see my family and then also to pick up with seeing my new girl friend, Pauline.

Having said that, I did not always go home, as much as I missed my Mum and Dad and Pauline. One weekend, Mick and me decided that we were going to have a weekend in London. Mick knew a couple of girls in London and he had arranged for us to meet them. This involved getting permission to stay with my Nan, my Mother's mother. They lived in Tottenham, North London, and even though we never saw them very often, I thought the world of them. They agreed for me and Mick to stay with them although we had to rough it because there were no beds available.

After spending the Saturday in London, we arrived back at my Nan's house. My Nan and Grandad were Irish and their kitchen table was always covered with a newspaper opened to the race meetings which is what they used to enjoy taking a bet on.

The big problem with my Nan's house was that they did not have an inside toilet. The toilet was in the back garden. I am afraid that a 17 year old lad who has had couple of sherbets waking up at all hours of the night is not going to go for a stroll down the back garden just to have a Waz. Especially when there was a perfectly good sink and tap in the kitchen.

I had instructed Mick not to worry about going out to the garden in the middle of the night, and that as long as he ran the tap, it was game on to use the sink in the kitchen. We had both used the sink during the night and thought that we would escape being found out. But first thing in the morning, whilst I was tucked up under blankets on the floor, I could hear my Nan talking to my Grandad. Nan was not amused but I could hear my Grandad saying something like, "They are only young lads, leave them alone". Needless to say that when we left after the weekend, we never went back again!! By the way, I can not remember what happened with the girls either.

I did really well at the college and thoroughly enjoyed it. Even though I had been in trouble, I still felt that the staff thought kindly of me. If you were one of the chosen ones, you could be selected to serve a dinner in what was called The Bamboo Room. This would be on a night time (Instead of going ashore) where you served Silver Service to some senior staff in the various shipping lines. I was lucky enough to get chosen. This was quite scary because it would have been the first time that I had had to perform the task of a Silver Service Waiter to people I did not know, and potentially someone who could be important to me.

The Bamboo Room was one of my last duties at the College and one which, when it was finished at least, I thoroughly enjoyed. Ten weeks after the first Moon landing, and us newly recruited Peanuts all meeting for the first time, we left the college to await a letter from a company to offer us jobs. We never knew if we would ever see each other again. It was a great and interesting experience.

Anybody who has had to work and rely upon a team of people the way we had to at the Peanut Factory will know that strange feeling when you all have to separate and go your separate ways. We were all very pleased that the course had been successfully completed and yet there was the new fear and excitement of not knowing what was going to happen next, but it was time to move on to the next chapter in our lives. Just like listening to "Old Service" personnel though, it is a time that will always be in our hearts with pride and without any regrets.

Chapter Ten

Lost at Sea

Having returned successfully from the Sea Training School I was now back in Torquay living in the *Abbey Hotel* waiting for a letter to arrive to tell me whether I had been offered a job with any of the Mercantile Companies. It was only a matter of days before I received a letter telling me that my pool would be Southampton. This meant that whatever ship I was going to serve on would have Southampton as her Home Port. Anyway they also gave me a date for joining a ship called The Royal Mail Steamship, *Windsor Castle*. This left me a short time at home and so I was able to continue trying to get to know Pauline better and prepare myself for leaving home once again.

One day in October 1969 I left Torquay, still seventeen years of age, suitcase in hand, just like Paddington Bear. I was making my way to Southampton to join my ship. By the way, my joining instructions merely told me where to report to and which ship I was due to join. I had no idea where I would be sailing to or how long I was going to be away for. Was I going to be away for a few weeks or for a few months? I did not even know at this stage whether the *Windsor Castle* was a passenger ship or a cargo ship.

I found my way to the Union Castle House which was located in Canute Road in Southampton. I joined one of many queues to get to a reception desk. I had to produce my Seaman's Card and my Union Card as well as my joining letter. Eventually I reached the reception desk where someone told me that I was to report Berth 104 where the *Windsor Castle* was. All I remember now is that I reached Berth 104 safely, but it seemed like a very long walk with my suitcase in hand. In front of me was one of the biggest and magnificent ships I had ever seen in my life. The hull was lavender and the funnel was red and black. Just across from us on a P&O berth was the newest addition to their their fleet, the QE2. I tell you, the whole thing seemed surreal. I couldn't believe that this was all part of my life. It scared me just a little.

A little bit of information about the *Windsor Castle*: Her length was seven hundred and eighty four feet and her gross tonnage was thirty seven thousand, six hundred and thirty nine tons. She could carry two hundred and forty first class passengers and six hundred and ninety one tourist class passengers. There were one hundred and two deck crew and three hundred and nineteen catering crew. Although she carried all these passengers, her main function was as a Royal Mail Ship between the UK and South Africa and her most precious cargo was the bullion that she carried on every trip. Most of the passengers outward bound were emigrating to or visiting relatives in South Africa.

The *Windsor Castle* was also the Flag Ship of the Union Castle Shipping Company and therefore was proud to have the rank of commodore as the captain. He would have been one of the shipping companies most experienced captains.

It was paramount to the shipping company that the mail between the UK and South Africa arrived on time. The only delays would have occurred during severe weather storms. There is a really amusing and interesting account when a Union Castle mailship, outward bound for South Africa, was leaving the calm waters of the Solent at the time of Royal Navy manoeuvres in the English Channel. The mailship's captain was interrupted on the bridge by a signal received from the Flag Officer of the Royal Navy Squadron. It informed him that his ship was impeding the exercising of His Majesty's Fleet. Without a moments hesitation, the captain dictated his reply: "And you, sir, are impeding the passage of His Majesty's mail." At this, ships of the awesome Royal Navy opened up their columns to make way for the steamship.

As I got closer to the ship I spotted a gangway which I promptly began to climb. One of the ships policemen (they call them MA's which stands for Masters at Arms) spotted me and asked me if I was crew. When I replied in the affirmative, he gave me a bollocking and told me that I should be using the crew gangway. I had been trying to board using the passengers gangway. A good start to my epic journey!

Down I went one gangway and then up I ascended the crew gangway. Another MA was at the top of this gangway who proceeded to check all of my credentials. There didn't seem to be much consideration that this was my first trip and that I was excited and bricking myself all at the same time. This chap was so used to his job that my considerations did not reach his attention.

At the top of the gangway the official told me that I was to report to the Purser's cabin who would sort me out. He gave me several instructions how to get to the Purser's cabin, but that didn't quite work out. He told me to proceed along the deck to the steps and then to go down the steps, turn left, turn right etc. etc. I was absolutely ages trying to find where I was supposed to be going. By the time I found the purser, having had to ask directions from other crew members on the way, I was getting into a right old flap.

Having found my way to the Purser's Office, he booked me in and sorted out the paper work required for me to join the ship. One of the most important items that had to be arranged was what they call an Allotment. The purser assured me that as a respectable and responsible son I would surely want to send my mother home an amount of money each month, even though I wasn't living with them. This was arranged at £8 per trip. My job for the next six weeks was to be a Bell Boy in the Tourist Class Restaurant. The purser also allocated me a cabin number. Directions were given to me to get to my cabin which included going up and around several decks and stairwells to actually get there. Needless to say, I was wandering around the corridors of the ship for a very long time again before someone was kind enough to actually guide me to where I wanted to be. I also had no idea what a Bell Boy was or what my job would be. Happy days.

I was soon to find out that life on board was not as simple as that. I was sat at a desk in a cabin where there were two bunk beds. Four lockers were also provided. By this time I was utterly miserable. When you board what they call a Dead Ship, there is no atmosphere at all. All I had was my loneliness and above that, I still didn't know where the ship was sailing to or how long I was going to be away from home for. Of course I was now wondering what sort of characters I would end up sharing my cabin with.

Whilst I was sat on a chair in an otherwise empty cabin and feeling increasingly sorry for myself, the cabin door opened and three lads came in. In a choice language which I will leave to your own imagination, I was asked what I thought I was doing daring to be in THEIR cabin. I explained that this was my allocated cabin as given me by the purser. They told me to fuck off and to try the cabin next door. I later found out that these lads were laundry boys (i.e. they were responsible for doing the ships laundry, including for the passengers). This encounter did not do much for my confidence and excitement.

I thought it best not to argue at this stage as I was unsure on what was expected from me. I found my way in to the next cabin which was also empty and again sat on the chair by a desk. There was another knock on my cabin door and someone was delivering mail. I had been sent telegrams from my Mum and Dad, which included my sister Aileen and my brother Terry. I also had a telegram from Pauline and also from Joan and Norman. I was twiddling with my St Christopher and I was just about ready to burst into tears. I was thinking to myself:- If one more thing goes wrong I am off this bloody ship like a shot and they won't see me for dust. I really had had enough. I was at an all time low and feeling completely vulnerable and lonely. I was in tears wishing that I was not here and instead in the comfort of my home with my Mum and Dad.

Whilst I had my back to the cabin door and with my emotions running wild, the door opened and I heard a voice say, "Bloody hell Bert is that you, I didn't know you were joining this ship". When I turned around I saw that Mick Shaw had not only been allocated the *Windsor* but now it looked like that we would be in the same cabin. It was such a relief to see a familiar face. After this encounter, the tables started to turn and I was to gradually settle into the ships routines. I have to say that Mick was just as pleased to see a familiar face as I was. My confidence started to return although I still had no idea what I was supposed to be doing next. Bear in mind that I was also on a big ocean going liner and at this stage I had no idea where in the world I was sailing to or for how long I was going to be away from home.

Mick was a bit more knowledgeable than me, having lived in South Africa, and was able to explain to me that we were sailing to South Africa and the trip would take five weeks and four days. We would depart at precisely 4pm on a Friday afternoon and arrive back in port at Southampton on the early morning of a Monday. Well I didn't even know where South Africa was, let alone Cape Town, Port Elizabeth, East London and Durban as our ports of call along what is known as The Garden Route. I had a lot to learn.

Writing letters became a bit of a pastime whilst at sea. My sister Aileen had bought me a writing wallet which contained my pen, writing paper and envelopes. This came with me on every trip (I still have it to this day). I did give it to my brother Terry several years later when he followed me into the Merch, but he has since given it back to me. It was fabulous to receive a letter from family and of course Pauline to fill me in on what was going on back home in the six weeks that I was away. The letters were delivered to the pursers office at each port that we docked and it was just a question of going to his office and asking if there was any mail for you.

Working by on a ship is when there are no passengers aboard, the main engines are not running and the crew are busy getting the ship ready for sailing. On top of this, crew like me and Mick were required to get to know the ship and find our way around. It was hard to imagine what was in front of us at this stage as there was no atmosphere on the ship at all. We used to go ashore in Southampton in the evenings for a drink, even though we were under age, to pass the time away. When we got back to the ship, the Master at Arms was always at the top of the gangway to make sure that crew who were underage, did not bring alcohol on board the ship. This is why we often made friends with older members of the crew until we were old enough to get our own booze on board.

Mick and I were given different jobs. I was given the role of Bell Boy in the Tourist Class Dining Room. What this meant in reality was that I had to be at the beck and call of all of the Stewards. I could not become a Steward until I had attained the age of 18 years old when I would then become a "Rating".

Being a Bell Boy was not all that bad, especially when we were under way, but at this stage I had to report to the Tourist Class Head Waiter. He was a big Irish man by the name of Paddy McAuley. I was responsible for ensuring that all condiments on all of the tables were always full. This alone was very time consuming, but I couldn't wait until I was a Rating and old enough to run my own tables. Every steward was given a table of six and a table of four each sitting. There were two sittings for all meals including breakfast.

As a Bell Boy there were limited ways in which we could earn a little extra money. Obviously because of our ages and our responsibilities, our pay was not great. I managed to earn some overtime by working kiddies Teas and then Afternoon Teas. The Waiters also used to give a Dropsy (Tips) when we reached Cape Town, and again when we returned back to Southampton. The waiters themselves seemed to earn lots of tips by ensuring that their Bloods (Passengers) were kept happy. Bloods was a term used to refer to passengers, I have no clue why this was.

The problem then was, what did we have to eat? Generally when the Galley had cleaned up, there was very little for us to have. This left us with two alternatives. We either ordered extra meals from the galley pretending that it was for a passenger and then kept the food warm on the hot plate. This was not terribly satisfactory, even if you could have steak every day of the week. The other way was to "Drop" a Trainee Chef" to make our meals for us and keep them fresh. Of course this came at a cost. This meant that some of the tips that we received from the waiters, then had to be paid to the Trainee Chef. This was the way that chefs made their dropsies. It was a real merry-go-round with money. It was in one hand and out the other.

The Silverware was not supposed to be passed through the big press (one big washing up machine), but sometimes, time was really urgent and one of the operators would allow us to pass the silver through the machine. This came at a cost of course. You guessed it. We also had to pay them from our own tips. Our wad of money from tips was slowly being re distributed.

Outside of the restaurant, my other role was that of 'Runner" at lifeboat stations. Lifeboat drills were compulsory and had to be carried out once on the outward bound journey and once when we were homeward bound. All passengers and crew were given the number of allocated life boats and when the drill was called we all had to attend with lifejackets at the allotted lifeboat.

Once everyone had arrived, it was my task to run up to the bridge with a disc to say that everyone was present. That disc would then be placed on a board and the commodore would be able to see that the drill had been completed. Down I would run back to my station when the call would go out to say that lifeboat drill was complete. I would then have to run back up to the bridge with a different coloured disc to let the commodore know that all passengers had returned to their own devices. This doesn't sound too arduous except that the *Windsor Castle* had the title of having the highest bridge in all of the UK mercantile fleet at that time. For this I never earned any extra money, nor tips.

Chapter Eleven

Bon Voyage

And then the whole thing culminated in one of the most exciting times of my life. The passengers had boarded, the engines were running and it was 4pm on a Friday afternoon. I was so busy that I hadn't even realised that we had cast off and were on our 6000 mile journey to South Africa at an average speed of 22 Knots. When someone had informed me that we were underway, I looked out of the port hole in the galley and could see the shore line of the Isle of Wight with sea between us. I then began to realise that there was no escape and that I was being carried away on a journey and that I had no idea what was going to happen. I had butterflies, I was so scared and yet I was also so excited. I was at sea!!!

I was soon to learn that just because I was working in the Tourist Class Restaurant, this did not mean that the service to our passengers would be inferior to the First Class Passengers. The Head Waiter expected a high standard for his restaurant and his waiters, including the Bell Boys. The main difference was that in Tourist Class we had to run two sittings for each meal, whilst First Class only had one sitting. This gave a more relaxed and leisurely feel to meal times for the first class passengers.

In between each sitting, he would inspect the restaurant to ensure that it was ready for the "Bloods". This included inspecting the glasses for any smudges. The cutlery was silver and had to be shining, but in particular, the table cloth had to be immaculately clean. As you can imagine, after the first sitting, there were often small stains left on the table cloth. Many a time I have seen a steward gearing up for his second sitting when the headwaiter paid a visit. If the cloth was stained, the headwaiter used to just pull the cloth, cutlery glasses included, and throw it to the deck. The poor (Lazy) steward then had to quickly get a clean cloth and re lay his table before his next set of 'Bloods" arrived. Quite often this is when the Bell Boy came in to their own and assisted the Steward. The language from the headwaiter, in the absence of passengers, was not very polite either.

Our first stop was at Las Palmas. Having left Southampton on the Friday before, we would then reach Las Palmas the following Monday after having spent a couple of days at sea. Can you imagine how I was feeling at this time? I had never been abroad before and here I was, on my own making my own friends, doing whatever I wanted to do without Mum and Dad being there to guide me. Of course, over a matter of time this also included making my own mistakes and dealing with them in my own way. I had experienced being away from home before, but I could always run back home if I needed to. This was different. Very very different. Apart from going to Butlins in Mosney in Ireland many moons ago, this was my first ever trip abroad. I was seventeen years of age and I was without my Mum and Dad.

I managed to get a couple of hours off at Las Palmas and get a run ashore. I was with Mick and we explored as much as we could in the time permitted before Afternoon Teas. One of the 'must buys' in Las Palmas was a traditional dressed Spanish Doll. Someone must have made a fortune producing these things. Anyway I remember being compelled to buy one for Pauline. I also once bought a small wine barrel which were also popular. The barrel was only big enough to hold one bottle of wine but before you added the wine to the barrel, it was recommended by the seller to keep it filled with water for a while so that it would adjust accordingly to having something wet in it. I had bought this barrel for Pauline's Uncle Len and Aunty Doris who were two lovely people and also the ones who took Pauline in when she had fallen out with her Mum and Norman. They lived in Waltham Abbey in North London.

When I got home I presented the barrel to Doris and Len and they were very impressed that I had thought of them. I explained the business of having to fill it with water first. I perhaps should have filled it with water when I first bought it. In the not too distant future I met up with them both again and they were amusingly annoyed at me because they had put the water in the barrel, put the barrel on top of their TV as an ornament (It did look nice), but unfortunately when they got up the next morning the barrel was empty and the TV was full of water. Oh well, win some, lose some eh?

We had also been given the tip that it would be beneficial to buy our Bacardi from here. The trouble was that Mick and I were still too young to take alcohol on board the ship. We were able to get around this by asking our friends who were older ratings to take the alcohol aboard for us. In Las Palmas, we would pay ten shillings (50p) for a litre of Bacardi. The reason for buying our alcohol here was that the clubs that we were going to frequent in South Africa only sold soft drink. They allowed you to take your own alcohol in with you. The club would supply the glasses. This in effect meant that we paid a fortune for our soft drinks!

After our run ashore at Las Palmas we then had a 9 day period at sea. This time was magical and I loved it every trip. Because I was working there were times when the only way that I could see outside the ship was through a porthole, but to go on deck and to look out to sea with no visibility of land around us was just a dream come true. I knew that I was so lucky at 17 years of age to be here doing what I was doing compared to what most other lads my age would be doing. I appreciate that to some, this may be their worst nightmare, but to me, well, it has stayed with me for the rest of my life.

I have often heard people who have served in the military saying how their time serving, was such a special time for them. The discipline and having to rely upon each other was instilled upon them. Well, we were not Military as the Merchant Navy is generally a civilian career, but our discipline and the fact that we had to live with, and rely upon each other 24/7 was exactly the same. It was surely an environment for adventure and making good friends; friendship that would last for over 50 years.

Watching a ship leave port was also a very special occasion. Passengers would throw streamers to friends and family on the quayside. Both would hang on to their end of the streamer until the ship had drifted too far from the quay for them to continue holding on. This was always such a moving moment and sometimes it made me feel quite sad wondering if these people would ever see each other again. Quite often there would also be a band playing suitable tunes that would help create a very nostalgic atmosphere for all concerned.

There is a ceremony which most people have heard of known as The Crossing of the Line Ceremony. This requires all people who had not crossed the Equator before to undergo a certain ritual. Well events were held for passengers which were great fun. A telegraph pole would be extended across the swimming pool and passengers would sit on the poles and drag themselves half way across so that they were facing each other. Each would be holding a pillow stuffed with feathers. The idea basically was for them to have a pillow fight and would try to knock each other into the swimming pool. The contestants would also be in some kind of fancy dress, such as being a pirate, or a baby in a nappy, that sort of thing.

On the other hand, crew members had to endure much rougher and arduous ceremonies. I had heard some of the stories and I determined that I would not be a victim to this stupidity. Of course Mick had Crossed The Line before and so this did not apply to him. I caught hold of this concept and when I was asked if this was my first time for Crossing The Line, I would always reply with confidence, "No, I have been across loads of times before." It worked. I never did get caught for some of the barbaric rituals!!

During the 9 day crossing to Cape Town, there were times when I was on deck looking out to sea and observing the Flying Fish that would keep pace with the ship and swim alongside us. There were also porpoise who would do exactly the same thing raising their backs out of the water as they swam to keep up with the pace of the ship. It was as if they were providing us with an escort. The wonders of the sea are fascinating and at this time, I was part of that wonderment. I felt so honoured and humble.

Chapter Twelve

Prejudices

My first arrival at Cape Town was also so very exciting. I was actually down below in the galley doing some type of work when I heard someone say that we were arriving in port. I looked out of a port hole and I could see Table Mountain which looked enormous. The sun was shining brightly and the atmosphere around the ship was electrifying as some passengers would be disembarking at this point. I was pinching myself and thinking how did a nobody Gloucester Boy end up being here where I am right now. I couldn't wait to get myself ashore to explore. There were also a small amount of new passengers joining the ship who were travelling along the coast to either Port Elizabeth, East London, or Durban and so this would mean that we may have to get used to some new Bloods. This was the first part of the journey where the crew might be able to get some time off to take a proper run ashore.

We never had too long on the outward journey to go ashore as our stay in port was just one night. However, there was a cafe on the waterfront which ended up being a regular haunt for me and my pals to meet up. Mick wasn't doing the same job as me and so I would possibly not see him at all during the daytime. Whilst I was kept busy in the Tourist Restaurant, he was busy delivering telegrams and working the lifts and different other things like that. We did manage to meet up fairly regularly in the cafe at the end of the pier which was the common meeting place for everyone.

At this cafe, we met a few of the local girls and inevitably made arrangements to meet up on our down coast journey. The popular haunts were two night clubs. One called The Spurs and the other was The Navigators. These were to become our main night time activities whilst visiting Cape Town.

The Spurs had a balcony running along the top of it. From the balcony over the dance floor, was a net stretching the length of the room. These days you would probably think that this was for releasing balloons on a special occasion. But in those days, it was for catching sailors who had had an argument and were thrown over the side. The net would catch them and stop them falling to the floor and breaking their necks. During my times going backward and forward, I did see a few lucky sailors getting caught in the net.

This was my first time in South Africa though and I had never heard of Apartheid let alone understand all of the politics involved in it, but I would soon start to understand a little bit.

As I said, Mick knew Cape Town a little bit and was more aware of its politics having lived out there for quite a while. We had gone out, probably with a group of other lads, for a walk around Cape Town. Mick was explaining that we couldn't go upstairs on a bus because that was for blacks only. There were parks with notices saying either 'Blankes' or 'Non-Blankes' I soon learned that this meant "whites or non whites". This kind of changed my feelings a little bit whilst walking around and trying to take in the sights, sounds and smells of this beautiful new city. With the excitement within me, I was now also sensing a feeling of apprehension and possible danger. It was very difficult for me to try to understand. Apart from my friend trying to get a job in my Dad's pub, I had never encountered discrimination on colour grounds before.

Even the taxis displayed "Blankes or Non Blankes". Anyway we had been wandering around Cape Town for the first time for a while when inevitably, the Tonks bladder took hold and I required to have a leak. I spotted a toilet and just wandered in without reading any of the notices outside. Why would I? I came from Gloucester. I was at the urinal and I stood alongside a black man who was relieving himself, as I was. I did notice him looking at me strangely but by this time in my life, I never took any notice of it. I did the usual manly thing whilst holding my willy in my hand next to this stranger and remarked how wonderful the weather was outside. When I exited the toilet block, Mick was outside all agitated asking me what I thought I was doing. I just replied that I had gone for a waz. Mick then pointed out that I had gone in a Non Blankes only toilet. I was beginning to see the ugly side of this beautiful country, even on my first visit.

After leaving Cape Town, our next port of call would be Port Elizabeth, East London and then up to Durban. Each port was amazing in their own right. East London was probably the cleanest looking and relaxing place along the route. We managed to get ashore at each location but invariably we never had long because after all, we were supposed to be working.

Durban also is a really unforgettable place to visit. A brand new terminal was recently constructed to cater for the passenger liners. This was called Ocean Terminal. If I remember right, this meant that passengers could disembark as if they were on an aeroplane today, rather than have to negotiate the gang way which could at times be rather steep to climb up and down to say the least. We actually had two full nights here, as we had two full nights in Cape Town on the Homeward leg. Durban is where I encountered the Zulus.

The Zulus used to run a rickshaw service for tourists. They would be dressed in full ceremonial dress with the head feathers etc. They looked absolutely fantastic. We learned that we didn't always need money to pay them for a journey. Quite often they would take towels from the ship in payment. Game on! The *Windsor* used to lose a few towels going along the coast!! Of course we never used our own towels for this service.

Each Rickshaw would carry up to two people at a time. The Zulus trick would be to pull you along until they reached a downward hill. They would then jump in the air, and with their feet dangling in the air, would let the Rickshaw find its own way along the road, gathering speed as it did so. We were then free wheeling along the road with our heads practically a foot or two above the surface of the road. Whilst floating in the air, our driver would also be letting out some loud warbling noises in a kind of war chant. Quite exciting, exhilarating and on occasions, frightening.

You daren't try to just take a photograph of them either. Although I never had a camera at this time. If they saw a camera, they would start their negotiations for the price of you being able to take their photos. And who would blame them? I do wish that I had been more into photography in those days. There is so much that I can no longer look back on. Of course, digital photography was unheard of.

Unless your job required you to, the crew were not allowed to mix with the passengers on board the ship. Anyone who might perhaps have amorous inclinations with a passenger and then got caught in a passenger's cabin was charged with 'Interfering with the ships cargo' and then instantly dismissed, probably to be transferred to the nearest Union Castle ship when available in the direction of Southampton. Most of the crew like myself were having such a great time on board that this was definitely not something that we would contemplate in fear of ruining our careers.

Whilst on board, the crew used to meet and get entertained in the crew's bar which we used to call *The Pig and Whistle*. This got shortened to *The Pig*. As a 17 year old Bell Boy this was so frustrating, especially for me having been living in a pub back home and drinking whatever I wanted to. Under 18 years of age we were not allowed to drink alcohol on board the ship. This would result in instant dismissal. We therefore had to attend T*he Pig* drinking soft drinks. The favourite drink amongst the ratings appeared to be lager and lime. This may sound a strange drink, but when you think of some of the work that the crew carried out, this was a very thirst-quenching drink. I used to look at them whilst they were drinking thinking that I couldn't wait until I was old enough to partake of the same thing.

Amongst the crew generally, there was loads of talent. I have to say that The *Windsor* was very male orientated and so the talent was quite limited. We had some great singers and musicians to entertain us. Sometimes I think that some of the talent was probably better than what the passengers were getting. The only problem with this was that after nearly six weeks away from home, the entertainment started to become a little monotonous. And after a few trips with the same entertainment - what can I say?

Because I was in the Merchant Navy one of the obvious scenarios that I would have to encounter was the presence of the gay community. I was just a young lad who grew up in Gloucester and as far as I was aware, I had never encountered a homosexual before. We mixed together as you would expect us to, as we were working alongside each other all day and socialising with each other when off duty. Once the gay community knew that you were heterosexual they never hassled you, even when we were young 17 year olds. I remember one night when a crowd of us were drinking on board and generally socialising, when "Shirley" asked me if I was gay, and when I replied in the negative, she replied "Oh what a waste". I should have been flattered I guess. We were all just goods friends and that was that. To this very day I am not the least interested in the sexual orientation of a person. If they are a kind and considerate person, that does it for me.

Chapter Thirteen

Stormy Seas

I loved meandering around the coast of South Africa on board the *Windsor Castle*. The route up along the coast is commonly known as 'The Garden Route.' Cruising along the coastline almost felt as if I was on holiday instead of working. That is except when the Cape Rollers decided to rock the boat occasionally so to speak. On one such occasion whilst trying to enter the port of Port Elizabeth, we had encountered heavy swells which had begun to be felt quite strongly within the ship. We had already been delayed by a few hours from leaving East London because of adverse sea conditions. Unfortunately for us, because we were entering a port, the ship had had to take its stabilisers in. Stabilisers would normally have kept the ship from rolling about too much when the weather got too bad.

At this time I was taking a rest between lunch and afternoon teas which was the normal routine. My bunk was always the top bunk which is where I was looking out through the open port hole to where the sea meets the horizon. Another of my cabin mates was also on his bunk, although he had the bottom bunk just below the port hole. The port hole was open as the weather was so hot as they were all amongst the crews cabins. Our cabins were almost on the waterline. As I watched the horizon, the sky suddenly disappeared and all I could see was a wall of water. At the same time instead of laying on my bunk, I was almost standing up. In a split second the sea poured in through the port hole and into the cabin with a great gush and the water completely soaked everything within the cabin. As I say, I was on my top bunk looking out to sea but my poor cabin mate had been having a crafty sleep and was unaware of what was happening. He had a rude awakening as the sea poured over him from the porthole and he appeared to be slightly scared and nervous. He looked like a flapping fish out of water. Had it not been a bit concerning at the time it would have been rather funny to watch.

We could hear crashing and smashing going on all around the ship and knew that we were either in proper trouble, or at least there was going to be some serious damage. The ship rolled one way and then the other, gradually decreasing in the degree of listing until finally it became stabilised.

Apart from closing our own port hole, several of us ran along to the other cabins to make sure that everyone else had closed theirs as well. I then proceeded to my work stations to see what damage had been caused and to see what there was for me to do. On inspection of the restaurants and galley it was clear that a lot of crockery and glasses had been smashed. All of the tables that had been laid in preparation for afternoon teas had been wrecked and everywhere was just a right royal mess. The bar area was awash with the smell of alcohol where bottles had become dislodged from their shelves and just landed and smashed on the deck.

Would you believe that even whilst we were trying to re-lay the tables and to clear all of the glass and other debris from around the floor space, passengers were queueing to come into the restaurant for their teas as if they were unaware of how close the ship had been to actually rolling over into the Atlantic Ocean. It was a very good learning point for me to discover how the human brain can react so differently from one person to another. Of course they were the passengers and I was merely an employee of the *Union Castle Line* who was paid to ensure that all passengers were able to enjoy their journey with us. The whole incident was reported in the local newspaper with a headline of "Struggle to Catch Runaway Piano". The article described our dilemma with trying to enter Port but concentrated on a report of a piano coming loose in one of the lounges, which of course could have caused serious injury if someone had been unfortunate enough to get in the way whilst it slid from one side of the ship to another.

Whilst I am talking about passengers queuing up to get into the restaurant after this incident, it reminds of how much the South Africans enjoy their food. It was not uncommon for them to look at any of the menus presented to them, Breakfast, Lunch or Dinner, and just say, "Yes please, I will have everything." The poor stewards would collect the meals from the galley and then serve it to the passengers. This would include ALL of the different meats and vegetables etc. would be balanced on the same plate. The plates used to be piled so high that it was almost impossible not to spill food all over the place. This included the sweets, which could have some sort of pudding which required a custard, whilst at the same time, putting a portion of ice cream on the top of it.

As I have already described, the Head Waiter always prided himself on running a first class restaurant, even though it was the Tourist Class Restaurant. It was not too long before the headwaiter put his foot down and said that we were not to carry out this practice (All food stuffs on one plate) any longer. He would only allow a passenger to order one meal at a time. This required the waiters to be diplomatic and explain to the passengers that they could indeed have everything on the menu, as is their want, but they must be eaten separately and that the Headwaiter had banned us from walking through the restaurant with overloaded plates. Believe it or not, this did extend the meal times on occasions when passengers would take us up on the offer.

I remember once when we lost a lot of precious time on our journey because we had to search for a male passenger who had somehow become lost overboard. I can't imagine how this happened as the side rails were all standard height and it would have taken some type of effort to actually go over the side. When someone was lost overboard, the ship had to turn around which alone takes some time. It then has to travel for six miles in the opposite direction whilst zig zagging. It then turns around and zig zags in the opposite direction. That's my understanding of it anyway. I forgot to mention that we were somewhere around the Coast of South Africa in shark infested waters. The chances of finding anyone alive were pretty remote. By sheer luck we found the survivor all in one piece, after several hours of searching and so were able to continue with our travels. When the man was interviewed by the media when we reached shore he was asked what he was thinking when he saw the ship disappearing over the horizon. He replied that he was thinking, "I wonder what they are having for dinner tonight." Unbelievable!!

There was one other occasion that I particularly remember where the state of the sea made itself known to me. During another break from the restaurant I was laying on the deck taking in some lovely sunshine with a couple of the other Bell Boys, one of which was Mick

Shaw. We were somewhere around the South African Coast. The crew recreation area on board the ship was right up on the bow of the ship. On this particular occasion the sea was like a mirror without a ripple to be seen. The sun was pouring on to us and we were getting really relaxed before we had to report for duty once more. All of a sudden there was a small thump in the bow of the ship almost as if we had hit something except the ship just continued forward. Unbeknown to us a trough had opened up from nowhere and we had dipped into it. This caused a huge wave to break over the bow of the ship and to swamp the deck of the ship where we were enjoying our well earned spell of rest and recuperation. By the time we gathered our thoughts together and looked back over the side of the ship, the sea was settling down again as flat as a pancake with just the hint of a ripple. As that part of the ship could be seen from the bridge, we could only imagine that the commodore and the bridge personnel would have been able to have a right good laugh at our expense.

Chapter Fourteen

The Abbey Hotel

In between trips I had always gone back home to Torquay to see my family and of course to continue my relationship with Pauline. I had always loved going back home because The *Abbey Hotel* was a really busy pub. I even helped out on the front door sometimes when the pub was so full that Dad had to restrict entry. It would be that as two customers left the pub, the doorman could let two more in from the queue. Someone always had to be on the door and Dad had to sometimes employ someone to do it.

Dad got really worried and concerned at one time when the Queen had been visiting Torbay in order to Review the Fleet which is a really big occasion. This is where the Monarch literally sails up and down ranks of Royal Navy ships on the Queens barge. Any available ship belonging to the Royal Navy was assembled. This in turn meant that there were thousands of Royal Navy sailors itching to get ashore and have a good time once their official duties had been completed. I was not at home when this happened but Dad couldn't wait to tell me when I got home. As I said, there were restrictions on the number of people allowed in to the *Abbey Hotel*, this was because the main bar was on the first floor and consisted of one large room. Outside the pub, the local constabulary had deployed lots of extra police officers to control the situation and they were accompanied by the Provost, officers who are the 'Police' for the Navy.

The pub was packed and there were lots of sailors and inevitably, lots of local girls all in good spirit if not a little loud as you would expect. Dad had called time, which in those days was 10.30pm and everyone should have been cleared of the pub by 11pm as required by law. By 11.30pm the pub was still packed, sailors stood on tables and singing songs at the top of their voices. Dad became worried because he knew that there were so many police officers outside and he was more worried about keeping his licence for the pub than anything else.

Dad went out and spoke to someone from the local constabulary and was advised that provided the sailors were not causing any trouble, it might be prudent to just let them carry on and just try to clear them out without agitating them. I think that there was some sort of unwritten agreement between the Provost and the Local Police. This cleared my Dad as far as the licensing laws were concerned.

It had gotten around to 12.30am and Dad and his staff by this time were getting a little tired and really wanted to just get rid of them all. A sailor approached Dad and said to him "If I got rid of this lot for you in half an hour, is it worth a free drink tomorrow?". Dad told the sailor that he didn't want any trouble and that as long as the police were happy, so was he. Although if the sailor could get rid of the crowd in half an hour, without any trouble, it would certainly be worth a free drink.

Dad told me that he couldn't believe his eyes when he saw the sailor start to do a dance called the conga. He started this dance and moved around the room with people joining on the end of the dance queue. Lo and behold Dad watched as the whole pub disappeared within the half hour and were last seen doing a very large conga along the promenade of Torquay. I would love to have been there to see this. Trust an ordinary common matelot to come up with a simple solution to a big problem.

Apparently that sailor did come into the pub the next day to claim his free drink. Dad said he let him drink as much as he wanted because it had been such a relief to clear the pub that night but especially without any trouble being caused. He was a star, whoever he was.

Something else had also happened whilst I was at sea. Pauline had had some large disagreement with Norman and her mum Joan and had decided that she was now going to move to North London and live with her Aunty Doris and Uncle Len. I forget what the argument was about but I suspect that it had something to do with our relationship. Anyway, Pauline moved to Enfield where she remained, which of course caused me some difficulty when I only had 8 days between trips and I of course wanted to see my Mum and Dad and my brother and sisters at the same time. My trips home would now become split between seeing my family and seeing Pauline.

Generally, I would travel back home at the end of a trip. I needed to give my Mum some duty-free cigarettes and my Dad a bottle of something. Coals to Newcastle seems an appropriate saying at this time. Mum would have made a great chaperone. You can imagine how busy the pub was and of course that attracted mostly young people hell bent on having a good night out. A group that I must have gotten to know invited me out to one of the clubs in Torquay once the pub had closed. There was no reason for me to refuse and I fully intended to join them. When I told my Mum what my intentions were, she told me that if I did go out then she would have to tell Pauline that I was messing her around. I never quite understood her reasons for telling me this but I can confirm that I never did go for a good night out whilst on my own in Torquay.

You know how earlier on I had told you how my young brother Terry was abused by me and Edward Foote? Well his abuse did not end at that stage of his life. When my Mum used to work behind the bar, she often found that her life was too busy to waste time in tidying her own hair to present herself to the public. To assist her, she had started to use wigs which she could just pop over her own hair before dressing up for her customers.

Unfortunately she still did not find the time to tidy her own wigs up. My Mum realised that only a hairdresser could fluff her wig up enough to a presentable standard. But again, my Mum never found the time to go backward and forward to the hairdressers. However, she also had an ideal solution to her predicament. Good old Terry.

Terry was only about ten years of age when he was detailed off to put my Mum's wig on top of a polythene "head" to keep it in shape, and then to walk up through the main street of Torquay to the hairdressers for them to do whatever was required.

Poor young Terry has told me over the years how distressed he was having to carry Mum's head up to the hairdressers and then collect it again once it had been tidied up.

The strange thing is that if you were to speak to Terry today, he seems to be quite normal which is quite an achievement considering how he was brought up.

Chapter Fifteen

Mates

I had travelled about four trips on the *Windsor Castle* as Bell Boy when I turned 18 years of age and therefore became a fully fledged Steward. My next trip saw me signing back on the Windsor now being responsible for my own tables. One table of six passengers and another table of four passengers and for two sittings. I then had to change cabin which would mean that I would have to leave the companionship of my old cabin mates like Mick, who was a couple of months younger than me, and make new friends yet again.

I was lucky and fell in with some lads who would also remain my good friends for more than 50 years. They are Roger Ingram, Ricky Dodds and Chris Webb. Roger was a trainee chef and Rick and Chris were both employed in the First Class Restaurant. Poor old Mick, left to his own resources, was on deck when we landed in Las Palmas and some laundry boys were there also. The laundry boys had thought that it would be fun to fill some balloons with water and then throw them from the ships deck on to taxis and cars parked on the quay. You can imagine the damage that was caused to the cars when they did this. Unfortunately, the ship's policemen (Master at Arms) took the names of all of the lads who were on deck at the time and when it came to signing back on the *Windsor* for the next trip, they were all told that they could not be employed on the *Windsor* and should find another ship. Mick was really peeved but the "authorities" were not open to discussion. Mick then joined the *Canberra* and I never saw him again for a very long time. It is a strange coincidence how we met again in the future. More of this later on.

The cabins used to stink of all of the deodorants and aftershaves and hairsprays that we all used. Everyone sprayed Cossack on to their hair. This was in effect a man's hairspray. The aftershave was always Brut which was well advertised by Henry Cooper at some point. Can you imagine how much a small cabin must have smelled with all this spraying going on. The rule of the cabin was that if you ran out of any of the sprays, you just raided someone else's locker and helped yourself to their supplies. The same also applied to cumber bands. For anyone who does not know what a cumber band is, it is like a wide belt worn around the midriff thereby hiding the line between a shirt and the top of your trousers. We all preferred to wear them but we never really discarded them very tidily after a tour of duty. This sometimes required us to raid someone else's locker to find another one for our next tour of duty.

Rick was the cabin mate who brought his own record player on board. The record player would be placed on the desk area of the cabin. We continually played the same records it seemed, trip after trip. The most favourite two that I remember at that time were Simon and Garfunkel *Bridge Over Troubled Water* and the Beatle's *Let It Be* albums. On top of that we had groups like Marmalade which were played in the night clubs and I got on everyone's nerves because I kept playing *Baby Make It Soon*, which was a really corny song. This was also about the time that the Beatles had announced that the group was breaking up.

The record player would also be surrounded with beer cans, not just any ordinary beer beer cans though. No, these were Tennants beer cans and each one was printed with a scantily dressed lady in swimwear and each can showed the supposed name of the model. As you can imagine it became a hobby to try and collect each and every model that was shown on the cans. We would line the cans up along cabins desk.

This reminds me of how we sometimes used to get two cans of beer for nothing. The beer packs had to be manually brought on to the ship from the shoreside. To do this a human chain was formed up from the quay on to the gangway and into the cold store. The reward for assisting with this was to be given two tins of the beer. It didn't take too long as there were usually plenty of volunteers. Of course Bell Boys were exempt as they were not allowed to have alcohol on board ship. I have to say that when I was a Bell Boy, this rule never stopped me from getting an alcoholic beverage whenever I needed one. It also paid to get the ratings on your side by helping them out in the restaurants and then they in turn would supply the alcohol to the Bell Boys.

Helping each other out was the way that we all carried out our duties whilst at sea. This can be illustrated in one incident that has stayed in my memory for some reason. One of the "Queens" (the name given to the Gay community), whose chosen name was Sharon, was a steward in the tourist class restaurant and was engaged to his boyfriend. Unfortunately his boyfriend was serving on another ship. However, the *Windsor*, and the boyfriend's ship, were due to be in Cape Town both at the same time. When they managed to see each other, the boyfriend had told Sharon that he no longer wanted to remain with him and that their engagement was off. Poor old Sharon was in a right state and took to drinking and literally became a total wreck and was unable to carry out his restaurant duties. This put the head waiter in a bit of a spot but all of the stewards who were stationed around Sharon's table decided that they could look after Sharon's Bloods for a while until he was fit and could return to duty. The Headwaiter allowed this arrangement and at some point Sharon was back on form and undertook his full duties again.

To get to the Restaurant from the galley we had to enter a revolving door which would on occasions become quite entertaining, when a steward could be carrying quite a lot of plates and food on his tray. This would be when a poor steward had misjudged the swing of the doors and got himself trapped between a door and the wall. Food, plates and whatever else would crash to the floor and the crew in the galley would always find it to be hilarious and would shout and clap so that all of the passengers could hear them, whilst the head waiter would not be at all amused. There was a term we used for such an incident and that was when someone had "Thrown a Wobbly", and was another example where Bell Boys came into their own by clearing up the mess which allowed the steward to carry on looking after their Bloods.

The crew were sometimes treated to a film night in the crew's canteen. We used to be able to watch some of the most up-to-date films. The steward who looked after this side of the ship's routine was called a Pig Steward. The Pig Steward would arrange the mess and stack all tables up one end and then lay the chairs out for the crew to view the film. The film would generally start at a time where theoretically all stewards should have finished at their stations.

There were odd occasions when a crew film was scheduled to be shown, when the Bloods would just want to sit and talk well after dinner which would get really annoying as we couldn't leave them, or re lay the table around them to get ready for breakfast. Often we would strongly hint that we would appreciate it if they departed the restaurant so that we could go and watch the film. On one occasion a couple of male passengers had heard that I was wanting to attend a crew film and found it funny to sit at my table as long as they could, just to annoy me. Even my mates were lining up to get ready to help me to lay the table in a rush to get to the film. The two passengers chanced their arm just a little bit too long on this occasion and in the absence of the head waiter and his deputy, a group of us picked the chairs up that the passengers were still sat in and took them outside the restaurant and tipped them out. At this point I should say that the passengers were also game for a laugh otherwise we would not have got away with it.

On arrival back home at the end of a trip, my shore leave was now split between going back home to Torquay for a few days and then spending the rest of my leave in Enfield with Pauline at her Aunties. I really got on well with Pauline's Uncle Len and Aunty Doris as they were really great people. They were also very protective of Pauline as she was still only 17 years of age at this time, as was I. I always felt guilty only seeing my Mum and Dad for only a few days as much as I also felt guilty for only seeing Pauline for only a few days. My eight days at home became very busy all of a sudden.

Chapter Sixteen

Contraband

Mostly I would always go home to see Mum and Dad first and then travel back up to Enfield to stay with Pauline before getting the train back down to Southampton. I used to hate leaving Enfield to rejoin my ship. I had to catch the all night Mail Train which travelled overnight from Waterloo down to Southampton. The train was cold and because it was a mail train, it stopped at every station on the way down to Southampton. The train did not leave Waterloo until around 1am and would not get to Southampton until around 7am. By the time I got back on board it was time for me to start work all over again. The ship was still a Dead ship as this would have been a Wednesday morning and we did not sail until 4pm on the following Friday. Most of us crew would arrive back on board about the same time as we all had lots of preparation prior to sailing, but arriving back on board a dead ship before anyone else was there was very lonely.

Mostly I used to get a taxi from Enfield to Waterloo but on one occasion Pauline's cousin, Butch, offered to drive me there which meant that Pauline could come with us and see me off at the station for a change. The only proviso was that I was to pay for the petrol money which I was more than happy to do. On the way to Waterloo, Butch pulled in at a petrol station and started to put some petrol in his car, meanwhile, I decided to get myself a bar of chocolate for my overnight journey. I duly went into the petrol station shop and bought said chocolate. When we arrived at Waterloo I asked Butch how much I owed him for the petrol. He looked at me in shock and said that he thought that I had paid the cashier. I told him that I had only bought a bar of chocolate. He was so nervous that he was going to be put on the most wanted list for making off without payment. Anyway I gave Butch however much it cost and he called in to the petrol station on the way back home and had to confess to driving away without paying for his petrol. They were obviously understanding with his honesty. Worse things happen at sea as they say.

On one occasion I was sat all by myself at Waterloo Station waiting for the arrival of my train. The platform was practically deserted and cold. I had sat down to each a sandwich that had been prepared for me to eat while on my journey to Southampton. As I did this an old lady sat by the side of me and I never took too much notice until I heard a thump and saw her splayed on the floor in front of me. She had landed on her nose which was now flowing with her blood all in front of me and frankly, putting me off my sandwich. At this point I also noticed that she was shaking uncontrollably. Somehow, even though I was no First Aider, I knew that she was having an epileptic fit. I ran to find a policeman who I had seen strolling around the platform and explained to him what had just happened. He confused me when he asked me if the lady was a passenger or if she was a bag lady. Bag lady, what was a bag lady? I described the lady to him and went back to the lady but it was ages before anyone came to her and my rescue. I have to say that I was underwhelmed with the assistance forthcoming from the Constabulary.

My salary must have been quite good at the time even though it appears quite pathetic looking at my payslip from when I was a bell boy. The ladies fashion at that time was maxi coats and maxi dresses. On one of my trips home I bought my sister Dawn a maxi dress and Pauline a maxi dress and maxi coat, all at the same time. I was generous to a fault because usually I ended up going back on board my ship stoney broke and had to have a sub to help me get through the trip.

My journey from Southampton back to Torquay was usually undertaken by train. Roger, one of my new friends since becoming a rating also lived in Torquay and on one trip, his Dad had arranged to collect him from the port. He offered to give me a lift which I readily accepted. The only problem was we had both collected more contraband than we should have. For some reason, we had an excess of boxes of fruit and certainly more than we were legally allowed to bring ashore. We were concerned about being caught by the Customs officers who looked after entry and exit from the ports.

Both Roger and I decided to take a chance anyway and so when Roger's Dad came to pick us up in his car we smuggled the boxes of fruit into his car boot. I should say at this point that Roger's Dad was a policemen in the Devon and Cornwall Constabulary. He also held the rank of Detective Chief Inspector and he was completely unaware of the smuggling that me and his son were involving him in.

I was sat in the back of the car and Roger was sat in the front with his Dad as we exited the port through the customs station. Luckily for us the Customs had not bothered to search us. As we passed the Customs point and entered on to the main highway I stupidly breathed a sigh of relief and said, "Crikey that was lucky, thank God for that". Obviously Roger's Dad then wanted to know what I was talking about and so we had to come clean. Roger's Dad was really angry and annoyed at the pair of us telling us how he could have lost his job if we had been caught let alone any court procedures that may also have followed. Roger couldn't believe that I had confessed in such a fashion. Needless to say Roger's Dad never volunteered to pick us up again. For many years later Roger's Dad never ever forgot this moment in time and constantly reminded Roger of it, as Roger always reminded me, even to this day.

A further incident of smuggling soon put an end to my criminal career. When the ship was a couple of days out of Southampton on the homeward bound journey, the crew had to fill in Custom Declaration forms so that if we had any surplus of what we were allowed we would have to pay a Customs Duty on the goods. Alternatively, we could place our surplus goods into bondage on board ship and collect it when we sailed on the next trip.

Well I had gotten away with taking more cigarettes home than I was allowed for a few trips and never been caught, however this trip was to change my whole outlook on smuggling.

I had about 600 cigarettes surplus to my allowance. These were for distributing to my Mum and Dad as well as for myself. The ship was still a few hours away from port before docking. Unbeknown to me the Customs and Excise officers had come out to meet the ship early as they had reports of drugs on board. They had authority for entering cabins without permission and to carry out searches. To be fair I had tried smoking cannabis at one time but it never really effected me and I never really thought about it anymore after that and never tried it since.

Because they boarded the ship earlier than I had expected them to, I never had the opportunity to attempt to hide my contraband very well. To be fair, they knew where to look anyway. I was working up in the restaurant at the time when the Customs Officers found my surplus cigarettes and called for me to attend my cabin.

Subsequently, they gave me a choice of accepting a fine on the spot and having my cigarettes confiscated, or going to court and probably get a higher fine, it might take all day for the case to be heard, and still the cigarettes would be confiscated. Of course I was also keen to get home to my family because even though I was a born traveller, I still got a little bit homesick. To plead not guilty and then having to attend court could have taken all day. Time that I was not prepared to waste. I decided just to accept the on the spot fine which turned out to be for fifteen pounds. I was devastated and swore that I would never attempt to smuggle anything else again. On top of that, they confiscated all of my cigarettes as well.

Chapter Seventeen

First Class

Back on board the ship, Chris and Rick had been telling me how big their tips were as they were stewarding down at the First Class Restaurant. I had good tips where I was at the Tourist Class Restaurant but I became tempted to be working with Chris and Rick and only having one sitting instead of two kind of tempted me to apply for a move. I was accepted as a First Class Steward and it felt completely different from what I was used to. We still gave the same type of service, it was just that everything felt more formal and of course the restaurant itself was a lot more plush and comfortable.

I reported to The First Class Headwaiter and was given my station to work from and everything was ticking along really well. I was beginning to relax and enjoy myself. There was one particular night when dinner was over and two of my passengers had not turned up. All of my other passengers had disappeared and I had re-laid the table ready for breakfast. I was looking forward to retiring for the day when a man and his wife arrived at my table wanting their dinner. I was not happy. I took their order in as cheerful mood as I could muster and disappeared into the galley to collect their order. Unfortunately the galley staff had also nearly finished cleaning up for the night and the food availability was sparse. I had to take a lot of stick from the chefs who were now shouting at me as if it was my fault that I had two passengers arriving this late for dinner.

Whatever the man ordered was still available but the request from his wife wasn't. I took note of what was still able to be ordered from the galley and took the man's meal in to him in the restaurant. I started to serve him whilst at the same time explaining to his wife that her order was not possible and then explained what was on offer. At this point the man went berserk and started shouting me in the restaurant complaining that I had served him before serving his wife. It was so loud that the headwaiter had to come over and intervene. I think I must have retaliated to the man somehow inappropriately because he had wound me up. I was still trying to be professional, but I guess it did not work very well. The head waiter did resolve the matter in some way that I can't rightly remember now and I thought that that was the end of the matter.

Anyway at the end of that particular trip I lined up to sign back on the next trip in the First Class Restaurant and was advised that I had been reverted back down to the tourist class restaurant. My spin as a First Class waiter was short lived and only lasted for two trips. I didn't really mind as I was more comfortable down the tourist end anyway. This Gloucester boy knew where he belonged.

Chapter Eighteen

End of the Line

Meanwhile back home in the pub, Mum and Dad had also decided that they had had enough of being so busy in the *Abbey Hotel*. The stress and worry with it all proved too much for them. They had made some really good money for themselves but decided that money wasn't everything. They applied for and were accepted to take over the *Victoria Inn* back in Gloucester. The move would take place in December 1970.

I was due to be away at sea whilst they moved and so I asked my Dad if he needed any help. I said that I could take a trip off if he wanted me to and lend a hand with the removals. He accepted my invitation and so I just took the next trip off and helped the best way I could. I made one big mistake and that was that I had not informed my pool of my intentions and so I guess they had to run around and find a replacement for me. I was young and inexperienced and still had a lot to learn.

The move back to Gloucester went smoothly and Mum and Dad were happy to be back amongst family and old friends. The day came when I had to phone up my pool in Southampton to explain why I had not reported for the last trip on the *Windsor* and quite naively let them know that I was now available again for the next trip. Obviously they weren't very happy with me and told me that I could no longer be employed out of Southampton as I now lived in Gloucester. This meant that I could not rejoin my mates on the Windsor and that my new pool would be working out of Avonmouth.

Working out of Avonmouth would incur me having to work on cargo ships mainly as there weren't too many passenger ships from that port. Well I decided not to go back to sea and that was the end of my short lived Merchant Navy career. It was great while it lasted but 18 months was not enough for me. I was now jobless and wondering what I was going do now.

Not too many years after I left the Merchant Navy there was a steep decline in the use of British Crew as Fillipinos were happy to work for far less money than us. Jumbo jets had made travelling fairly cheap and certainly much quicker than ships. Instead of taking two weeks to get to South Africa you could get there in a few hours. On top of that, container ships were also coming into their own. Our type of ships would quickly disappear and cruising holidays with one class ships would soon be the norm.

Chapter Nineteen

Looking for a Job

I was now 18 years of age and I didn't have a clue what career path I was going to follow, I did not have any obvious skills that I was aware of even though I was prepared to have a go at anything that presented itself to me. I didn't fancy using my catering skills from the Merchant Navy because that type of business ashore took up too much leisure time and I wasn't prepared to put the hours in unless I was able to see some of the world at the same time.

At this time Dad did not have authority or budget to employ a full time barman and so he could only offer me a part time position as a barman. This obviously was not enough to satisfy my life style. By this time Mum and Dad had accepted that Pauline and me were serious about each other and had even by now become engaged. There was no big party or anything like that for the engagement, indeed opinion was still against us, everybody seemed to be advising us that we should not get married, by that I mean my Mum and Dad and Pauline's Mum and Norman.

Pauline was speaking to her Mum and Norman again, so much so that Pauline was allowed to move into the pub with me, albeit we were still not permitted to share the same bedroom. The only time that we could share together with just the two of us was if we "Stayed up for Coffee" once everyone else had gone to bed. Bearing in mind what time the pub would have closed and we had cleared up you can imagine what time of the night that that was. By this time Pauline had also found a job in Gloucester working in a supermarket on the check outs.

To help to make a little bit more money I was also working for a few weeks as a painter on a building site. One of the pub's customers had heard that I was looking for work and he gave me the opportunity to work with his son who was about the same age as me. I had probably just turned 19 years of age at this time. The painting involved painting inside some new tower block offices in Gloucester somewhere which were still under construction. To get to the rooms that we needed to paint I was required to walk along scaffolding on the outside of the building to access rooms where there were no other workmen around. This held one obvious problem for me as I have no head for heights. We had to be careful walking along the scaffolding as some of the planks were not actually resting on a pole and could easily tip you into oblivion if you weren't careful. I have looked at modern day scaffolding and it appears that much more thought has gone into safety including boards to stop tools or equipment falling from above on to some poor unsuspecting passer-by. I don't know how long I did this for but I suspect it was merely a matter of weeks. I quite enjoyed the job but it was never going to be my lifetime career. I was still doing the job of part time barman with Dad during my spare time.

Plans were also underway for me and Pauline to be married. Even though Pauline was now living in Gloucester with me in Mum and Dad's pub, Joan and Norman wanted her to be married in London and to be fair they were being very cooperative. They were paying for the whole thing and so to be honest I think I was probably happy with that. By the way, my religion had officially changed again to Church of England in order for the service to take place in London.

I remember getting my suit from Burtons and even then it wasn't a proper suit. It was one of them mix and match types where you bought the jacket and the trousers separately. I am not even sure that me and Pauline even paid for her wedding dress. I strongly suspect that was Joan and Norman's input again. It was going to be a big white wedding and would take place in Waltham Abbey and in the Waltham Abbey Church itself. All my Gloucester relatives were going to have to make arrangements for a coach to get them to the wedding so that they could all travel together. I probably should have been involved in making these arrangements for my family but I am ashamed to say that I probably did not have a clue what was going on.

In the meantime I still quite enjoyed working in the pub and Dad was soon able to offer me full employment as a barman. Pauline also used to work behind the bar by now. I had already had some good experience with handling customers during my Merchant Navy days, other than the time I got the sack from the First Class restaurant which we should forget about now. I soon began to realise that just when you think that you have met all the sorts of people that you could possibly meet, a new personality will emerge from somewhere and catch you off guard if you are not careful. Even at my present worldly age, there are still individuals who can surprise me for one reason or another.

Some of the regular customers were the worst that you could encounter. One of the customers once asked me for a pint of bitter which I duly poured out for him. When I gave it to him he asked me if I could put a shot of whisky in there for him. I told him that I could and he then said, "In that case do you mind filling my glass up properly the way it should be?" I was so annoyed with him. After all, the usual routine for a barman was to give the pint a small head of froth to make the pint look more presentable. On other occasions if you filled the glass to the very top, you couldn't get a head on the beer, they used to complain about this as well. Anyway in time, the breweries themselves caught on to this problem and instead of giving the customers pint glasses, they gave them oversize glassed which allowed for giving the customer his or her pint of beer whilst still maintaining a good head of froth. Further to that, the breweries even advanced to the beer pumps automatically giving a measured pint.

The end of a lunch time and an evening session in a pub were also interesting. There was no such thing as a glass washer and every glass had to be hand washed and then dried and shined up with a cloth. This took up to an hour after closing time on occasions. These were the times that the staff used to have time to have a good banter with each other and were probably the times that I most enjoyed.

Mum used to make loads of sandwiches and rolls first thing in the morning and then present them under plastic covers on the bar counter where they would sit all day if they hadn't been purchased. These came in handy at the end of the evening some thirteen hours after they were first made. I used to love eating the leftovers whilst we were cleaning up ready for the next day. This would obviously be completely unacceptable with today's hygiene regulations. The cheese and onion cobs were especially tasty at the end of the evening. Mum's most popular dish was her Ploughman's Lunch that she used to put together. She put so much cheese and whatever else on a plate that it was impossible to put anything else on it. I think she must have charged a very good rate because they were so popular with the customers.

Away from the pub duties for a minute, one of the biggest achievement for a young person growing up is to pass their Driving Test. Well I was already 19 years of age and so quite old to be starting to drive. I decided to take driving lessons and by coincidence, I had the same driving instructor that my Dad had had many years ago, remembering that he was a lot older than me before he passed his test. The instructor still used to have the same trick for getting his learners to quickly learn a "Hill Start"as he did when Dad took lessons with him. The Driving Instructor asked me if I smoked cigarettes and of course at that time I did. He then took my packet of cigarettes and placed them under the back wheel of our car whilst parked on a hill. He would then tell me to do a hill start and that if I didn't do it right, the packet of fags were going to "get it". This trick worked because Dad and me were very good at hill starts. This turned out to be a really useful driving skill, especially with some of the really old bangers that I used to drive. Dad tended to drive a lot of automatic cars which may have been an indication to either how much he liked his cigarettes, or how bad he was at hill starts.

It took me three attempts before I passed my driving test and once I had passed I couldn't afford to buy a car anyway. Dad was very good and he didn't mind me using his car when I needed to once I had passed my test. The day I passed and went back home to Mum and Dad to tell them the happy news, my Dad just threw me his car keys and said that's good, you can go and get some stock for me from the Cash and Carry now, that will save me going. I will never forget that feeling of being in charge of a car all by myself and without someone to advise me when I was not doing something correctly. The car was a Ford Classic and I have always thought how trusting Dad was to give me the keys to his car just like that. Everybody who has passed their driving test will remember the time when they were sat in their car all alone and without someone advising them what they should be doing. It was truly a magical experience.

As soon as I was able, I did buy my very own car. It was an Austin A35 with full leather interior. The smell of the leather inside the car was intoxicating and the car itself would be considered to be a very good collector's item in today's climate. Unfortunately, at the time I owned it, the car was not quite that attractive. It was a real wreck and had next to no acceleration at all, which was actually quite advantageous because the breaks were practically non existent as well. On one dreaded day whilst driving along by myself, I had hit a pothole and the whole of the back window just fell into the inside of the car thereby creating the first time that I had ever had air con.

Working behind the bar was great fun for a while. The downside really was the unsociable hours you were required to work whilst everybody else was having fun. Dad had some other great bar staff who we used to get on with, so well unfortunately I think the majority have passed on to the big bar in the sky now. God bless em. Tony Orlando and Dawn were high in the charts with their song "Knock Three Times" and this was continually being played on the pub's jukebox. Jessie Kermack was one of Dad's barmaids who I worked with a lot and whenever we were together we would play that song and when it came to the chorus line we would stamp our feet on the floor. That makes it sound like that it was just me and Jessie but it wasn't, quite often the whole pub would be singing away and stamping on the floor. They were very enjoyable days albeit the pub was always full of smoke from cigarettes. As most of us smoked in those days we never really noticed. I bet our clothes and hair must have smelled to high heaven.

It is much more enjoyable going into pubs these days. And if they continue with waiter service which a lot of pubs started doing during the Corona Virus when they were allowed to open, it will be an even nicer experience in my opinion. After all if you go abroad, that is how the majority of venues serve you with food and alcohol.

Just after Christmas 1971 the brewery that employed Mum and Dad asked me if I could look after one of their pubs in the centre of Gloucester for a couple of days. I was used to changing barrels and generally looking after a cellar and looking after the general running of a pub and so I agreed. The Landlord and Landlady had to undergo a conversion course to make themselves conversant with decimalisation which was to take place on the fifteenth of February 1971. I was still only 18, very nearly 19 and so it was very strange to me. I never had to deal with the money as the course was only local and the Landlord and Landlady could return back home at the end of the day. The course itself only lasted for two days.

One day, one of the older customers was sat in the corner of the pub nursing his pint of ale when all of a sudden he jumped up and started screaming that the enemy were approaching. He would then use his hands like kids do when they are pretending to have a machine gun in their hands. He also re-enacted the movements of throwing a hand grenade. Whilst a little shocked myself at the time, one of the other customers explained that this poor man suffered from what he called Shell Shock or rather by its more modern understanding of Post Traumatic Stress Syndrome as he had been in the last war.

After a while of working behind the bar in Dad's pub and doing the odd casual painting jobs I started to think about my future career. I did not see myself as being a forever Landlord. I couldn't put up with awkward customers or people who were out of their minds on drinking alcoholic beverages. Sometimes there is nothing worse than being sober yourself when there is a lot people around you who are affected through drinking alcohol. Not so bad probably if you are actually earning money from them but I was on a set wage.

Chapter Twenty

Police Recruit

Now I decided that I needed to explore what possibilities there were for me in the job market. One fine day I took myself in to Gloucester town with the thought of going into the local job centre. As I was walking around the town on my own I spotted a RAF Careers Office. In the window was a snowdrop (that's what they call RAF policemen and women) astride a very impressive motor cycle. I studied the content of the window for quite some time and my mind began to work overtime on what kind of career I might pursue. The only problem with that idea was that I do not like motor cycles but I was sure that there must be other tasks that a policemen in the RAF could do.

Unfortunately the RAF careers office was closed for some reason. Maybe it was a lunch break or early closing or something like that. Not being the most patient of people I decided that I did not need to wait for the careers office to open and that I could go immediately to the job centre to make initial enquiries into joining requirements and such like.

At the job centre I waited until I was called forward to speak to a man behind the counter who I was hoping would put me on the right path for the rest of my life. My question to him was, "How do I join the RAF Police?" at which point he started to look through his piles of information for all of the jobs being advertised in his shop. After much paper shuffling he informed me that the nearest RAF station to me was RAF Quedgeley and that they employed police there. He presented me with some forms to fill in which I did there and then and as I left the job centre he told me that some one would be in touch with me.

I didn't have to wait too long before I got invited for a written test and a potential job interview. The test turned out to be very basic and if you could read and write basically you qualified for initial employment. The only thing that confused me a little bit was that the man who interviewed me was an Inspector and didn't appear to be wearing the light blue uniform that I was expecting of an RAF

Officer. I was not too conversant with ranks in different police forces at the time and so this did not phase me too much. The Police Force that I had inadvertently applied to join was the Air Force Defence Constabulary and so I just assumed that that was another name for the RAF Police. Anyway, we parted company and he informed me that I would be notified in due course as to whether my application was successful.

Whilst all of this was happening around me, arrangements had also been made for quite a big wedding, mine. There were a lot of logistical plans that needed to be made to get married. One of the convenient things also about getting married at Waltham Abbey was going to be that Pauline's Dad lived in Enfield which is only a stones throw from the Abbey, and Charlie, that is Pauline's Dad's name, was going to give her away at the church.

Chapter Twenty One

Getting Married

On May the 15th 1971 Pauline and I were married and I have to say that it was a well organised affair but I am not sure what input I had in it. That is probably how it came to be well organised in the first place. I suspect that the mother of the bride (Joan) would have had the reins and that she would have done her very best to ensure that the day went without a hitch. I have to say at this stage that Joan and me got on with each other really well. I had and still do have a lot of respect for her even though she has unfortunately now passed away. She always tried her best to ensure that me and Pauline were looked after. So much so that she often used to pass us an amount of money and tell us not to let Norman (her partner) know just in case he wanted to give us a bung on his own behalf.

Before the up and coming wedding I had held a stag night in Cheltenham. This consisted of my Merchant Navy mates of Rick, Chris and Roger. True to form I am sure that we had a really good night and I distinctly remember getting very hungry during the evening and asking for a Scooby Snack. Every bar we went in to we asked for the Scooby Snack because we thought that we were very funny, obviously on reflection some fifty or so years later, that seems really corny. Never mind, we enjoyed ourselves at the time and thought that we were hilarious, especially after having downed some ale.

In Cheltenham at the time of my stag night there was some event going on around the Green in the town. There were marquees and tents abound that were selling food and drinks and I think some form of entertainment. My stag party had already had a skinful and at one point all we needed was to have a waz. True to form instead of looking for a gents toilet in one of the local pubs, we found a secluded place behind one of the marquees. There were lots of electric wires laid along the ground but it was dark and there was no one around so we saw no potential problems with this. We were wrong. There were wires all over the place hooked up to generators. Whilst we were all stood side by side doing the manly thing and relieving ourselves over these wires, all of the light in the neighbourhood became fused and the whole area was left in pitch darkness. The sound of music playing through the loudspeakers became silent and I am not sure if this was actually our fault or a total coincidence but we always thought that it was. Anyway it gave us all a good reason to have a good laugh before we did a runner and continued on our journey.

The wedding went as planned and was quite a big affair. The coach had arrived safely from Gloucester and all of my invited family and friends were present. During the end of the evening, an altercation had occurred between Joan and my Mum. I suspect that alcohol may have been a factor in the argument. To this day I still do not know what the argument was about and quite frankly now so much time has passed and the people concerned are no longer with us, I will never know. The argument resulted in Mum and Dad and the rest of my Gloucester family leaving the reception a little earlier than expected. I felt really bad about that but I was being encouraged by everyone to stay at the reception and let the day finish on a good note. It was my wedding day and I had a responsibility to all of the guests but my heart was being pulled in caring for my Mum and Dad. I also had a responsibility for my new bride.

By all accounts the Gloucester coach, after leaving Waltham Abbey got completely lost around London and ended up going round and round all of the well known landmarks. Back then of course the M25 did not exist and the main route up to Waltham Abbey would be around the Great Circular Road. I had to travel that road many times after this and I can tell you that it was pure chaos. Anyway the Gloucester family did not get back until the early hours of the next day and they were all thoroughly exhausted. I can imagine my Mum and Dad saying to each other, "Never Again".

Chapter Twenty Two

Recruits Course

Eventually I was notified by the Air Force Defence Constabulary that I was to attend a six week induction course at HM Naval Base in Portsmouth on the 1st November 1971. I was still a bit confused not only with the colour of the uniform of my interviewing officers, but also the fact that I was now going to a Naval Base to learn how to become a RAF Policeman. I am probably not the fastest greyhound on the track but something did not seem right to me.

Come the day I had to travel from Gloucester to Portsmouth. I had not been given a uniform at this stage and so I was blindly going into my new career with the feeling of trepidation and also a bit of, "What the hell is happening here?' I will keep my readers in suspense no longer and fully admit that I had joined the wrong Police Force. In my defence this was not totally my fault as I had told the man in the careers office that I definitely wanted to join the RAF Police.

To complicate matters even more, the Police Force that I had originally applied to join had ceased to exist as it had merged with two other police forces, the Admiralty Constabulary and the War Department Constabulary to form the Ministry of Defence Police. This merger had occurred on the 1st October 1971 just a month before I became physically employed with them. I just thought, "Oh well, let's see how this pans out, I can always quit and join a *proper police force* if I want to later on".

During my training time at Portsmouth we were taught a lot of current Law and Procedures that we were required to know as well as basic gun handling drills. We had to learn everything parrot fashion in those days. At nineteen years of age I reckon that I was then the youngest officer to have ever joined the Force. I was still only nine and a half stone in weight with a fourteen and a half inch shirt collar.

Firearms were an important part of our training. In fact if you failed the Firearms training for some reason then you would have failed the course all together. The main guns in use at the time were the old .38 Revolvers. This was definitely different from my original expectations. I couldn't see that they would let me ride a big motorbike firing a revolver as I drove along.

Also after the first week of travelling back and forth from Gloucester to Portsmouth I met with another of my fellow recruits who lived in Worcester but was going to be employed at the Research Establishment at Malvern in Gloucestershire. Well any way he told me that as long as I contributed to the petrol than he would take me back and forth to Portsmouth. He only had a beaten up old mini and he had to keep the windows open all of the time because they kept misting up because it was so cold. I used to freeze on those journeys but it was better than catching a train each way. Even though I had been used to being away from home from my Merchant Navy Days, I still hated it when I had to leave everybody, especially as a newly married man.

After successfully completing my training I was stationed at RAF Quedgeley in Gloucester which was very convenient for me. Pauline and me were still living in the pub with my Mum and Dad except that officially I could no longer be employed in the pub as it was against Police Regulations. I had also still not been issued with my full uniform such as my raincoat, great coat etc. The first day that I was due to report for duty was a complete stressful affair. The uniform consisted of blue shirts with detachable collars for constables and sergeant ranks. I have no idea why this was. Was it so that you could wear a shirt for a month and only have to change the collar now and again when you thought that it was dirty? I honestly do not know. What I do know is that when you are rushing about trying to make yourself presentable for the first occasion of turning up for duty, the detachable collar is not your best friend. The back of the collar was attached to the back of the shirt with a stud and then the front of the collar was also held together with another stud. You are then required to put a tie around the collar and do it up and then to fold it down to look something like a shirt collar. The shirt collar itself I think must have been made with very thick cardboard and was almost impossible to fold down. For my first day of duty, which was the usual nine to five reporting duty, I was practically in tears with my bloody shirt and already felt that I should have joined a different police force.

Quite often the stud in the shirt would break and then the trick was to sew two buttons together but you had to make sure that you got the length of cotton between the two buttons correct or else they didn't work. Sometimes if the collar was not fitted correctly, there would be a gap between the collar and the shirt revealing the wearers bare neckline. The shirts were truly awful. The shirts themselves were worn by both constable and sergeant rank and then if you ever reached the dizzy heights of promotion to sub-inspector, you could then be issued with a white shirt which had its own collar. There was an incentive to try for promotion all on its own. That is how you could tell an officer at a distance, if you saw a white shirt, they were the senior officers. Years later when the rank of sub-inspector had been dispensed with and I was to get promoted to the rank of Inspector, all ranks were issued with white shirts and there was not a blue shirt or a stud button in sight. There is no justice in this world.

It was a couple of months after starting employment within the Force before they even gave me an issue rain coat. I am not sure what the problem was with acquiring my full uniform. I can only assume that it was my skinny stature that was causing problems. In the interim one of the officers I worked with allowed me to use his police cape which although officially redundant, kept the rain off me and I could put my hands in my pockets to keep warm without anyone knowing. I wish we had kept the cape as part of our clothing as it was really warm and it had a Lion's head on it as a clasp. Probably a collectors piece today.

My original salary on joining the Ministry of Defence Police was £1,005 pounds per year. There was no such thing as police rent allowance for my Force at this time and as a matter of fact, women were not even allowed to join. Women would later start to employed within the Force from 1974. At that time the starting salary was still not brilliant for a man of my age and we were barely able to survive. Out of my monthly take home pay, I was still able to pay my rent (Pauline and me had moved out of the pub by now and were living in a flat that we had found in Tuffley, Gloucester), as well as getting a car on tick which was an old Austin A40. My take home pay at that time would have been about £70 or so. There was police accommodation that could be provided if there were any available, but police officers still had to pay their own rent.

It wasn't just the Law that police officers in this new force needed to adapt to but also the merging of the three different police forces. Between the different police forces there were variations on many different procedures that were carried out. The new Chief Constable was recruited from the Admiralty Constabulary and so much of his indoctrination in that force was carried over to the new force. This did not meet with the approval of many of the serving officers from the other two police forces. Because much of this was known before the merger, each force was desperately trying to promote officers from their forces to try to get a leg hold within the new force.

Because the Law had not long changed from the Larceny Act to become the then new Theft Act of 1968, many of the "oldies" found it difficult to adapt. As an arrogant recruit to the job who had just learned all of the new legislation in parrot fashion, I found it hard to understand why long serving officers did not understand the current law. It wasn't just the Theft Act but the Criminal Law such as Criminal Damage and others were also in the process of change.

Whilst I was serving as a police officer at Quedgeley I obviously could not be employed behind the bar in Dad's pub. This was strictly against police regulations and would have easily been detected by anyone. In fact I should not have been moonlighting anywhere. But times were hard and we needed more money.

Chapter Twenty Three

RAF Quedgeley

One of the pub customers used to have a contract going around MOD establishments emptying their bins. This did not include Quedgeley. As I have already indicated, the salary of a copper was not that good and I was open to earning a little more legitimate monies. He offered me a job on the dustbin lorry which included RAF Innsworth and other establishments that I cannot now remember. They were obviously all around the Gloucester area. I was very nervous when I took up this pursuit in case anyone found out that I was a MOD Policeman, but the pay was good and enhanced my present salary. I was working shift work by now and so the bins had to meet up with my availability.

RAF Quedgeley was a rather strange place to work. I cannot go into much detail about the goings on of it other than to say that the majority was a maintenance unit for the whole of the RAF. This meant that the unit helped to supply everything from knives and forks to hospital equipment as well as spare plane parts. Obviously all of these items were considered to be attractive items and could easily be unlawfully acquired by the work force. So it was required that the police carried out regular searches of people leaving the establishment. Another part of my task was to check the inside of these buildings during nights and weekends. The sheds were enormous and creaked and groaned when you were alone inside them. The imagination could easily run away with you and put you on a very nervous standing.

One dark night I had finished inspecting the inside of one such building and was just securing it when a voice said me, "Good morning Constable Tonks". It was the Deputy Senior Police Officer who was an Inspector and he was just carrying out a random night visit to his officers. I nearly jumped a mile in the air. In those days I was not routinely armed with a firearm and so the Inspector got to live another day.

We did not have personal radios during this period and our only form of communication was through beacons throughout the patch that we were on. If our headquarters needed to speak to us, they would telephone the site that you were on. A light would flash on an outside telephone which the patrolling officer would then see and then go and pick that phone up. Back at HQ, a switchboard operator, who was also a policeman, could see your location because as soon as you picked a particular phone up, a shutter used to close on the switchboard indicating which phone was being used. Likewise, if you used a telephone from your patch, a shutter used to close on the switchboard also indicating your exact location.

During this time the IRA were very active on the mainland and we had to call in at regular intervals at certain locations to prove that we were safe and sound. This was required all through the night and so there was no opportunity to shirk your responsibility, even if you wanted to, as each call had to be meticulously recorded by the operator. Being the still early days of policing, our main form of defence were a wooden baton and a whistle. If you failed to make a call at a given time a patrol team would be sent to your location to check that you were OK.

Very early one morning when daylight had just about risen, I saw a man on a pushbike cycling around the site I was on, towards the boiler house. I assumed it was the boiler man arriving early for duty. The only problem was that no one had told me that he was on my patch and this annoyed me. I contacted the main control room to complain and they told me that they were unaware of anyone else being on my patch and duly sent a sergeant and two constables to help me look for the man. I had already checked the boiler house and there was no sign of anyone being there. After an hour or so of searching the area we concluded that there was no man on a bike within the restricted area that I was in. I was later told a story that some years previously, one of the old boiler men had had a heart attack and died in that very same boiler house and there had been several reports from various people, not just police officers, who believe that they had seen him cycling towards the boiler house. That was the story, make what you will of it.

Typically I wish that as a young 19 year old recruit I had taken more notice and interest of the old hands who had been in the job for lots of years before me. Before the formation of the Ministry of Defence Police, a month before I physically took up employment, all entrants would have had to have attained at least the rank of sergeant in whatever service that they may have left to join the present force. The Admiralty Constabulary, War Department Constabulary and the Air Force Defence Constabulary were generally second careers for long serving military personnel who needed to have a second career. I think that this is why the present force was sometimes referred to as "Dad's Army."

Most of the constables that I was working with had been Non-Commissioned Officers in one of the three services. This was very evident sometimes with the medals or ribbons that these men were allowed to wear on duty. It was very strange to me to have a sergeant or an Inspector approach a constable and still salute them and call THEM "Sir!" This is not what I had been taught and I definitely did not understand what was going on at the time. The reason for this was that the constable would have had a higher rank when they were in a service or that their ribbon indicated that they were superior to the officer by way of military action. This was something that I had to come to terms with but did not fully understand at this stage of my career. I had a lot to learn.

I did have one very embarrassing moment shortly after having taken up employment at RAF Quedgeley. I nearly forgot to mention this one. I had undertaken my initial induction training with another officer and I had now been left to look after myself. I had been given my full uniform and I was full of confidence although maybe just a little bit apprehensive in case something was to happen that I could not cope with on my own. Anyway this little incident happened around eight o'clock one morning.

I was on traffic duty as the road into this particular area of the site very narrow, so much so that when a bus was travelling along it, it became a one way street. I had to look out for any buses that may be coming off the main road to travel down the site road. When this happened, my responsibility was to stop any other traffic trying to leave the site so that we did not jam the road up. Needless to say I saw a bus starting to leave the main road and I duly stopped all other traffic from moving on to the same road. As the bus passed by me the driver tooted his horn in appreciation. I was so chuffed with my good work that I waved back at the driver. The bus stopped quite rapidly and the driver leaned out of his window and asked me what was wrong. I then had to explain to him that I was merely acknowledging his appreciation. From that moment on I recognised that it was not only not necessary, but potentially quite dangerous to wave at individuals whilst trying to direct traffic.

There was the odd occasion when I did not have a car to travel to work with. I was living about five miles from work and so would sometimes have to revert to a pushbike. This may sound OK to many people today but in those days, the work place did not supply lockers for clothing and definitely not any facilities for showering once you arrived at work. Because of the various locations that we had to work, it was not possible to leave your uniform at any particular spot. This meant having to wear the uniform that I would be working in all day with the exception of putting a civvy jacket on over the top. The different weather conditions gave me very different problems.

On one particular day I had no transport to get to work. One of Dad's customers told me not to worry as he would drive me in. I had no problems with this until one of my colleagues clocked me being brought to work by the customer. He warned me that this particular reprobate was well known to my colleagues and had been arrested on more than one occasion for nicking from our establishment. I knew that Dad's customers were sometimes a bit iffy, but I did not expect the embarrassment to protrude in my direction.

There was another complication in that my days at RAF Quedgeley were numbered as the MOD were reducing the number of policemen at that location. The rules were that I could apply for my top three preferences for places I wanted to move to. If I was unsuccessful for any reason in all of these choices then the Force would allocate me somewhere else to serve, possibly somewhere that I did not particularly want to be. Some locations were as far away as Scotland and that was much too far for me to leave my Mum and Dad and the rest of my siblings. My first choice was an establishment in Hampshire called Bramley near Basingstoke. I had to wait and see if my application would be successful or not.

Chapter Twenty Four

Starting my Family

Meanwhile on the 30th May 1972 my eldest son was born at the Gloucester Maternity Hospital. The Maternity Hospital had by now moved away from the old Gloucester Infirmary where my Mum used to work. My sister Dawn kept me company in the waiting room whilst I was waiting for him to be born. Fathers were not encouraged or even able to attend the birth of their children at this time. Albert was eventually born either very late at night or at the very early hours of the morning I don't remember exactly but it was around that time of day.

When we were allowed to go and see mother and child I was so excited to see that he was a boy. There were no scans available to tell you the sex of the baby beforehand. Agreement had already been made that a baby boy would be called Albert after me, my Dad and his Dad (my Grandad), and then Roger Christopher Richard after my old Merchant Navy mates. This Albert would become the fourth generation of eldest sons being called Albert and this made me really proud and pleased to be able to break the news to my Dad. I know when I broke the news to him that he was so proud and couldn't wait to tell his own father. I can't say that my Grandfather showed any sign of excitement over the name but I am pretty sure that deep down he would also have been just as proud as my Dad and me were. We had the story of the four Alberts with a photograph of us all published in the local paper called the *Gloucester Citizen*.

At first we were all concerned over baby Albert's health as he had been born with a clicky hip and we had no idea what the implications of this meant to his long term health. He had been put into in a splint which was in place to keep his legs wide apart. Apparently a clicky hip was not uncommon and merely meant that the ball and socket joint on the hip had not yet fully developed. The splint would only remain in place until his ball joint had developed satisfactorily. As you can imagine, with us being so young and this being our first child, we were the normal worried parents.

Baby Albert meanwhile had been released from hospital with

Pauline and we went back to our flat in Tuffley. Joan and Norman had come down from Cambridge to stay with us for a few days to see the new baby. Unbeknown to me, Pauline had made arrangements for baby Albert to sleep in a cot in Joan's bedroom instead of ours. Looking back with years of wisdom now, I can see that their reasoning was to enable the pair of us, but more so Pauline, some quiet time to get a good nights rest. Unfortunately at the time and with my lack of experience, I was none too pleased with this. It was my first born and I was really looking forward to having him in our bedroom with us. This arrangement continued in to the next night and by this time I was getting really agitated with the whole scenario. Pauline was trying to quell me with the fact that her Mum was only with us for a short while and then we would have the baby all to ourselves.

Unfortunately on the third night my patience snapped. I was on a 2pm - 10pm shift and I had a really humdinger of a row with Pauline. I wanted my baby with me not sleeping in another room with Pauline's mother. I became so angry that I punched the living room door with my fist. This was a big mistake as when I went to work at two o'clock, I could hardly drive as my fist had swelled up and was hurting like hell. I was never so stupid again I can tell you. It can really hurt when you are trying to show how macho you are. Anyway when I came home at ten o'clock, Joan and Norman had gone home and I was not welcomed home with open arms from Pauline. The atmosphere was very cold. Pauline said, "I hope you are satisfied now, Mum and Norman have gone home early thanks to you and they are also feeling guilty for causing a row." Whilst at work I had thought about this incident all day. Yes, I was feeling guilty and so I hope everyone else is feeling better now!!

I had not been home from work very long when the telephone rang and it was my Mum wanting to speak to me. Joan and Norman had stopped off at the pub to explain to my Mum and Dad what had gone off and to say that they were really sorry. Mum had convinced them not to go home but to stay with them for the night and that she would have a word with me and see if we couldn't sort things out. Anyway, it would have been about 11 o'clock that same night that me and Pauline put baby Albert in his cot and drove up to the pub to see everyone. Needless to say that we all made up and dare I say had a bit of a laugh over the whole thing and then Joan and Norman came back home with us. Baby Albert slept in my bedroom with me though!!

On another occasion when I was left holding the baby on my own so to speak, Pauline had gone out one night with a friend of hers to the Bingo, leaving me in charge of Baby Albert. This did not phase me at all but it did turn into a bit of a fiasco. To start with I have to tell you that this was all pre-disposable nappy days and we, especially me, had to learn how to put a towelling nappy on him. Of course this was further complicated with him having to wear the plastic splint for his clicky hip.

We used to have to soak soiled nappies in a bucket of "Napisan" before washing them in order to keep the nappies white looking. On this particular night baby Albert had indicated to me that he needed a clean nappy on which I proceeded to do. The nappy was just wet and so this was an easy task for me. Shortly after having given him a clean nappy, he indicated to me that he needed another change. This time the nappy was soiled and required me to work a bit harder to complete the operation of changing his nappy again. I must have taken some time doing this because just as I was putting the clean nappy on him he peed so high in the air that it nearly caught my face, and he again had another wet nappy. By the time Pauline had come home from the Bingo I had four dirty nappies all piled in a corner waiting for her attention. It was bad enough with towelling towels as today it would have cost me a fortune in disposables.

Chapter Twenty Five

Bramley

After a few months of my application being submitted I was told that I was to be posted to the station of my choice which was CAD (Central Ammunition Depot) Bramley in Hampshire. This pleased me as it was not too far for me to visit back home or for my Gloucester family to come and visit me. The move took place not long after Albert was born, certainly within a couple of months. We were to be offered police housing available not far from my place of work which I could reach on my pushbike.

As a young man now with a family it was still exciting being independent of Mum and Dad. The quarter that we were allocated was in Coopers Lane which was adequate and up to standard for military accommodation. This was still in the days of no central heating and indeed, the old metal windows were still being used and not double-glazed I might add. During the winter, they were just as cold as the housing that I had grown up in. Ice appeared ovenight on the inside of the windows in winter. Baby Albert had been attending the Basingstoke Hospital about his clicky hip and over a period of time he was no longer required to wear his splint.

Because we were a sensitive establishment and given that the IRA were being rather active over here, all officers were duly armed for their tour of duty. I was now 20 years of age and I am not sure that this made me feel particularly any safer than normal. I have to tell you that the Central Ammunition Depot (CAD) consisted of two thousand acres of woods and railway lines with lots of ammunition storage sheds placed strategically around. There was not one single street light, or any other light to be seen on a night time. Officers were supplied with a spark proof torch so that we couldn't accidentally ignite any ammunition which we were reluctant to use anyway. To put a torch on in an otherwise pitch black unlit area would merely draw attention to any unwelcome customers to exactly where you were. It was surprising how your eyes to get used to the dark after a short time of not being subject to any lighting. I found that my peripheral sighting was especially useful and I think under normal circumstances, when there was no fog or mist around, I could see for an extremely long way and would have been able to detect any undue movement. My only concern was that if someone was around with nefarious intentions, they would know that I was somewhere on patrol, I would not necessarily know that they were there.

One of the constables who I served with at Bramley had been part of the drop at Arnhem during the second world war and he was one of thousands who had been dropped short of their intended target which was made in to a film at some point - *A Bridge Too Far*. I should have asked him and others like him so many questions had I not been so ignorant as to their past. I don't know if they would have been happy or not to talk about themselves in this way, but I really do regret not pressing them for a lot more information which today, I would have found fascinating and interesting. I guess this is similar to the reason why I have ventured to put pen to paper now about my own experiences in life. As my son Bertie said in his introduction, if we don't ask now, when they are gone, it is too late.

After a few months serving at CAD Bramley, a vacancy came up for a Dog Handler. I will talk a bit more about this later but the thought of doing something slightly different really excited me and so I applied for the post and to cut a long story short, I was successful. I was sent to the Royal Army Veterinary Corps Dog Train ing School at Melton Mowbray and was allocated a brilliant German Shepherd named OPEL. The dogs all had tattoos to show that they were military dogs and OPEL had 2C43 tattooed into his left ear. The 2 indicated the year that the dog had been acquired by the military (1972) the C indicated that he had been bought within the UK and the 43 indicated that he was the 43rd dog that the military had bought from the UK that Year.

I took great delight and pride in being a dog handler. It was also good company when performing an 8 or 12 hour shift when all you saw was the shift sergeant who visited your beat twice a shift. This alone was a well regimented procedure that was designed for the benefit of both the sergeant and the constable. On whatever shift you were on, there were regular times for meeting up with the sergeant at regular locations. By this time we were issued with Bantam Radios which were quite large and cumbersome. They also had really long whip aerials which you had to be careful with in case they took someone's eye out. The sergeant would meet at a particular place at a particular time and you were expected to report that your beat area was "All Correct." He would then check your pocket book to make sure that it was up to date and would then make an entry that he had visited you at a certain location and the time that he met you. He would also duplicate this entry into his own pocket book. When he returned to station, he would then make an entry in the Occurrence Book stating that he had successfully visited all officers on their beats and that they had all reported everything as being correct or otherwise.

One early morning, I am talking about two or three o'clock in the morning, I was patrolling with Opel when he indicated to me that he was not happy with something unusual. I had been a dog handler for a little while by then and so was fully aware when the dog was trying to tell me something. In the early hours of the morning, and when no one else should have been in the area the dog was particularly sensitive. I could also now hear a rustling noise myself along the perimeter fence line. I radioed through to my Control Room and informed them that I was investigating a noise along the fence line. I kept Opel on his lead for the time being and slowly made my way towards whatever was causing the disturbance.

What I did not tell the Control Room was that I had drawn my .38 revolver as a precaution and was ready to use it. To take such action required a full report to be submitted and then an inquiry would have taken place. I wasn't in the mood for any of that. As soon as I got near the fence I could see what was causing the disturbance. One of the cows in an adjoining field was scratching himself up against the wire meshed fence. I immediately called in to the control room who had already dispatched a vehicle with a sergeant and two constables to check the noise out with me. I met up with the sergeant and explained the goings on but omitted the part where I had drawn my pistol. I don't think that I would have lived that one down. Anyway my dog, me and more importantly, the cow survived without any injury.

Chapter Twenty Six

On Parade

One of the traditions for policemen when reporting for duty at that time was to report fifteen minutes before your allocated tour of duty and to "Prove your appointments." We were never paid for this extra fifteen minutes every duty that we carried out, we always called this "fifteen minutes for the Queen." During this fifteen minutes we were given any relevant information including the terrorist threat levels and any known information regarding terrorist activity. We were expected to stand up when the sergeant entered the Parade Room and we had to open our pocket books to today's date which had to be prepared before hand. Across the page of the pocket book we had to drape our police whistle and a working pen and in our other hand we were to produce our wooden truncheons for inspection. This procedure was further enhanced on a night shift when we had to also produce a working torch.

The sergeant would also inspect our uniforms to ensure that trousers were properly creased and shoes were polished. The trousers were serge and were awful to keep creased. One trick was to rub soap along the inside crease of the trouser before pressing them with a hot iron. This made the creases particularly sharp.

The uniform trousers were supplied with a special long pocket for holding our police truncheons which were the old fashioned wooden ones that are depicted in all of the old films. Occasionally an officer might forget part of his appointments, such as his truncheon. After all they were a real health risk and I had heard where officers had fallen over or something similar and actually ended up with a broken leg because of the positioning of the truncheon. Officially, if an officer had to draw his truncheon for any reason he was meant to submit a full police report as to the reasons why. One day I had paraded for duty and realised that I had forgotten my truncheon. When the parading sergeant got round to me to inspect my appointments I pretended that I was in a bit of a fluster and instead of withdrawing my truncheon for inspection, I had put my bicycle pump down my trouser leg and pretended that it was my truncheon. I am not sure if the sergeant was actually fooled or if he just did not want to get into the whole thing of making me go all the way back home to collect the truncheon.

The arming up procedure was not so strict, particularly by the standards that were to be later introduced to the Force. We would all draw a revolver from the armoury and then stand in a row with the gun "broken" to show that it was not loaded. The sergeant would then issue each officer with five .38 rounds of ammunition which officers would then load the guns with and then holster them. The guns would actually take six rounds but we were to always keep the top chamber, the one nearest to the firing pin, empty in case we dropped the gun or something like that and then have what is called a Negligent Discharge of the bullet.

Eventually the type of weapons that we were to be issued with were modernised and I have fired a few different types, including a sub machine gun, (9mm Walther Pistol and also the SA80 Rifle). Some years later an officer was killed during a normal shift arming up action and this highlighted the inadequacies in the procedures that we were employing. Our procedures had already been tightened long before this incident but it drew attention how a possible lack of concentration could have serious consequences. There is a National Police Standard which was introduced many years ago which all Police Officers now have to follow.

CAD Bramley used to accommodate what were called European Voluntary Workers (EVW's). These were all men who for whatever reason were unable to return to their homelands after the second world war and sometimes called "Displaced Persons." They were all Polish. I wish that I had found out a bit more about them at the time but the majority of them only spoke in their own language. I became really sorry for them because from my understanding they were unable to visit their families in their own countries and therefore had very little contact with other people from their native lands. We were regularly called to attend their accommodation where they had usually been drinking too much alcohol and ended up fighting with each other. We also had a couple of occasions of suicide by hanging which were also quite upsetting, especially if you had gotten to know them a little bit. All of them were employed within the establishment to perform menial tasks just to give them a wage. Whenever there was a need to talk to them we had to get an interpreter in to act as an in-between for us.

It was some time now since Pauline and I stopped living in the pub with my Mum and Dad and we still had the move away from Gloucester to contend with. Mum started to get worried about me because she said that she thought that I was beginning to look very thin. At 19 years of age I weighed nine and a half stone and wore a size fourteen and a half inch collar on my shirt. This was my natural condition but my Mum started to buy me something called Complan in order to try to beef me up a bit. She also used to buy me loads of cakes and doughnuts to try to fatten me up. I used to eat regularly and so there was no underlying reasons why I was so thin. I had always been thin all through my growing up years and so I do not know why my Mum was so concerned about me. I wish that I can be thin now as after all those years of eating cakes and things like that, I now struggle to get the weight off me. I gave up Complan many years ago.

We had transferred to Bramley in Hampshire during 1972. Bramley is a really nice little village set in a rural setting with hardly any facilities other than a pub and a corner shop. The pub is called the Six Bells and lies opposite the only convenient corner shop for miles around. Basingstoke and Reading were our main towns when we wanted to go for a big shop and each lay around 10 miles in opposite directions.

Chapter Twenty Seven

Constable Hard Up

We used to mainly go to Basingstoke rather than Reading as our bank was also there. Just around the corner from the Married Quarters was a small railway station where you could catch a train to either of the destinations. The trains ran regularly and so during the times that I did not have a car, the train was a good alternative, except when doing a monthly shop of course.

The pub was quite popular with everyone and was generally a good meeting place. My Mum and Dad used to like coming with us to the pub when they would on a rare occasion visit us. They could not come that often obviously as they were running their pub at the time. One time when my Dad came down he found out that the pub also acted as a Lodge for The Buffalo's (Buffs) which they call a poor mans Masons. Dad and my brother Terry were already members of the Buffs and encouraged me to join. I was reluctant as they had gotten themselves a bad name within the Police. It was deemed that Buffs looked after one another even when on duty and were afforded all of the cushty jobs, similar to the way that the Masons had received such biased opinions within the service. Anyway I relented and joined them and when it came for my inauguration, Dad bought a coach load of other Buffs across from Gloucester to support me and join in for the evening. I have to say that I did not get any favourable treatment on or off duty just because I was a Buff.

Even though the pub was a popular, if not the only place to meet up with anyone, there was just one more place that was even more popular amongst the police contingent of CAD Bramley, and that was the Police Club which was in the grounds of the Ammunition Depot, but outside the security fencing. This was a particularly useful and popular watering hole due to the low price of the alcohol that used to be served there. The club was subsidised by the MOD as we never had to pay any rent for the building or even any electric bills. The club was not allowed to make any profit at all and were only allowed to cover the cost of the alcohol. There were days when you could walk into the club, usually on a special occasion and just say "Drinks are on me" and then proceed to buy everyone present a drink. The bar bill on these occasions still did not amount to a great deal. The only downside to the police club I suppose was that it was further to walk to than the *Six Bells* but it was worth it, especially when money was a bit tight.

The Club had a full size snooker table and was very popular. If someone was already playing on the table you would just put some money on the table to show that you were reserving the next game for yourself and whoever you were with. Sunday afternoons were always fun in the club. The Sub Inspector and the CID Sergeant used to get to the Club really early (The Sub Inspector had his own keys to the Club) and would always be playing on the snooker table when the Club opened and so there was no chance of getting on the table until they had finished their games.

The Club steward was always a serving Police Officer, in fact running the Police Club was his full time job. can you imagine this, the steward was an officer who had been in the job for many years and so was on the top rung of the incremental scale, whilst younger officers like myself were on shift working and earning quite a bit less.

The Club also benefited from a much larger room which was used for functions such as a social evening or a farewell do. There was no need to drive a car as there was a bridge in the Married Quarters area which used to cross over the Main Line Railway and drop you down into the outer perimeter of the Depot where the Club was. Inevitably this was the choice of transit. It was actually a lot further in distance to drive to the Club than it was to walk. We could take guests into the Club providing that we sponsored them and signed them in and out of the Visitors Book.

The Club had to close after lunchtime during the weekends or in the evening. When it was open during the week, it was the responsibility of the patrolling Sergeant to come into the Club and ensure that it closed on time and then check the building once everyone had gone and then lock up and return the keys to the Police Post. Sometimes if there was a special event on, and depending who the Sergeant was, he would turn a blind eye and allow you to continue with any celebrations for an extra half hour or so, unfortunately there were also other Sergeants who would demand that we closed dead on time. Spoilsports.

We also used to have a Police Officer whose job it was purely to look after the dogs and kennels. Our man was called "Topper Brown". He was a big drinker and could down quite a lot of pints in an evening. He was a single officer and lived in his own accommodation not too far from the depot. He always used to drive his Hillman Hunter even after a night of heavy drinking and no-one seemed to think too much of it. One evening after having had a good night at the club, and whilst driving home, he rolled his car into a ditch along the main road just outside the depot. All of these roads were country lanes without any street lighting. The sub Inspector had been following him home in his car (he probably was also over the limit for drinking). When he saw the car in front roll. He first of all obviously made sure that the kennel man was not injured and then between them they made arrangements for the car to be pulled out of the ditch. That was the end of that little scenario. Definitely not complying with today's standards. Please do not judge us by today's standards and try if you can to think of a time when drink driving was not such a serious crime. Seat belts were not necessary and smoking inside any building was the norm.

Most Police officers used to cycle to work and there were two reasons for this and none of them was to particularly stay fit. The first reason obviously was that those who lived in Married Quarters like me were only about a mile away from our place of work and therefore it was a waste to use petrol just for this purpose. The other reason, and also the best reason was that we were allowed to claim "cycle mileage" whilst at work. What this meant in effect that we were able to claim 2p a mile for the first so many miles after which we could then claim 1p per mile. There was even an official claim form which a sergeant had to sign every shift to authorise the claim.

The majority of the Depot was criss-crossed with railway lines and wooded area and a few tarmac roads in between. However every officer used to be able to cycle 20 miles per shift, at least that is what the claim form said. Obviously there was no way for a sergeant to confirm this exactly, in fact they also used to claim the cycle mileage and so they just used to sign the claims off. It sounds petty now but that used to give an extra £5 or so a month. Luvly Jubbly! What is even more amusing is that even when I became a dog handler, I still claimed the mileage. It is true that my dog used to run alongside me whilst I cycled but I think the poor dog would have been completely knackered if I had kept that up for real. That was only on an 8 hour shift, there were a lot of 12 hour shifts around for whatever reason. I think that there was even a scheme where the MOD would give you so much towards buying a bike for yourself and then you were deducted so much a month out of your salary to pay for it.

I remember once doing three months of 12 hour shifts without having a day off. I was not the only one as the Force found themselves being widely used during the IRA threat times, depending on the Alert status. At one time I remember a Directive being issued by the Chief Constable that no officer was allowed to work such long hours as they should have at least one day off during the week in order to get some family time in. This was before we joined the Common market with its EU Working Time Directive. This did not stop the Chief Constable wanting officers for detached duties at various locations and so his directive on overtime was often ignored. At least the Chief Constable was covered if anything had gone wrong because an officer might be exhausted!!

Chapter Twenty Eight

Two More Sons

On the 13th March 1974 my second son, Tony, was born in Basingstoke Maternity Hospital. On this occasion I did not have the company of my eldest sister or in fact anybody, I was all alone. It was now acceptable for fathers to witness the birth of their children if they wanted to and I was duly invited to remain for the duration. I had heard many men say that it was such an emotional time for all concerned. As I had dipped out of seeing my first child being born I was determined to stay through all of the happy event this time. I stayed at the "non working end" whilst nurses, doctors, midwives or whatever they were, got on with the job in hand. And then someone was saying out loud "here it comes, its head is just coming out". Remember that we did not know the sex of this child. As soon as I heard this exciting announcement, I decided that it was best if I disappeared and came back shortly, which is what I did. I just couldn't bring myself to witness this tremendously emotional affair and so some might say, I missed out again.

On the 21st November 1976 my last son was also born in the Basingstoke maternity hospital. Again I had to endure the whole process of pregnancy and here I was again awaiting the birth of another child, again still not knowing what sex it was. Poor me. We had reached the point where the nurse had stated that the baby was being born and so I had to decide what I was going to do. Should I go or should I stay? This time I decided that I was going to man up and see the whole thing through. I watched as the baby was being born and eventually and without any trouble, my third son was born. I manned up as best as I could and managed to burst out crying with emotions that I did not know existed. I was so pleased that I had hung around to witness the birth of my son Alan. I now regret that I hadn't been allowed or had ducked out of seeing my other sons being born. I want to say now that all of my sons have always made me proud not just now, but whilst they were growing up, although there were one or two exceptions which I will tell you about in a while.

It was somewhere around this time that Pauline also had to go in to hospital to investigate some lumps on her breast. We had seen a consultant and in true fashion he had told us the worse case scenario where it may be breast cancer. Pauline had to sign a form where it stated that if, whilst carrying out the exploratory operation it was found that the lumps were cancer, they would continue, if necessary, to remove the breast. This was a big deal for us as we were both only twenty four years of age. Women did not get breast cancer at this age. Luckily enough, it proved not to be cancer but it had still put us through that pressure when cancer is looming in the background.

Chapter Twenty Nine

The Fostering Years

It was 1974. I had been in the job for three years and females were now allowed to join the Force. This was quite a revelation in a male dominated workplace. Bramley never received any to work with us as there was a slow roll out of them and they were obviously being posted to establishments where there was a larger influx of female workers who may need to be searched by female officers. Up until then, whenever we were required to carry out searches on females, we generally requested the assistance of a female union rep or someone of a similar status. They would carry out a search in private, obviously and then just inform us if there were any suspicious circumstances, and we would take it from there.

This was also the year when the MOD Police gained parity on pay and conditions with our Home Office colleagues. We could also claim a rent allowance which was not available to us before. If we didn't claim a rent allowance we were allowed to live rent free in service accommodation. You can imagine that this was a big boost to our finances at the time after having to pay rent all these years.

For some reason we still never seemed to be any better off financially. I worked lots of 12 hour shifts, I did detached duties to places like Rushmore Arena for Military Tattoos, Farnborough Air Display and various other events. I was earning lots of money at the time, I was living rent free and still I was always short of money. I suppose having three children did not help. To make things even more complicated for us, we had decided to foster children after seeing an advertisement in the local paper about two young girls needing fostering due to some family crisis. Pauline and me applied to become foster parents and we were accepted.

The two girls that had been mentioned were obviously more in need of immediate fostering and we had a few hoops to go through before we could be accepted as foster parents. I also had to apply for permission to take in foster children as I was living in service accommodation, the application was accepted and approved. Whilst living at Bramley we did foster many children, at one point we had accepted three foster children all at the same time who were brother and sisters as we did not want them all to be split up. There are some uninformed people around who might think that they might like to foster children in order to earn a little extra money. I can tell you that if you ever think this way then you are very much mistaken. Having one extra person in your house for some time is more than enough but to take in three like we did, we were bloody saints!

Not all foster children are well behaved. Unfortunately we encountered children who kept running away, to others who were angry and would cause damage inside the home. Bad enough if it was your own house, but we were living in Police Accommodation and had to answer for any damage caused, as well as paying for it to be put right.

The other thing about fostering children is that you have to give them back. Admittedly there were times when we couldn't wait to give them back, but at other times it was hard to let them go. There was one girl we had stay with us for quite a few weeks, I think her mother was in hospital for some reason and her dad needed to work and there was no one else available to look after her. I remember her being really lovely and polite and all that, but the day came when she had to be returned back to her mum. We were asked if we would like to take her back ourselves or if we wanted the social services to do it. We decided to take her back to her family as they were not too far away. When we took her back, we found that she lived in a house that we considered to be "not up to scratch". There was cat poo in the kitchen and the whole house was a right smelly mess. We were offered a cup of tea but we declined. We felt so bad taking this lovely little girl back to live in what we considered to be a right shit hole.

When we got back home we phoned our social services contact and described what we had just witnessed and said that we were anxious about he girls health and hygiene. The social worker asked us if the girl had been happy to see her mum. We described how the girl had run up to her mum and gave her a cuddle. The mum had also cuddled the girl and was emotional to get her back. The mum also kept thanking us for looking after her daughter in her hour of need. The social worker then pointed out the facts of life to us. She explained that even though the conditions that some people lived in were not perhaps up to our standard, that did not detract from the fact that the children were loved and that the children loved their parents. That was the over riding factor in any loving situation regardless of anything else. This has stuck with me for ever when I find it oh so easy to pass judgement on the way other people live.

Like I said, on top of all this I was still always skint and sometimes did not even have enough change in my pocket to go and get myself a pint down the pub. This is why when a civilian friend of mine who lived on the service accommodation site asked me if I wanted to help him out with a bit of painting I was quick to accept. He also worked for the Ministry of Defence but in the Department of Environment which meant that he went around carrying out repairs for the MOD as well as being a painter and decorator. He had got a private job painting the doors and windows of a couple of big houses around where we lived and wanted some help. I explained that I was happy to help but I had this small problem of not being able to handle heights which also included ladders. I was alright up to about the fourth or fifth rung of a ladder. I will call this man Colin, mainly because that was his name, but I will not use his last name. He explained that he was happy to do all of the ladder work if I could stick to the downstairs window and doors, this included rubbing them all down and then painting them. After assuring myself that I would not be working anywhere where I might be recognised as a copper I restarted my career in painting.

Chapter Thirty

My Second Career (Not)

All was going well and Colin and I made a good little team and I was earning a small amount of cash in hand. The houses that we were working on were really tall and sometimes Colin would ask me to "foot the ladder" whilst he was at the top of it painting a gable end or something. I started to feel a bit guilty about this because he was paying me a wage but all I was doing was standing at the bottom of the ladder. I said to him at one time that I wanted to be brave and have a go at climbing up the ladder and earn my money by doing a bit of painting. Colin was obliging and agreed to let me have a go. With the paint kettle in one hand and my paint brush in the other I started to climb the ladder. After a few minutes I had nearly reached half way up the ladder but my whole body was shaking and I was beginning to realise that I needed both hands to hang on to the ladder which wouldn't leave me any more hands to actually do the painting once I got to the top. Colin could see what was happening and I suspect was also getting a little bit restless and suggested that he could have finished the job in the time that it had taken me to get half way up the ladder. I agreed and with relief came back down the ladder and let Colin get on with the painting.

A further incident whilst I was with Colin occurred one day when he had completed painting a section of a gable end, but needed to replenish his paint kettle in order to carry on. He had obviously come down the ladder and disappeared to get his fresh paint. Meanwhile I was looking at this tall ladder leaning against the gable end and decided that I would be helpful and just move the ladder along a bit to where the painting needed to be carried out. I had seen Colin move the ladder loads of times by now, he was even smaller in stature than me, and so I had great confidence that there was nothing to it. I put my shoulder under one of the rungs and commenced to move it along the wall. To my horror the top of the ladder all of a sudden became very heavy and I was wrestling to maintain a balance with it. I was losing my battle very quickly and inevitably the ladder took advantage of me and became top heavy. It crashed down into the next door neighbours garden. Poor Colin came rushing around the corner with an ashen face to a scene that must have been very scary for him. I was tangled up around the ladder which was laying across the next door neighbours garden. Lucky enough the next neighbour was not at home and so they had no requirement to know what had happened. Colin helped me back to my feet and resurrected the ladder against the wall. I had to explain to him that I had only been trying to be helpful and we decided between us that this was not a good idea and that perhaps I should ask Colin first whenever I wanted to be helpful. It was only about ten minutes or so after this that the next door neighbours returned home and parked their car exactly where me and the ladder had come to rest along their garden.

Chapter Thirty One

Tales of Bramley

The year of 1976 was one of the hottest summers on record. I was still serving at Bramley and Alan had just been born. My pay day was always the last working day of the month and we always had more month left over after using all of my salary. On this particular day it was pay day and we needed the money desperately as usual. There was no internet banking or anything, in fact thinking about it, no one had even heard about computers. The only way to get any cash was to go into your local bank and to cash a cheque. Not having my own car at this time we managed to scrape enough money to get me a one way ticket on the train to get into Barclays Bank in Basingstoke where it was my intention to withdraw some money which would also include my train fare back home. There was no such thing as buses either in Bramley where we were living.

It was a boiling hot day, absolutely scorching when I got the train in to Basingstoke. I used to be quite trendy and I wore flared trousers which were fashionable as well as a pair of cuban heel shoes. My attire is relevant as I will now explain. When I produced my cheque to the bank teller, she told me that my salary had not yet been paid into the bank and so she could not let me have any money. I told her that this is the day when my salary was always paid into my bank account and that perhaps it just isn't showing yet and perhaps she could just check it out for me again. Her reply was the same as before and she was adamant that she could not issue me any money. I explained that I lived nearly ten miles away in Bramley and that I had no other way of getting back home and that perhaps she might just be kind enough to at least issue me with my train fare home. She would not agree to any of this and so I started my ten mile trek back home on foot. It did not take long before my Cuban heels became obvious as not being a good walking shoe. I was walking along the main road back to Bramley from Basingstoke and I can not remember now whether I tried to hitch hike or not, the bottom line is that I ended up walking the whole ten miles back home. Somewhere along the road I had had to take my shoes off and walk in my socks as the pain in my feet had become unbearable.

It was many hours before I reached home and the sun was still belting it down. I had been missing from home for hours and even my neighbours had become aware of my absence. When I reached home Pauline was standing outside with our friends Barbara Bovingdon and her husband Gerald. They took one look at my dishevelled state and all burst out laughing especially when I told them that I had not even been successful in withdrawing any monies from the bank. I had to soak my feet for ages in a bowl of water and I was not too happy, particularly with Barclays Bank. It was not very long after this that I changed my bank.

There was an Explosive Ordnance Detachment (EOD) attached to CAD Bramley. For the uninitiated this is what the Bomb Disposal Team was called. They had an area inside the Depot especially for themselves for practising on certain scenarios that they might encounter. They had plenty of call outs during this period as most people in our environment were conscious of the security situation with the IRA. The EOD would fly red flags around a restriction Zone when they were using explosives to ensure that anyone would not enter that particular part of the Depot whilst they were working. They would set off explosives inside vehicles to study the effects on the vehicles.

This is how an opportunity presented itself to me when I needed to scrap my old car. When we had transferred from Gloucester to Bramley, I had an Austin A40 which like my old Austin A35 would be a collectors item today. The car had given up the ghost on me and so I needed to scrap it somewhere. It was going to cost me money to get a scrap merchant to collect it from the Married Quarters and as I keep saying, money was tight. I offered the EOD the car for them to practice on, they came and inspected it and decided that they could use the car for their practice. They duly collected the car and it is not untrue to say that shortly after they had taken possession of it, it went like a bomb. They literally blew it apart, but I never had the opportunity to witness the affair. At least I could say that my last car went like a bomb!!

Another time when I was patrolling near to where the EOD

explosive area was, I was fully unaware that they were working. There were no red flags flying and my mind was probably wandering about winning the football pools or something else just as exciting. I had Opel with me when all of a sudden there was this mighty explosion. I instantly realised that the EOD were obviously working and even though I was unaware that they were working, I was still a safe distance from them. As I continued forward with my patrol a car bonnet all of a sudden landed no further than 30 feet away from me. It had been blown up by the EOD and landed a bit further out of their safety zone than they had anticipated. I made a phone call to their location as soon as I could and explained what had happened. They retrieved the car bonnet and that was that. I never made any complaints because them lads were under enough pressure without me adding to it.

During what we called silent periods (Weekends and Night shift) the Control Room used to call every officer on his beat every hour to ensure that they were safe and sound. It used to go something like this:- "Control to beat 1, come in beat 1." The Officer on Beat 1 would then answer, "Beat 1 all correct," and then the control room used to continue along all of the other beats. One early morning in the middle of winter, I had been out patrolling and was due to go to one of the Police Lodges for my meal break. I entered this particular meal room where another officer was already there. He had the heating on full and it was really hot and stuffy after coming in from the freezing cold. I had sat down and my dog had settled down under the table, even though the dogs were not officially allowed in the Police Lodges. I had my cuppa and whatever I was eating and had hung my radio up on the back of the door of the lodge. Unintentionally, because of the oppressive heat of the lodge, I fell asleep.

This was the early hours of the morning and I had put my feet up on the table whilst I had relaxed a little bit too much. All of a sudden all I could hear was "Come in Beat 1" when I realised that the Control Room was calling me for a security call. I attempted to jump to my feet and to reach the radio in order to give my expected response to the Control Room sergeant. As I tried to stand up I soon realised that I had pins and needles in both legs and that all other feeling had disappeared from them. I collapsed in a heap on to the floor and was unable to reach my radio. The constable who had been in the room when I had first arrived was also still in the meal room and soon started to complain to me about all of the noise that I was making. I had to ask him to hand my radio down to me so that I could return my security call before the sergeant started to take any further actions. I never let myself get into a situation like that again.

CAD Bramley had a Chief Inspector in charge of the contingency of Police Officers. He was a person of rank who we rarely got to see unless we were in trouble for something or other. Whenever we were close to a person of Chief Inspector rank it was always routine to throw them up a salute. The criteria for saluting was that the officer should be in uniform and that they should also be wearing a hat so that they could return the salute to you.

I was on a duty one day which required me to carry out a gate duty. This was a gate to the depot which allowed employees to enter and exit. The gate was only open for about an hour or so mornings and evenings as it was considered to be a courtesy gate and just for the convenience of employees so that they did not have to travel all the way around to the main gate. One evening the Chief Inspector was driving out through the gate with his wife by his side. I have to stress that he was in his own private car and was definitely not in uniform. I kind of nodded to him as he left the depot only to hear his car come to a sharp stop and it was now reversing into my direction. The Chief Inspector wound his window down and with a very red face shouted out to me "Don't you salute a senior officer when you see him constable." I replied: "I thought I was saluting out of respect of the uniform and rank sir not out of respect of the person". Even as I say this now, it doesn't sound like a good response to a senior officers question. Needless to say I was in the dog house and the next day had to endure a strict bollocking not from the Chief Inspector, but from the Inspector as it was obviously below the Chief to have to sort me out.

Chapter Thirty Two

Hong Kong

Whilst we were living in Bramley, Pauline's Mum and her partner had moved to Hong Kong for a few years. Norman was quite high up in his job which was something to do with tunnelling. Back in England he had some part to play in the digging out of much of the London Underground. In Hong Kong he had a lot of responsibility for the tunnelling for the New Mass Transit Railway which required him and Joan to locate themselves there for about three or four years. They both came and stayed with us in our married quarters in Bramley so that we could take them to Heathrow Airport when they had to depart these shores.

This presented us with a golden opportunity to have a great holiday. Indeed, Joan and Norman had challenged us to find half of the air fare for me, Pauline and the three boys and that they would then foot the other half. The air fare was going to cost £1,200 and so we were required to find just £600. Bearing in mind that we were always skint and never able to save a penny, this was going to be a major challenge for us. Anyway with lots of skimping and effort we did finally manage to get our air fare together. I had managed to get 28 days off work on Annual Leave by saving some leave from last year and bringing forward a week from next year and all sorts of faffing around but in essence, we had a whole month to look forward to in Hong Kong. My police dog Opel would be taken out on more regular exercises by the kennel man.

The day came for us to travel to the airport, Heathrow. None of us had ever been on a plane before. Alan was still in a cot and not yet walking and so Albert and Tony would have been around five and three years old. The year would have been early 1977. Because we had never travelled on an airplane before we were obviously not used to the requirement to check in and all that that entails. Although we had gotten to Heathrow in plenty of time we had not been savvy enough to get ourselves checked in as soon as possible. This resulted in us booking our seats fairly late in the proceedings. It was not really until we boarded this massive Boeing 747 that we realised the importance of checking in appropriately. Our seats consisted of Pauline in a wide row where a cot could be placed for Alan to travel in, Tony was in a row behind Pauline, I was behind Tony but in a different aisle and poor Bertie was in another seat next to complete strangers further on to the back of the plane.

I had approached a stewardess with our predicament and she then tried asking other passengers if they were willing to swap seats so that we could at least sit closer to each other. Apart from this being our first plane ride, it was also a very long journey which required a stop at to Frankfurt and then Bahrain on the way out. No passengers were willing to take pity on us and so this was how we had to travel to Bahrain, after which there was some capacity for changing seats and being nearer each other.

As the plane started its take off procedures by taxiing and life belt drills from the cabin crew my heart was in my mouth. I felt so miserable and anxious for the sake of the kids without their Mum or Dad being able to hold their hands on this occasion. I don't know about the kids but I could have done with someone holding my hand. All of a sudden there was the roar of the engines as we began to take off and I still did not know if this was normal or not. We had picked up speed and I could feel the rumbling of the planes tyres speeding across the tarmac. All of a sudden the front of the plane started to rise into the air and it felt as if my back was going to scrape along the runway and then we were in the air. I couldn't see out of a window properly and so I was almost becoming a little claustrophobic. Then once the plane was airborne, the noise of the engine all of a sudden went quiet and I was so concerned that we were just about to fall back down to earth. of course we weren't and this was just a normal standard and successful takeoff. As soon as the lights went off giving us permission to smoke, the inside of the plane soon became full of people chuffing away on their fags.

Bertie has a memory of that plane journey that I did not recollect but he reminded me about it since starting to write this book. He had been sat near the back of the plane next to a gentleman who was also on his own. Bertie was about five years of age or so but seems to think that the man may have had an accident in his pants. The man who had been sat next to him was carried away by the flight crew and we never saw him again. Apparently the man had died in flight whilst sat next to Bertie.

When the time came for our return journey back home after a month of living in Hong Kong, we made sure that we checked in at the airport with plenty of time to ensure that we all had seats next to each other.

The landing coming into Hong Kong was quite an experience. It was night time when we landed at Kai Tak airport. This airport had been reclaimed from the sea and so jutted out into the water. As we landed there was water either side of us. One slip and we would have been in the sea. Because the runway was so close to the town, they were not allowed to display any flashing lights for any product advertising. Also when we did take off on our way back home there was limited air space because of the mountains in front of the runway which meant that all planes had to perform a steep curve when taking off which was also quite unpleasant for inexperienced travellers such as ourselves.

I enjoyed Hong Kong which was rather overwhelming for a boy out of Gloucester. Stanley Market was one of our regular destinations whilst moving around. You could get everything you wanted from here including chickens and frogs. Because there was not many facilities for cold storage, food such as chickens and frogs were sold live and not ready wrapped in plastic covering. Fish was also included in this. When shopping for any of the aforementioned you merely pointed to the animal you wanted and in front of your very eyes it would be dispatched and presented to you to take away, still warm. Not for me this way of buying my meat I have to say.

Live birds in cages also seemed to be quite popular and I believe that canaries or some other such bird were considered to be lucky to have in your home if you were a Chinese person. There were cages of these birds everywhere you walked along the market.

The other strange thing about this market was that it was very close to the airports runway. When the massive planes were coming into land, they would fly almost feet away from the rooftops of the buildings belonging to the market. You could literally see the pilots and passengers as the planes glided overhead with their engines roaring for slowing down to land.

On one occasion we went to visit a couple who had until recently been our next door neighbours at Bramley, David and Carol. David was a corporal in the army and had been posted out to Hong Kong not too long before we had gone there on holiday. When they had become aware that they were due to be posted to Hong Kong and as they had met Joan and Norman while they were visiting us it was obviously discussed about meeting up once they were all there, which they did.

From one of their windows in the married quarter that they had been allocated, you could see the runway of Kai Tak airport even though it was quite a few miles away. What was fascinating though was watching the airplanes taxi across the runway and then build up speed for their take offs. They were heading straight towards the married quarters and then they had to take a sharp turn to their left in order to avoid the hills and mountains just behind the quarters.

Joan and Norman actually lived on Hong Kong Island itself which was much nicer than Kowloon as it was quieter and less populated. They were living in a high rise flat overlooking the Island and in the direction of Kowloon. It was also interesting the shanty towns that could also be seen from the living room window. Joan and Norman lived in a very nice accommodation and even had an amah to do all of their housework. Looking out through the window you could see people living in little tin huts which were all packed close to each other. The locals did their clothes washing in a little brook that ran alongside their huts. The contrast between wealthy and poor was staggering. Even with the rather archaic conditions that they lived in you could see the children going to school in the mornings and they were all spotlessly clean and their clothes immaculately cared for. They did leave you wondering how the hell that they managed to to this in the conditions that they had to live in.

Our favourite haunt for a few hours each day was the beach at Repulse Bay. Norman had been able to take some time off work while we were there but obviously could not take a whole month off. He had a car and so we would generally go to Repulse Bay in the mornings before the sun got too hot and then when Norman came home in the afternoons we would go for a tour around Hong Kong and Kowloon.

On one occasion whilst we were on the beach, a group of Chinese people seemed to be filming in the area for something or other. They had spotted Albert and Tony, who as I said were only a few years old and both had blond hair at the time. The film crew came over to us and asked us if we would mind if they filmed them as apparently the Chinese were fascinated with blond haired children. They did tell us why they were filming but it escapes my memory now. I know that we signed some papers, written in English and they promised to send us a copy of the film that they were making. Needless to say that we never heard from them again.

The kids were loving the beach thing as you could imagine and one day they were playing with one of those inflatable balls. There was a very gentle wind blowing which had taken hold of the ball and blown it in to the sea. It didn't look too far out and so I decided that I was capable of getting it back for them. Did I mentioned yet that I am not a very good swimmer? I entered the water and did a few breast strokes to get to the ball which by now had blown a bit further off shore. I turned around and then realised that I was further out than I was really comfortable with. My heart did start to beat a little faster as I could see that no one had taken any notice of me whatsoever. I started to have a mini panic but realised that I had to overcome my difficulty and as soon as I could, I put my feet back on the sand. Life was carrying on around me and no one was any the wiser as to my distressing time that I had just been involved in.

When Norman was not working we did a tour of The Peak which was reached by way of a tram. I think that it must be one of the steepest tramways in the world. It was so high and all I could think of is what would happen if we started to roll uncontrollably backwards. The view from the very top was astonishing and looked all over Hong Kong and Kowloon for miles and miles. After a day of sightseeing we took the kids home and arranged for the Amah to babysit for us whilst the adults went out to the Jumbo Restaurant for something to eat. As we sat down there were tanks of fish swimming around as if they were part of the decoration, but it transpired that they were actually the bloody menu. We had to point at a fish that we liked the look of and within the space of about forty minutes it was freshly cooked and on your plate for you to devour. The whole thing about food on this holiday was gradually turning me in to a vegan. (I never became a vegan by the way).

The other thing about going to Hong Kong was that we took an empty suitcase or two with us because buying clothes over there was so cheap. I don't recall how much advantage we took of this because when we got back home we were going to be skint again.

Almost every where you went around Hong Kong you would see signs prohibiting people from spitting on the floor which to us sounded rather absurd. That is until one day we were following a rather nicely dressed young lady, all dolled up to the nines. As she was walking in front of us we could hear her clearing her lungs and then she let forth a mouthful of gunge into the side of the road. The lady stopped looking so nice after that.

Anyway as far as I remember our flight back home after such an interesting holiday was uneventful. We managed to all get seated together and we all had a brilliant holiday and were going back home with astounding sun tans. The holiday was over and now we were going back to our humdrum way of life. We were never going to be able to afford a holiday like that again.

Chapter Thirty Three

UFO's

By the time that I was 21 years of age, the age of parental control had changed to 18 and so when it came to my 21st birthday I was actually on a 2pm - 10pm shift at work. It was still a bit strange not having any family around us to celebrate such events, especially as we were still so young. I had already missed out on celebrating being 18 years of age and now this was another milestone in my life which went by unnoticed.

I had a couple of strange happenings during my patrolling days at Bramley. The first was when I was on my own, remembering what I have previously said about how dark the establishment was without any artificial lighting. I had been looking to the stars and noticed a group of about three or four lights high in the sky circling around each other. What was also strange was the way in which they were all moving. They were not floating through the air but were in one spot first and then they would shoot to a different location. As in a jerky movement. I watched them for quite some time. The sky was completely clear and there was very little breeze if any around me. As I watched them, one of the lights headed straight up into the sky and in a flash had disappeared and the other lights took suit and swiftly followed the first one. I did mention this to other officers on duty but no-one else had observed the lights as I did and so that was the end of that. I do believe that there is a strong likelihood of some other form of life up there beyond our own universe.

When I was on a patrol I would sometimes team up with another patrol and another incident occurred when it was very early in the morning and the daylight had started to break. The Dawn Chorus had started up and again the sky was clear and it looked like being another nice day. All of a sudden me and Ken, that was the other officers name, stopped patrolling and there in front of us in the sky was a very large bright light, and no, it was not the sun. Neither of us spoke for a minute or so as we then observed this ball of light suddenly head away from us at a great speed and out of sight. We looked at each other in bewilderment and couldn't believe our own eyes. We confirmed with each other that we had both seen the same thing but no explanation was ever forthcoming. Perhaps we should have reported the sighting but that particular location seemed to attract these type of sightings on a regular basis.

My kids also had some fun memories of Bramley one of which was how we had managed to set up an agreement with the corner shop to allow them to go to the shops for our cigarettes, especially when we never had any money to pay for them. Being able to get cigarettes and other items from the corner shop without having to have any money was particularly useful until pay day came, provided that I could get access to my salary from the bank of course. We still used to use cheques a lot in those days as obviously there was no internet banking or anything like that.

Apparently one of the not too fondest memories of my eldest son Albert was when he and Tony were upstairs in the married quarter in one of the bedrooms. For some reason they had decided to stand up at the window so that they could be seen by their friend Gary Hewins who was standing in the front garden. They were stark naked and thought that it would be extremely funny if they both took a pee against the inside of the window, which they proceeded to do. Gary who was the same age range as my two, about 5 or 6 years of age, thought that their behaviour was hilariously funny and was having a good old laugh with my two pervert boys. Unbeknown to them I had walked up the stairs and had spotted what these two reprobates were up to and took swift action to stop their enjoyment. I had slapped both their arses whilst they were still stood at the window. Gary had apparently felt that playtime was over and that he better go back to the safety and confines of his own house. I do not remember much if any of this incident but it certainly left an impression on the boys in more ways than one. Obviously I do not condone my own behaviour now.

When we lived at Bramley I had started a little hobby which proved to be liked by too many people. That is the art of home brewing, both wine and beer. The beers I made were not from the kits that you could buy in the local shops. I found out that wine could be made from anything. My very first wine that I ever made was from tea, just ordinary tea. It tasted rather pleasant and that lead on

151

to making many more different tasting wines in the future. One of my most famous wines was made out of elderberry which was made from the berries that I would collect within the depot. I once gave my brother in law a bottle of this and a couple of years later whilst around his house he offered me a drink. He told me that it was a port and asked me if I liked it and when I said that I did, he explained that this was the bottle of elderberry wine that I had given him a couple of years ago. I have to say that it tasted just like a good shop bought port.

Unfortunately for me my mischievous kids also took a liking to my beers when I was not keeping an eye on them. Both Albert and Tony yet again were of the age to be utter rascals and had sampled my wares when I was not around. Again I do not recall this time but I am informed by the pair that this is how they learned to drink at a very early age, on one occasion apparently becoming slightly drunk.

Chapter Thirty Four

Dog Trials

Meanwhile back at work I remained a dog handler. I took an interest in the Army Dog Trials which took place at Melton Mowbray in Leicestershire every year at the Royal Army Veterinary Corps (RAVC). To get backwards and forwards to Melton Mowbray from Bramley I was allowed to use the Police Mini van which was part of our vehicle fleet at the time. All of our vehicles where I worked were owned and maintained by the army and we more or less had to take whatever they gave us. The distance from Melton Mowbray from Bramley is roughly 140 miles and the mini van probably had a top speed of 50 mph. Also the early day mini vans were not that comfortable for the drivers. I had to lean right forward when changing gears and after such a long journey my back would really ache.

I loved the trials which included agility, obedience and man work. Man work included the ability for the dog to chase a villain and then to bring them down to the floor. They did this by being trained to go for an arm from behind a running villain and their weight, along with the momentum of the chase would do the job nicely. My dog Opel was very good at all aspect of this type of work even though we never won any prizes. It was just great fun to train a dog up to a very high standard.

Our dogs in those days were not classed as Police Dogs as they are today. They were bought and trained by the military as Security Arm True Dogs. By today's high standards they would not now be considered to be a suitable Police Tool in a police locker, which is why many years after I stopped being a Dog Handler, the Ministry of Defence Police started to breed their own dogs and now comply with the requirements of recognised National Police Dog handling. They also started to use Belgium Malinois instead of the German Shepherd because of the German Shepherds inherent hip displacement problems

On one trials competition, one of my fellow dog handlers, Geordie, came along with me with his own dog, also to take part in the trials.. I have to explain that the RAVC at Melton Mowbray even though they looked after the army's dogs, their main interest seemed to be with the horses that they bought and trained. Don't get me wrong, they had dedicated staff for the kennels and the dogs but they seemed to boast more about their horses than they did their dogs. Anyway one day me and Geordie found ourselves with a bit of spare time on our hands and so decided to take our dogs for a leg stretch into the fields opposite from where we were. It was a hot sunny day and as we meandered along this field we came upon a hedge which was throwing a small shadow across it. We decided to rest our dogs in the shade for ten minutes as well as taking a break for ourselves. Geordie liked to smoke his pipe and I was a cigarette smoker and so we both made ourselves comfy and lit our own particular weed.

We had been talking about something frivolous when we could hear something like drums approaching us from behind the hedge. Funnily enough the ground was also vibrating ever so slightly. All of a sudden two or three horses came floating above our heads having jumped over the fence that we were leaning against for shade. The riders never spotted us and we had to scarper out of that field as quick as our legs would take us. Even the dogs did not have any chance to give us any warning. If we had been discovered in that field with our dogs we would both have received a right old rocket.

I always hated the accommodation procedure at the RAVC as we were treated just as if we were in the army. The procedure was that we would rock up at the main gate where we would be checked to make sure that we were expected. We would then go straight down to the kennel area to get the dogs kennelled, watered and fed. Then back up to the accommodation area where we would drop off our suitcases on to an old army bed. The room was a dormitory type accommodation inside an old tin Nissan hut. There must have been around twenty beds to each hut with ten beds either side of the room. The flooring was old brown linoleum which we were expected to take a turn in polishing each morning. I can't imagine even suggesting to today's Ministry of Defence Police Officers that they were required to do this sort of thing (and I wouldn't blame them - I wouldn't do it either). After offloading our suitcases we would then report to the Quarter Masters Store where we would be issued with a mattress, a couple of blankets, sheets and pillows. It always took a couple of trips as the mattress proved to be a touch too much to carry all at the same time.

On completion of our visit to the RAVC we then had to return the same to the QM's stores which would be inspected for any unwanted stains etc. It was all very regimental which is why a lot of Police Officers did not volunteer to return there for whatever reason. I just liked the trials which is why I took all of the garbage that came with it. Even the huts were dilapidated. You could literally look through the top of the hut and see the stars on a nice night. On one occasion I remember one of the wooden windows just falling out where it had rotted. The whole place truly should have been condemned years ago.

When Police Dogs started to be introduced to the Ministry of Defence Police, the RAVC did not want to train them. There was always a jealousy that my Force were starting to have requirements for dogs that they were not able to support. This again is why many years ago the Ministry of Defence Police eventually took on responsibility for themselves with regards to Police Dogs. I have to say that today's standards are not recognisable from my days in handling dogs but the improvements are much for the better. All dogs are now home kennelled which is the main procedure which I wish that I had had when it was my time.

Like all young coppers I was as keen as mustard and really excited to be in my job. I had been lucky in that I was not required to complete my two years probation before becoming a dog handler and so I was in my element.

On one particular cold, dark and miserable night, I had reported for my normal duty and carried out my regular patrols around the area I was detailed off for. The evening weather was miserable and damp and I was suffering from a cold with runny eyes and nose when I met the patrolling sergeant for our normal rendezvous. On seeing me he asked me if I was alright to which I explained to him about the cold that I had. I also stated: "I might as well be at work feeling miserable as being at home unable to sleep etc.", perhaps in my naive way doing my bit for a bit of brown nosing as well. I did not get the reply that I thought that I might get. Being an old hand he replied back to me: "Well if it was me I would rather be suffering in comfort than being out here in this weather at this time of morning". He then signed my pocket book and bid his farewell without too much more chatter. I guess that he didn't want to catch my cold.

To make matters even worse, the police hut that was my base for the night did not even have an inside toilet and the toilet itself was a dirty old Elson bucket in what can only be described as a shed by the side of the police lodge. (For those who are unaware of what an Elson Toilet is, it is literally a bucket with a lid and a small amount of strong disinfectant poured in the bottom). This was emptied on a daily basis by whoever the depot staff were responsible for such things. Comfort on duty this was not.

Chapter Thirty Five

Train Accident

We moved from our original house in 49 Coopers Lane that had been allocated to us to another Married Quarter just around the corner at 12 Coopers Lane. I can't remember now why we did, but can only guess that there were more bedrooms in the house that we moved to. Our new accommodation was still very dated and without central heating. The mainline railway from Reading to Basingstoke ran directly at the back of us with a chain link fence between us and the rail track. It was also the main line to London and so it was quite a busy track. As I have said before, Bramley had its own railway station where the local trains used to stop and indeed we used it regularly for getting backwards and forwards to Basingstoke or Reading.

On the 4th or 5th November 1974 there was a terrible accident at this crossing. A group of people travelling on one of the local trains had alighted when the train had stopped at Bramley. Now the usual practice would be for the train to depart the station before passengers were allowed to cross the railway line to exit the station, but on this occasion for some reason the people did not follow this practice. Instead they walked behind the train that they had been travelling on and walked straight in front of a freight train travelling in the opposite direction. Three people were immediately killed and body parts were sent into the back gardens of some of the married quarters. There was a railway attendant in the rail box who was observing everything act out but had no way of notifying the poor passengers. There was no barriers to stop people from making this mistake and also no tannoy system to talk to anyone. The railway attendant in the box that day later became the father-in-law of my brother in law who had met his daughter when visiting us. He was affected by the accident forever and retired from his job with British Rail.

Chapter Thirty Six

Don't Take the Tablets

One very stressful incident that occurred happened one sunny morning. Pauline's brother, Barry had started living with us for a little while and even had a job working in the Ammunition Depot. I forget what job he had. Unfortunately Barry still wet the bed and was taking tablets prescribed by the doctor to help him to get over this problem. Barry had gone to work and I was still in bed one morning when Albert walked in to my bedroom and told me that he had had some sweets and that they did not taste very nice. Albert would have been two or three years old at this time because he was so small and could not reach any cupboards. He showed me the bottle that the so called sweeties had been in and I then realised that he had taken some of Barry's bed wetting tablets. I did not know how bad the tablet might be and I also did not know how many he had eaten.

I jumped out of bed and made a drink of salty water for Albert to drink to try to make him sick but we could not ascertain how long ago he had taken the tablets. I phoned the local doctor and she obviously advised that we take Albert straight to Basingstoke Hospital, which we did. Albert at this time seemed quite normal and showed no signs of any ill effects. I should not have wasted time in contacting the doctor as I now realise and should have taken him straight away to the hospital.

We walked quite calmly up to the reception desk and explained the situation and then a doctor came out to see us. At the time I was carrying Albert in my arms and still without any obvious signs of ill effects. All of a sudden Albert went into a fit and became rigid in my arms which is when the doctor took him from me and there was a panic all around whilst a team of doctors and nurses disappeared with Albert into a cubicle. We were fully aware then that this was clearly a very serious situation and couldn't have been any more frightened than we were.

Pauline and I were in a waiting room and had telephoned our families as there were none living around us. By this time a doctor had come out to see me and Pauline and broke the news that Albert was in a grave condition and that we should prepare ourselves for the worse. Joan and Norman had driven from Cambridge to Basingstoke in record time to be with us. I also remember that my sister Dawn and her husband Richard also came down to be with us. Everyone was so distraught with the prospect of losing our little Albert. Barry in particular, for obvious reasons was almost unconsolable.

On one or two more further occasions we were told by a doctor that there was very little that they could do because the tablets had entered Albert's blood stream. I can not explain the feeling at that time. I guess you would never understand that feeling entirely unless you have been through it yourself.

It was many hours later when we were told that Albert's stats appeared to be improving and that if he survived the next twenty four hours, then he stood a good chance of surviving. We obviously never went home from the hospital as we needed to be with Albert and it was the next day we were told that he had survived his ordeal and that we could actually now take him home. We couldn't believe that yesterday he was literally at deaths door and here we were now being able to take him back home. Albert left the hospital as if nothing had happened as he was fully fit again without any side effects. We were so lucky that he never suffered from any after effects.

Needless to say I went straight out to town and bought a medicine cabinet for the bathroom. This was the second occasion that I had experienced a child taking substances from somewhere in the house. The first having been my sister Aileen when she had drunk paraffin all those years previously. I am happy to say that little Albert thrived after his ordeal. Although Barry had felt guilty because it was his tablets that Albert had taken, in reality, it was our fault, me and Pauline, for not ensuring that our own children could not have access to any such substances. Lessons were learnt that day for sure.

Chapter Thirty Seven

Lessons Learned

Bramley was a steep learning curve for a young man such as myself. One incident always sticks in my mind which although a learning point, also makes me chuckle to myself on occasions. I was in the kennels with another handler, either at the beginning or end of our shift, I forget now. He had fallen out with one of the other handlers and was having a right old moan about him. He kept saying things to me like: "He is a right prat though isn't he Bert?" and that sort of thing. Because I hadn't actually disagreed with what he was saying, I suppose that I had unintentionally passively agreed with him.

I hadn't fallen out with or disliked any of the handlers and so I remained impassive whilst he was speaking to me. Or I thought I had. Some weeks later I ended up working with the other handler and he was not in a good mood with me. At some point he put me up against a wall and shouted at me that the other handler had told him that I had agreed with everything that he was saying about him. I tried to explain my predicament and that I did not want to fall out with anyone and that on top of that I had not said anything about anyone. Anyway that was my lesson learned. Being impassive and letting someone else talk nastily about someone else without disagreeing with them sometimes sounds as if you are agreeing with all of the detrimental comments. It's a hard life trying to be neutral sometimes.

Having moved away from Gloucester there was no family close at hand. I was working regular shifts which in the early days consisted of quick changeovers. This meant that I would come off a night shift at 6am and would be back on duty at 2pm the same day. This allowed the shift system that we were operating to work. The change of shift day like this would always be on a Sunday. I remember this affecting to a great detriment one Christmas when the Christmas day fell on a Sunday. I had a young family and on this particular occasion had two young sons at home. I still had to do the quick swing that I have just mentioned. In affect this meant that I had no time at home on that day. I had finished my night shift at 6am Christmas day and then had to have a sleep, open Christmas presents, have my Christmas dinner and report back for parade for duty at 13:45 hrs the same day. Absolutely diabolical!

Chapter Thirty Eight

A Changing Force

The Ministry of Defence Police was changing much faster than any other Police Force that existed. I had joined just one month after the amalgamation of the three other Forces - War Department, Air Force Department and Admiralty Department. In 1974 women had been allowed to join and we were permitted to have a recognised police livery on all of our vehicles as well as wearing the chequered head bands on our caps. Police helmets were also introduced as well as Rent Allowance and there was also talk about changing the way that we procured and trained our police dogs. It was a very exciting time for everyone in the Force at that time. We were the third largest Police Force in the Country with over 6000 officers across the UK.

Also around 1977, I had passed the promotion board to become a sergeant. I had tried a couple of times previously but not quite made it. We had to take three separate written exams consisting of Law and Procedure, General Police Duties and Knowledge and Reasoning. Having passed each of those exams we then had to sit before an Area Promotion Board chaired by an Assistant Chief Constable and if we got through that we were allowed to sit the Central Board which would be chaired by the Deputy Chief Constable. It was quite an achievement at the time and I was only 25/26 years of age. I would have been probably the youngest Sergeant in the Force at the time even though my promotion never came through until 1979 when I was 27 years of age.

However, I was in a real dilemma and at a fork in the road as they say, in my life. I had become a little disgruntled with my job. I had enjoyed my detached duties to large events like the Farnborough Air Show, the Aldershot Military Tattoo, there were even some Royal Events that I helped to police at various locations. Therefore I had applied to join my local Police Force which was the Hampshire Constabulary. I was not the only copper wanting to change direction at this time as we now had a few younger people like myself in the Force. Some joined the Hampshire Constabulary and my next door neighbour, Mike Dillon, joined the Metropolitan Police. I had attended Winchester which was the Hampshires Headquarters and had been lucky to pass their entrance exam which I had to take as we did not have any transfer agreements between Forces in those days.

The problem now was that we had attained wage parity with the Home Office Forces and I was now just about to get promoted to sergeant. This meant that MDP officers would effectively earn the same wage as our Home Office colleagues as well as having the same rights with allowances such as housing allowance. I had three young kids at home and I was still financially struggling to make ends meet. I could either take the promotion and stay in my present Force, even though I would be expected to relocate to another station, or I could accept the Hampshire offer and start from scratch all over again, including being on probation for another two years. As history has shown us, I decided to take the money and the promotion and stay with the Ministry of Defence Police.

Chapter Thirty Nine

Promotion

So I continued my career in the Ministry of Defence Police. I do not regret my life choice in staying with the job that I knew fairly well by now. Let's face it, had I changed my career, my life and the lives of many people around me would be completely different to what they are now and have been in the past. I found the challenge of responsibility in a higher rank very exciting and sometimes a little bit frightening. My main problem was that I was still very young to be in this position. I still had to contend with officers who had completed a career in one of the armed forces and now here I was at 27 years of age and up to this point the majority of my experience was in Dog Handling. I like to think that I had the personality to be able to cope with some of the stresses that I would encounter. I was quite often not as hard skinned that I might have appeared to my colleagues but I was able to hide the fact that sometimes I was frightened to death of having to use my rank. The theory is that if you have to use your rank to achieve something, then you should not have been promoted in the first place.

On my promotion to the rank of Sergeant I was posted to a station titled, RNAD Priddy's Hard which was just across the water from Portsmouth Naval Base. RNAD stands for Royal Naval Ammunition Depot. Priddy's Hard was almost a sub station to another RNAD establishment close by called RNAD Bedenham and between us we were responsible for arming the Royal Naval Fleet moored at Portsmouth before they set sail to wherever they were going. We became particularly busy during the Falklands War in 1982

On my transfer to Priddy's hard I had been allocated a Naval Quarter in an estate called Rowner which was one, if not The largest Naval Married Quarters Estate in the whole of the UK. I ended up living next door to officers that I worked with, and naturally became friends with them and their families. The quarters were centrally heated and this felt quite luxurious to us. The houses were really basic but all were in good condition. There was a set of shops within walking distance and even a take away Chinese that felt brilliant having spent the last 7 years in Bramley with literally nothing around for miles other that a small corner shop and a pub.

I had not been promoted for very long and also relatively new to my new station when I had to deal with my first situation in my new rank. I was on a 2 - 10 shift and I was responsible for just 4 other officers on duty at that time. Two of those officers were my next door neighbours. I was expected to carry out a supervisory patrol which would have required me to meet up with the officers who were on patrol. I had to call another officer in to replace me in the office whilst I went out on patrol. His job was to monitor the radio and telephones. I had been patrolling for some time and had not met up with any of the patrolling officers as yet. I have to say that I was enjoying my own patrol looking out across the water and listening to the rattling of the ropes on the sailing boats that were moored nearby. Something I had not been used to in Bramley.

At the other end of the establishment was another Police Lodge which was for the officers at that end of the establishment to take refreshments when required. There was always a well known rule that officers should stagger their refreshments and that someone should be out on patrol at all times. I walked through the door of the police office and two officers were sat relaxed in their chairs with a television set on to a programme that they found very interesting. As I walked in they hardly acknowledged me let alone stand up and apologise for not being on patrol. This was the first encounter that I had with supervisory responsibility. My first reaction was anger for the fact that the officers had not shown respect to my rank, and I do mean my rank and not me personally. I was not used to such a blatant disrespect for a supervisory officer. It was a far cry from my days as a constable at Bramley. Secondly, I knew that they would have been warned that I was out on a supervisory patrol and so should have prepared themselves accordingly. To me this was an attack on me personally. It was saying to me that, "You may be a sergeant but you are not going to have any control over us." This again was something that I was not going to be able to ignore without some repercussions.

I walked towards the plug that the TV was plugged into and pulled it out of the socket. I then ascertained to see if any of them was actually on a refreshment break, bearing in mind that the two of them should not be on a break at the same time. I also asked who the TV belonged to and then told the officer concerned that he was to get rid of it immediately. Obviously I then continued to advise the officers that they should be on patrol and that the next time that they met me on duty, they should report that their patrol areas were all in good order. I was not naive enough to think that this stopped any of them from watching TV when they were on duty, but it did establish what I expected from the officers on my watch.

I was still able to socialise with these same officers when we were not on duty and indeed our wives all got on with each other. When I was not on duty I was called by my first name and when we were on duty I was called by my rank (at least to my face - I am sure I got called lots of other things besides but this never worried me). I think that in today's police forces almost everyone is called by their first names and I would have found that altogether unacceptable and so I am glad that as I write this, I am happily retired.

I was only at Priddy's Hard for about two years when I had passed my exams for promotion to Inspector rank. I had also sat the Promotions Boards and passed those as well. I was really pleased with myself as this was the quickest time that I could have been promoted as it was mandatory to serve at least two years in the rank of sergeant before even applying for further promotion. I was not promoted straight away but I was transferred to a larger station just up the road from Priddy's Hard called RNAD Bedenham. This in effect meant that I had more officers under my control and had a bigger area to police. We had two sergeants on duty at a time. One was a patrolling sergeant and the other was what we called the Duty Station Officer. We were also classed as a Group Station and we were responsible for several other establishments including the Royal Naval Air Station Fleetlands, another establishment at Dean Hill which was about an hours drive from Bedenham as well as Lee on Solent, from where the Navy ran their hovercrafts. We had to monitor the radio calls from these stations and ensure that they were all secure and being ran correctly. It was quite a responsibility.

RNAD Bedenham had their own police club which also accommodated all single accommodation for officers not only from our own set of stations but also from the Royal Naval Dockyard at Portsmouth. The police club became a regular haunt for us as it was really cheap alcohol but with a good atmosphere, snooker table etc. Not long after my arrival at Bedenham, the single officers accommodation had been refurbished at great expense and even the Chief Constable was invited down to officially open it all.

Shortly after being posted there, I was on patrolling duties with another Constable when I was informed from the Control Room that a telephone call had been received from a mother of a single officer who was accommodated at the police club. The mother was concerned for her sons welfare after having been contacted by him to say that he and his girlfriend had split up and that he was deeply depressed over the whole thing. The officer was stationed over at Portsmouth and after enquiring from there whether he was on duty or not I was informed that the officer was off duty. I attended the officers accommodation at the police club which was closed at the time in order to speak to him and confirm that he was fit and well.

When we arrived at this officers room in the police club, he did not answer his door after I had knocked on it. There was a glass panel above the door of this officers accommodation which appeared to have been blacked out by holding some sort of flame to the glass. After all attempts to find out the whereabouts of this particular officer we concluded that he could very well be in his room. A peep through his keyhole only revealed a room which was very untidy and had clothes and belongings thrown all over the room, but no sign of the officer himself, although we could not see all of the room. I banged on the door and called out his name several times with no response. I then decided that for welfare reasons, I was going to have to attempt a forced entry into his room after making sure that there were no spare keys anywhere. The officer who was with me was not keen on this idea as the Chief Constable had only just sanctioned this new accommodation, as I say at great expense.

If you have ever tried to break a door down you will know that it is not that easy (unless you have the "persuader" that is in common use these days). Anyway I did manage to get hold of a sledgehammer and proceeded to smash away at the door handle end of the door. As the wall was only a framed plaster board construction, the other end of the door gave in first. I must admit it did look a bit of a mess. Having gained entry to the room It soon became apparent that the officer was not at home anyway.

It transpired that the officer was actually at one of the local pubs drowning his sorrows and when he got back to his room, he was not entirely amused or even in agreement with my actions to check on his welfare. In fact he put a complaint in against me which ended up not going too far. The Chief Inspector who was in charge of the detachment had words with me and explained how he also was not pleased with my actions. His deputy, who had the rank of Inspector also had words with me and told me that he had no problems with what I had done and not to think any more about it. I never heard anymore after that and so I guess everything was OK in the end.

Chapter Forty

A Daughter Arrives

It was around this time that my Chief Inspector had to interview me and inform me that I had been invited to be given my promotion to Inspector in return for being transferred to the Force Headquarters at Empress State Building in London. This would have meant moving my family to live in London and I would then have had to commute daily to get into work. I believe that the accommodation in those days was at Mill Hill which was army accommodation. I had talked this over with Pauline and came to the conclusion that we would not be able afford to live in London. We had recently bought our first house at Bridgemary, near Fareham, and this was already stretching our pockets to live. Therefore I turned down the posting and ultimately, promotion for the time being.

In the mean time, away from work, we had continued with the fostering of children from the local council. It would have been late 1980 when I had been on a 2 - 10 pm shift at work. I returned home to be told that the Social Services were bringing a baby to us who had been rescued to a Place of Safety and asked if we were prepared to look after the child for a while. Obviously we had said yes and shortly after I had gotten home from work there was a knock on the door. When I opened the door our Social Services contact was stood on the doorstep with a small bundle which turned out to be a thirteen month old baby girl called Kelly. We were never really told the full circumstances regarding Kelly being brought to us and generally speaking, we did not need to know.

We were required to let Kelly's parents see her on a regular basis at the offices of the social services. This was quite hard on occasions as Kelly's Mum and Dad were very immature and only very young albeit in their 20's. It was a real privilege being able to look after someone so young who was in need of a safe environment to live in. Who would know at that time that this little baby would end up staying with us for ever and then being adopted into the family legally. Our three boys were very good about accepting the new baby although as she got older, they did tend to wind her up on many occasions. Mind you they wound each other up as well and so this was no big deal really.

After turning down my promotion to Police Headquarters, the Force seemed to forget about me for the next two years or so. Because I was one of the younger sergeants in the force at the time I was chosen to work alongside the Provost and Security Services located at RAF Rudloe Manor. I was attached to them for about ten weeks in all. My job was to remain in civilian clothing and to tour MOD establishments within England and Wales testing out their security arrangements. This was an interesting duty although it meant being away from home during the week and returning home on most weekends. Some of the testing required me to climb over barbed wire security fencing at all hours of the early morning, even where guard dogs were on patrol. I was not that keen on that. Also all of the MOD Police at these establishments had become routinely armed with firearms due to the rise in IRA activity and eventually it became unfeasible to carry on with this type of security testing.

Dad in uniform.

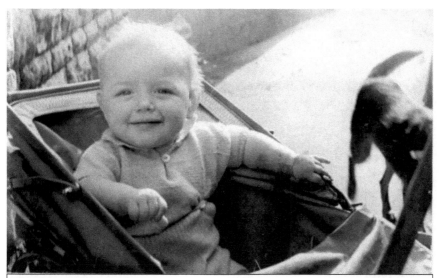

Myself as a baby in a pram.

As a toddler with my Dad.

My boyhood friend Edward Foote, with my sister Dawn and our cat Tiddles in her arms taken in the front garden of Avening Road, White City, Tuffley..

Myself, Aileen and Dawn

Myself, Dawn, Nan, Aileen and Terry

Me with my teddy.

This is me at the Finlay Road School in Gloucester.

Aileen, Terry, myself and Mum at Wainlodes Hill, Gloucester.
Below: My sisters Dawn and Aileen with my Dad, me and little brother Terry.

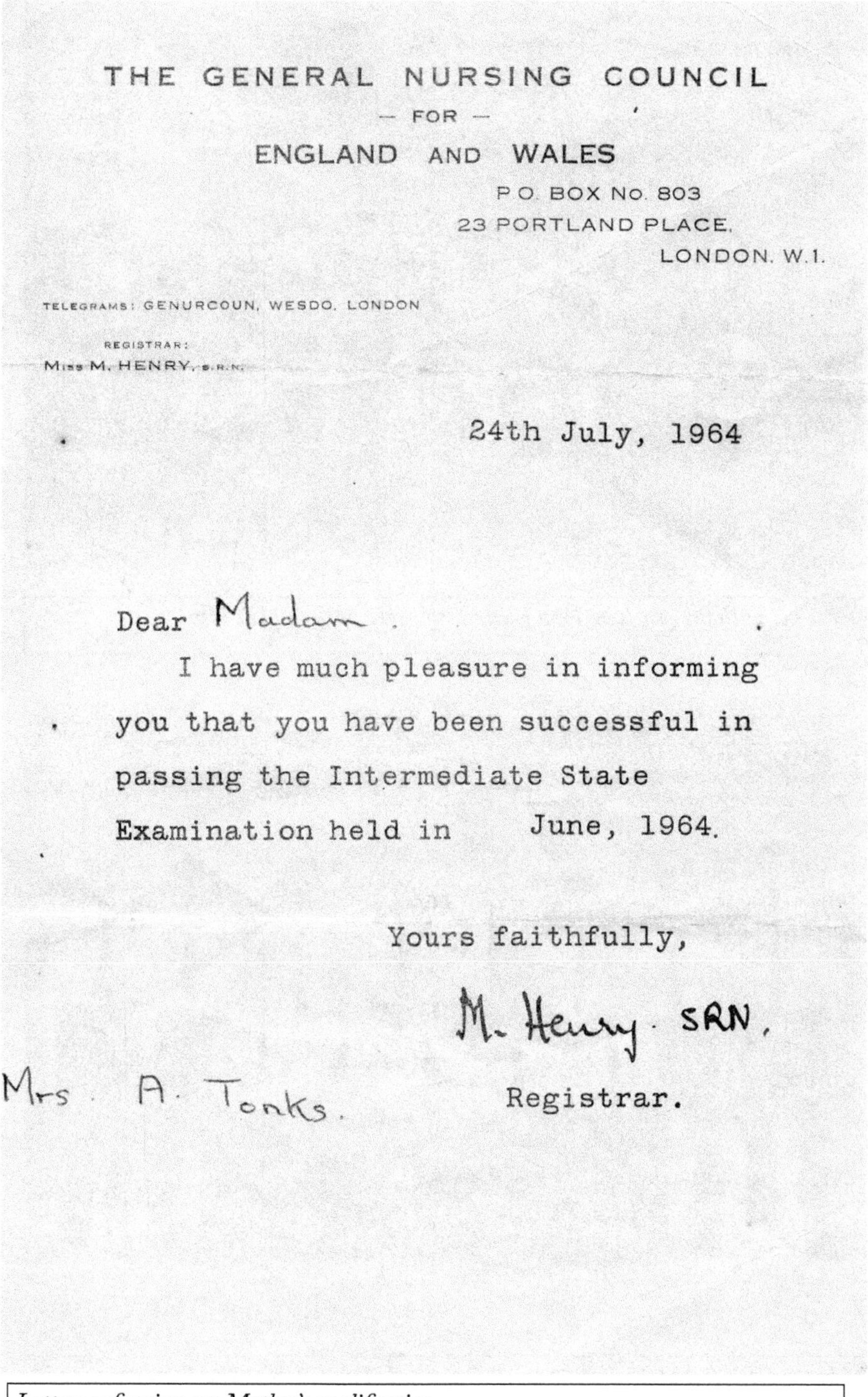

THE GENERAL NURSING COUNCIL
— FOR —
ENGLAND AND WALES

P.O. BOX No. 803
23 PORTLAND PLACE,
LONDON. W.1.

TELEGRAMS: GENURCOUN, WESDO, LONDON

REGISTRAR:
Miss M. HENRY, s.r.n.

24th July, 1964

Dear Madam.

I have much pleasure in informing you that you have been successful in passing the Intermediate State Examination held in   June, 1964.

Yours faithfully,

M. Henry. SRN.

Mrs. A. Tonks.   Registrar.

Letter confirming my Mother's qualification.

177

At school with Brother Ken. I am fourth from right in the middle row.

My class (L class) at Training School Gravesend. I'm back row 2nd from the right & Mick Shaw is seated on the right side at end of row (just in front of me really)

W.A.E. 14
(formerly Form F.)

ACCOUNT OF WAGES
(Sec. 132, M.S.A. 1894)
Keep this Form as a Record of Your Nat.
Insurance (see note overleaf) and Income
Tax Deductions.

Name OF SEAMAN

TONKS.   ALBERT.

Dis. A No. R 8746.

Name of Ship and Official Number	Class	Section	Income Tax Code	Rating	Ref. No. in Agreement
R.M.S. "Windsor Castle" London - 301167	U. C.S. G.S. List U.E.L.	A or B	>	BELL BOY	268

Nat. Insurance No. ....
Contributions commence
Monday 15-12-69   (Date) 22-12-69

Date Wages Began	Date Wages Ceased	Total period of Employment		Allotment Note given for		
		Months	Days	Amount	Date 1st Payment	Interval
17-12-69 / 18-12-69	26 - 1 - 70	1	10 /9	£8·0·0	25-12-69 15-1-70	Weekly Monthly

A. EARNINGS		£	s.	d.	B. DEDUCTIONS		£	s.	d.
ges including Saturday afternoon at sea compensation		32	—	—	Advance on Joining				
....months @ £.... ....per month					N.U.S. Advance				
10/9 days @ £.... per day					Allotments		8		
Increase in Wages (Promotion, etc.):					MMs				
From....to....(....Months @ £....per month					MMMMMMM				
(....Days @ £....per day					Pension Fund....No.				
From....to....(....Months @ £....per month					XXXXXX 8x				
(....Days @ £....per day									
					Union Contributions:				
					....7....weeks at....4/-		1	7	4
Overtime....hours @....per hour					Nat. Insurance (Voyage):				
....hours @....per hour					8·7 weeks at 17/8		3	19	11
Leave and Subsistence brought fwd....days					Nat. Insurance (Leave):				
Voyage Leave....5....days					....weeks at....				
Sundays at Sea....					Graduated Contributions First Deductions		12	13	11
Total....5....									
Leave taken....		£	s.	d.					
Balance due....days @ £....per day					Wireless Messages				
Subsistence....5....days @ £. 5/3 per day		1	6	3	Postages				
					Tobacco		4	4	6
....lete as (Carried forward to next voyage					Wines				
....essary (Paid—to be shown in Earnings Column		37	6	3	Stores				
					Canteen				
First Total Earnings....		42	15		Cash Fines & Forfeitures		10	10	·
Overtime or Compensation Pay									
Less Reduction by £....p.m....antis....days....					Income Tax		9	9	·
Gross Earnings....		80	1	3					
Deductions....		36	17	5	Graduated Pensions				
Final Balance....		43	3	10	P.64 Additional Tax				

ADJUSTMENTS	£	s.	d.	£	s.	d.
Add						
Deduct						

Voyage
67

	£	s.	d.
Total Deductions	36	17	5

National Insurance (including any related to
leave) paid to 1-2-70

K. UNDERWOOD, Purser

....Signature of Master.

SEE OVER

Here is my pay slip as a bell boy after a trip on Windsor Castle from Southampton to South Africa

In Cape Town with Table Mountain behind me

R.M.S. WINDSOR CASTLE

As a waiter in Tourist Class Restaurant on board Windsor Castle with passengers.

Here I am sitting on the dock next to Windsor Castle beside the dock at Cape Town.

I had just passed my driving test. I am here at the wheel of my Dad's car..
Below: Mum at the bar of the Victoria Inn.

Portsmouth: MOD police recruits course. I am in the back row, far left.

Dad on the submarine HMS Alliance at Gosport.

Left:
Here I am on a dog handling course at Royal Army Veterinary Corp Melton Mowbray with my dog Opel.

Bottom:
my son Tony on his kennel mans course in RAVC Melton Mowbray.

In my sergeant's uniform after promotion with my younger brother Terry in his constable's uniform

While on an Inspector's course we visited Bentinck Colliery.

Chapter Forty One

Greenham Common

During 1981 the UK government had agreed to house the American nuclear cruise missiles at a location known as Greenham Common in Berkshire. The MOD Police had been tasked in protecting the UK government assets and to become a buffer between UK civilians and the American Service personnel. This had aroused a group of women in particular to protest against nuclear missiles altogether. Unfortunately their protests were not peaceful and often ended up with someone getting hurt, including the policemen on duty. The American military police officers did not have any authority to deal with British Citizens. This is why the Ministry of Defence Police were deployed mainly within the wire of Greenham Common. Because of the scale of the protests, a few different police forces were required to assist outside the wire. Outside the wire were Thames Valley Police, Metropolitan Police, a small number of Ministry of Defence Police as well as Hampshire Police. The Thames Valley and the Metropolitan Police also deployed their mounted branch.

Like all demonstrations that take place in this country, there are always activists who are hell bent of causing disruptions and even with the intent of getting themselves arrested. Sometimes the tactics were to get as many people arrested as possible which would not only deplete the number of police officers available at the scene but also to clog up the judicial system at the courts. Also, if the activists could get themselves arrested, this also gave them their day in court as they would always plead not guilty of whatever offence that they were arrested for. This also then afforded them the extra publicity for their cause.

Bearing this in mind it was not always advisable to arrest the protestors for minor offences. Without boggling your mind too much, this was also pre the Police and Criminal Evidence Act of 1984 and we were operating under what was known as Judges Rules which actually gave the Police Forces a bit of extra scope. One method used by all police forces at the time would be to arrest the demonstrators and commence to transport them to a police station several miles away for charging. On the way to the police station a decision would have been made to not charge the persons concerned. The protestors would then be dropped off miles away from Greenham Common and informed that they were no longer under arrest. It was then up to them to find their own way back to wherever they wanted to go. This was well before mobile phones and such like communications and made life really difficult for the demonstrators and certainly kept them out of the way for a couple of hours which was the main plan. This plan was really effective for a while until a court case decided that this would amount to kidnapping by the police and this practice had to cease with immediate effect. This type of action by the police was addressed in later years in the Police and Criminal Evidence Act which then stated that offenders had to be taken to the nearest Designated Station for charging. Luckily this was not so in the early days of Greenham Common.

There was no such thing as peaceful protest. One tactic used by the demonstrators would be to slide a metal sheet under the back wheels of a vehicle aimed at the gates of Greenham Common. They would then accelerate the vehicle with the clutch pressed in and then abruptly let the clutched out. The speed of the metal plate hitting the gates was horrendous and would have decapitated any officer who was in the way. All officers were briefed on these tactics and knew how to avoid injury. Another horrible practice by the demonstrators would be to sew razor blades into the inside of their clothing. This meant that when they were arrested and then searched by the arresting officer, that officer was in great danger of injury from the blades. Sometimes, the women would even cover themselves in their own excrement to make it very challenging for arresting officers. The camp lasted for many years whilst the cruise missiles were kept there. They called themselves the Greenham Common Women's Peace Camp. I can tell you that they were anything but a Peace camp. The women who were permanently camped at Greenham Common were nicknamed "The Smellies" by the Police officers who were regularly deployed there.

I did quite a few duties there over the years and the money that the officers made was quite lucrative. We were working a minimum of 12 hour shifts and then having to be accommodated either at Aldermaston or another MOD establishment called Burghfield.

As usual the accommodation was basic and the food not very good but there was great camaraderie amongst the officers which made everything bearable. We never really had many officers who complained about the conditions that we had to endure because that would have made life miserable all round for everybody. Besides which most of the detached officers were volunteers and knew that they would get a big pay packet at the end of the month.

On one occasion whilst I was on duty at Greenham Common I received a message that an officer from the the Thames Valley Police had been looking for me. Apparently my old mate from the Merchant Navy, Mike Shaw, was a constable in the Thames Valley Police and had heard somehow that I was on duty. Unfortunately we were unable to meet up at that time but we have talked about that occasion when we were both on the same policing operation at the same time.

As if Greenham Common was not enough to contend with I was also tasked with taking a coach load of officers from Gosport and Portsmouth up to an establishment then unknown to me. It was an American Air Base called RAF Wethersfield. Little did I know at that time that one day I would be promoted to Inspector and actually be in charge of the UK policing there, as well has holding a Customs Declaration giving me the powers of a Customs Officer. Again there was meant to be a mass demonstration about an American Air Base being stationed in the UK. At that time the Air Base did not even have a security fence around it. It covered a very large area and had an operational runway. The American Service Police were again present but were informed to keep out of the way. This time the lead police force was the Essex Police. They were deploying officers on scramble motorbikes in the event that protestors might get as far as the runway which was entirely possible without any physical barrier other than a few coppers trying to block their path.

I was detailed off to be in charge of a van load of officers at the top end of the runway. We were overlooking a farmers field that had been ploughed up. There was nothing to be seen for miles. I had heard over the radio that down at the Main gate, there had been some disturbances and some small demonstrations had taken place I sat next to the driver of our van and we were smug that we had travelled all this way just to sit in a van looking out across some nice looking farmers fields. The officers in the back of the van were having a banter with each other. Others were smoking or generally taking life easy.

All at once either my driver or myself noticed some movement in the field in front of us. We kept observing for a short while until the movement became a vision of what must have been a couple of hundred demonstrators heading towards our location. We literally had to wake some of the officers up in the van who had decided to get some shut eye after such a long day of nothing happening. Radio Comms were not that brilliant but I deployed all of the officers from the van towards the fence line and radioed the situation back to our headquarters and asked for immediate assistance as it was clear that we were going to be easily overwhelmed.

Within a short space of time the demonstrators were knocking on our door and I was able to speak to some of them. Meanwhile, as always, another contingency of demonstrators had taken it upon themselves to head towards the runway to set up some sort of camp. The Essex Police on their Scramblers were kept busy, but they obviously did not want to carry out any arrests as this would have soon depleted their numbers which was the aim of the demonstrators. Our backup had also arrived and eventually we were able to minimise the disruption to the Air Base. Obviously all flying for that day had been stopped in anticipation of today's events. It was a long day. Most of the day had been spent with me and my officers being bored rigid and then all of a sudden we were running around like headless chickens. We did manage to save the day with very few arrests. It was advised that all detached officers should avoid any arrests as this would been very inconvenient to get the officer back up to the appropriate court. We therefore had an arrest strategy where only local officers would do the arresting for any offences committed.

Chapter Forty Two

Medmenham

Two years after my promotion to sergeant, I was sent on a Sergeant's Promotion Course. I was a bit put out as I was thinking that this was a bit late now, having completed my two years probationary service in my present rank. I had to go to RAF Medmenham which was our training establishment then as well as our overall MOD Police Headquarters. Medmenham is just down the road from Marlow in Buckingham and is a very rich and prosperous area to reside. As usual for us, the local pub was a good two miles walk up the main road and as the idea was to partake of alcoholic beverage, there were not many volunteers to drive us all to Marlow for a night out.

I had to attend Medmenham many times during my career on different courses. It was a rather horrible place to have to stay. Of course if you were rich enough to live there permanently it was a quaint place that was popular with the well to do. Unfortunately when you were billeted in MOD accommodation life was not that great. It was boring other than going to the police club in the evening after we had been fed in the canteen. Many officers took their own bottles of alcohol and just stayed in their own rooms for the duration. I was not wealthy enough to afford my own bottles of booze and so usually ended up at the police club where the beer was as usual very cheap to buy. It also allowed you to mix with the rest of whatever course you were on at the time.

The biggest problem was that these were the days before mobile phones as I have mentioned a few times before. In the police club, there was the only public telephone for the students to use. It was a pay phone. Of course everybody wanted to phone their loved ones every day and I was no exception. The problem was that the bar did not always have enough change for the telephone users and although the alternative was to reverse the charges, you could not always get access to the telephone because it was constantly in use. Some officers would hog the phone for absolutely ages and you would end up getting really annoyed at them. There was the odd occasion when I would not be able to get on the phone at all during the evening even though you had to constantly have your eye on it to see when it had become vacant. This meant going to bed in the evening without catching up on how the rest of the family were coping without you, and to hear any problems that may have arisen whilst you were away from home. To be fair, this was also the same problem when I was working away from home at any other job that I was on. Being a family man, as I like to believe that I have always been, this did mean that I spent many nights going to bed with a guilty conscience because I had not contacted my family back home. This was not conducive for a good nights sleep and indeed for completing the rest of whatever course or duty I was having to attend. Each time I was away from home, my marriage became more and more strained for one reason or another.

It was rather strange being away on a Sergeants Promotion Course after I had already completed my two years probationary service in the rank of sergeant. However I was not the only officer in this position. We were quite a motley crew and some of the promoted officers were from the CID. One of them was an officer called Tom Wallington who was a big and very brusque chap. Sadly he died a few years ago now. He had already served for many years previously as a RAF Policeman. I got on with him. As usual our accommodation was a dormitory and there was about ten of us accommodated in each dorm.

One night Tom Wallington and his mates from CID had gone out for a drink in Marlow. I had stayed within the police club at the Training School. Tom's bed was in the same dormitory as mine. For some reason it became a good idea to grab hold of the Station cat that was a regular visitor to the dorms and coax it to settle down in Tom's bed. This included using some cat food and a lot of persuading. I could hear Tom and his mates coming back from his night out and as I was already in my bed, I turned around and pretended to be asleep and then await the repercussions. Tom was a bit worse for wear after his nights drinking and had obviously made to get into his bed when I heard a string of verbal obscenities. I was trying not to let Tom see me laughing. All of a sudden I was flying through the air as Tom had realised who the main culprit was and had upended my bed with me in it. The dormitory was in uproar as everyone was in on the prank and could see what had happened. Years later, Tom would become a

Superintendent in my Division and to be honest, I don't think that I was ever his favourite person after that.

It was about this time that my brother, Terry, had decided to join the Ministry of Defence Police as well. Terry had also joined the Merchant Navy after me and incidentally had also attended the National Sea Training School at Gravesend in Kent a few years after I had left. He had by now left the Merch after incurring a back injury and had to be flown back home by his shipping company from New Zealand. Having recovered sufficiently he then followed me into the MOD Police. Meanwhile my Mum and Dad were still publicans in Gloucester.

Mum and Dad's customers were what you might call a bit rough and ready. Some had been in trouble with the police for various reasons including assaults and drugs. There was one chap called Archorn who was a biker with a big beard and long black scruffy hair. He was actually a nice chap when you got to know him, and more importantly when he got to know you. His claim to fame was when he had been arrested by the police on one occasion and as he was a violent person when upset, they put him in the back of a police van with a police dog. When they came to open the door to the police van, the dog was apparently cowered in the corner. Apparently the dog had taken a bite out of Archorn and so Archorn had bitten the dog back.

The customers soon learned that Terry and me were MOD police officers. This caused some conversations to take place. Dad use to tell everyone that Terry and me were trained in street fighting rather than the usual Judo and Karate crap. He told everyone that we could fight dirty and with such energy that we could take anyone out if we needed to. Strangely this approach seemed to keep the customers mainly in check and me and Terry never really experienced any bad behaviour from the customers.

I do remember one young fellow one day getting a bit unsociable when my Mum was behind the bar. I was not working behind the bar then as I would have gotten into trouble with my job. I didn't need to do anything though, as my Mum just walked the other side of the bar, grabbed hold of this young man and commenced to smack him around the head with her hands while marching him out of the pub all on her own. Nobody upset my Mum and got away with it. Let's face it, I never did so why should they? She was also very good at using street language to get her point across. After all she was Irish. I just stood behind the bar watching events evolve and nobody, not even this chaps mates, dared to interfere with his expulsion. It was fun to watch.

Chapter Forty Three

The Falklands

Whilst I was serving down in Gosport during 1982 we became very busy as tension throughout the country increased. This was the year of the Falklands war and the whole of the Naval Fleet were called upon to defend the Island. The atmosphere down in Gosport and Portsmouth was really exciting with the television and other media was full of the activities at this time. My kids can still remember the atmosphere down there at the time. They had met some Argentinian children who were given accommodation in the Naval Quarters whilst our military trained their Naval personnel how to work the ships that we had just sold to them, prior to them trying to take the Falklands off us. A bit cheeky don't you think?

Whilst we were living down in Gosport we had managed to get a mortgage on our first house. We had moved up to Bridgemary, still in Gosport which was convenient for the kids schools and for me to get to work. Invariably I would walk backwards and forwards to work as this then left the car for Pauline's convenience, besides which I liked to get the exercise. The kids school was also a short walk away from our new house. I know that getting a mortgage on the house was stretching us financially, as usual, and cost £22,000 which is nothing in today's money, but it was still a great achievement for us back then.

There was a small set of shops just around the corner from us as well which was a bonus for us. The boys managed to join a local football club and Bertie, because he was older, did particularly well and was in a regular team. When I was not on duty I used to enjoy running as a regular exercise and I used to take the boys for a run around one of the fields close by. I remember Alan was only small and found it difficult to keep up with us bless him, but he persevered and completed his laps that I had set out. Today Alan is a keen runner and can run for miles at a time and even belongs to a running club. However, the boys main hobby remained skateboarding.

Even though none of the kids particularly excelled at school, they were all very good students and always attracted complimentary remarks from all of their teachers. I was always confident that their personalities would allow them to achieve whatever they wanted to do in their future life and they have proved me correct. Tony was the only one who had to be coaxed rather more than the others. There were occasions where either me or Pauline would take him to school and he would just follow us back home. We would get back to the house and there he was walking behind us and refusing to go back to school. It was his Nan, Joan, who came up with the idea that if we took a plant in for his teacher and then asked her to detail Tony off for the responsibility of watering the plant, this might give him some incentive to remain at school. This tactic seemed to work for a while at least.

Apparently one day when Alan was out with some of his mates around the Bridgemary shopping area, he had entered the local Co-Op. He did not have any money and he would have been around 8 years old or so. Inside the shop he had spotted some custard cream biscuits and something called Monster Mash and so decided that he would take them without paying. However this act of thievery did not go unnoticed. Alan has told me since that the manager of the Co-Op lived a few doors away from us and had seen Alan take the items from his shop. The manager then came and told me about it. I then marched Alan back to the shop to apologise and to pay for the items that he had taken. On top of that, I had, shamefully today, pulled Alan's pants down and gave him a smack across his bare backside. Alan has told me recently that this definitely stopped him from stealing anything in the future.

Chapter Forty Four

The Poor Force

The MOD Police have always been the poor cousin of the Police Service. We don't get any local funding for any initiatives and we have always relied heavily upon the service station that we policed to supply us with accommodation, vehicles and other such things. It was their responsibility to issue us with suitable vehicles and to maintain them. Most of the time the vehicles were adequate and liveried to show that they were police vehicles. On the other hand we sometimes were supplied with vehicles that could only be described as completely inadequate and inappropriate for a police vehicle.

One such vehicle was a Royal Navy Ford Escort Estate supplied with Police insignia and a airhorn that fitted on top of the vehicle roof. Officers used to have fun with the airhorn when cleaning the vehicle. They would aim the hosepipe down the horn so that when it was activated it sounded more like a strangled dog. One day I had to respond to one of the other MOD establishments nearby after a call that a fire had broken out in a dormitory and that persons were still inside the building. I was with another officer who was the driver on this occasion. We entered the public road and my driver put his foot flat to the floor. We managed to get about 50 mph from the old wreck and there were other vehicles on the road in front of us. I think there was a 40 mph limit on the road anyway but as we wanted to travel as fast as we could, I activated the airhorn. Unfortunately the vehicle had only been washed that morning and so only half of the horn was working. If you can imagine a police vehicle sounding something like nee nah, neee nahhh! Well then, all we had was nahhh, nahhh, nahhh! It was very embarrassing, so much so that I turned the siren off and took a chance on getting through the traffic. As it happened we had a false alarm and when we got to our destination we found everything to be normal and no action required from us. Someone had broken a glass alarm somewhere I believe, just for fun. Well if they had observed the way we had reacted to the alarm, they would have had some fun alright.

I liked Gosport and we had made some very good friends there, some of whom still lived in the married Quarters on the Rowner Estate. My best mate at the time was Andy Chatwin and Pauline got on well with his wife, Yvonne. Andy and I used to regularly play squash in the courts down in HMS Dolphin, and for the few years we lived in Gosport we had set up a 5 a side football team for the MOD Police. Every year we entered the MOD Police tournament at the Nuclear Establishment at Aldermaston. It was a great knockout competition where teams entered from all around the UK from different MOD establishments. We travelled on a daily basis and either managed to play on our Rest days or we were allowed Annual Leave so that we could represent our station. We never won any titles but we all enjoyed the event. The families never came to watch us play and I quite do not remember the reason for this. In the end it just became a lads day out playing football.

I also had a friend named Rob Thomson who was in the Navy and was employed on submarines, not the nuclear type. He was employed on Sonar and had to learn how to recognise loads of different sounds whilst the submarine was submerged. He was very handy to me as he did not smoke and therefore was able to get me his ration of "Blue Liners or tobacco on a regular basis. Blue Liners was a name given to cigarettes supplied by the navy to their personnel and had a blue stripe running down them to show the customs officers that they were "Crew Cigarettes." This was slightly illegal but we both agreed not to tell anyone.

One day his submarine hosted a Christmas party for members of the crew with their children. Rob and his wife Lisa did not have any children but they invited me, with Pauline and the kids to attend. It was fascinating for the kids as we had to climb down the ladder from the hull into the bowels of the submarine. As you might expect with submariners, all went well for a while until they bought out some Christmas cake. Before long the cake along with any other food stuff was being hurtled through the air at each other. We did not need to have taken the kids with us really. The whole cabin area became a right old mess until someone took control and put a stop to the proceedings.

Once everything was back under control the crew simulated a boats dive for us. This meant that all of us in the bowels of the submarine could experience the feeling of the boat actually submerging. To allow this they had to turn all lighting off and then to put a red light on. A klaxon was then sounded to announce a dive. The submarine then sank down a couple of feet as we were obviously still tied alongside and I don't think Health and Safety would allow us to enact a real dive. It was a very enjoyable time with everyone and the kids thoroughly loved it, I enjoyed the experience myself.

Another friend of mine was also on submarines and his name was Paul. When my Mum and Dad used to visit us from Gloucester, my Dad always enjoyed the company of Paul or Rob. The main reason for this was that my Dad used to be a Stoker Mechanic in the Submarine Service. Dad managed to arrange for Paul to get him some submariners working shirts. This was a blue shirt and I think they were called Number Sevens, or something like that. Also the submarine that my Dad had served on, HMS Alliance, had become the centrepiece of the Naval Museum at HMS Dolphin in Gosport and is still there to this day.

I went to HMS Dolphin with my Dad on numerous occasions so that he could go and reminisce onboard his old boat. When I went on board with my Dad, there was a member of the museum staff who was tasked with showing us around. As we were walking around my Dad announced that he had served on her. The guide, who was also an ex submariner anyway, was really interested in what my Dad had to say about the boat.

Just up the road from the establishment that I was employed in, was RNAS Fleetlands. This establishment looked after the running of the helicopters used by the Royal Navy. RNAS stands for, Royal Naval Air Station. I was a friend of the Inspector who was in charge of the policing there.

Fleetlands ran a couple of clubs for the workforce there and they used to organise a few social gatherings. One of these was a Gentleman's evening which obviously included several lady strippers. I almost reluctantly, agreed to attend one of these evenings with several colleagues for a Lads Night Out.

The drinking and the camaraderie made for a great evening and then the ladies started to perform. The majority of it I found to be very funny and entertaining especially having consumed a few alcoholic beverages. Then one of the ladies said, "Has anyone never attended a strip performance before?" I knew that this was not the time to start telling the truth. Unfortunately for one young man he put his hand up. What a fool?

They were all rather good looking ladies who were all completely undressed. One went over to him and walked him to the middle of the floor so that everyone could see the action. They then undressed him and made sure that his excitement was visible to everyone. They then stood over him and commenced to squirt cream all over him and then just left him in the middle of the room whilst they walked 'off Stage'. The poor young man then had to stand up, clean himself off, and then go and sit back down with his mates.

I do not know how I was supposed to feel, but I felt total humiliation on the poor lads part. To me there was nothing exciting or erotic about any of this. Was this my upbringing coming in to play? I don't know. All I know is that I did not enjoy any of the evening other than having a drink with some mates. I did not need the rest of the show. I am not a prude (I think) and I accept that others may have found this performance to be funny. For me, it was just all too humiliating.

Chapter Forty Five

HMNB Portsmouth

It was at this time also that I had to start a 4 week course for promotion to Inspector. I was required to attend the Derbyshire Constabulary Headquarters at Ripley in Derbyshire This again did not do much to bond my marriage. I had started to have suspicions regarding Pauline and a friend of mine. I can not remember all of the details now, but I felt that there was reason to suspect that my marriage was not all as it should be.

Every weekend that I came home would end up with me and Pauline having a row before I returned to Ripley. I used to leave home and drive up to Derby with nothing else in my head but the fact that I thought that Pauline was cheating on me whilst I was away from home. It was a long and lonely journey and one which I would have done anything to get out of, but I had no choice at this time. On top of that, the course itself was demanding and required lots of study as it would eventually lead up to a Diploma in Supervisory management which my job required me to have attained.

After living in Gosport for four years, I eventually had notification that someone in Headquarters had "forgotten" that I was still awaiting my promotion. I had an apology from someone at my Area Headquarters and was immediately offered my promotion to an establishment called P & EE Shoeburyness. This was a Proof and Experimental Establishment which also accommodated a subsidiary of the Nuclear establishment at Aldermaston. Because of this I was required to be Positive Vetted before I could be transferred. In order for me to get my promotion whilst I was awaiting the vetting process, I was informed that I would be temporarily transferred to HMS Portsmouth in the rank of Inspector. Luckily this did not require a move of accommodation and I was able to travel daily to my new place of work.

There was an establishment on the Gosport Side of the water called the Royal Clarence Yard. In practice this was where the Naval Ships were supplied with all of their victuals but also where a police boat would pick up police officers residing over in Gosport to take them to their place of work in the Portsmouth Dockyard. So this is how I used to travel to get to work rather than drive all around the M27 to get to the dockyard.

My position in the dockyard was not an enviable one. I was only there temporarily but I was still in charge of a whole section of officers which also included a Marine Unit. Because I was only temporary, I was not really in a position to make many changes to any of the working practices that I might have wanted to. Generally, I was really just treading water awaiting my vetting to come through so that I could take up my permanent appointment at Shoeburyness.

Whilst I was working at the Dockyard I did pick up some experience as I went along. One of them was when the Queen and Prince Phillip were going to board the Royal Yacht Brittania and I was the Duty Inspector on duty for this occasion. The reason for the Royal party to be boarding the Royal yacht escapes me now but the moment is still stuck in my memory. The yacht was tied up at its moorings and had recently undergone a refurbishment. She looked resplendent with the gold leaf shining so bright along her length. Her Majesty and Prince Phillip arrived at the gangway and obviously everything had been organised with regards to the height of the tide and so on so that it was not too steep for the Royal party. They both passed within an arms length from me but my job was not to look at them, but to ensure that the area around them was safe and secure and I took that responsibility very seriously and so I never got to look at them whilst they boarded the Royal Yacht. Most policemen on Royal Duties will tell you how they were on duty on such an event and never actually managed to view the Royal party as their job was to look into the crowds for any nefarious activity, not to just observe the Royal party. If you look at police officers working today during such events, you will see that they are always facing the crowds and not looking at the main event.

When I was on a night shift, I would normally go down to the boat section and patrol along the Solent with them. I must admit that we used to stretch this brief and would often traveller to the Isle of Wight for a look around. This was so especially when the round the Island race used to take place whilst I was there. We also had an American Aircraft Carrier moored out in the Solent because it was too large to enter the Portsmouth Naval base. Our job was then to protect the Naval Assets for the Americans and this usually required and extra police boat and crew to be put on duty. I loved all this side of my job and I was in my element at this time.

Eventually my vetting came through and I was given a date to be transferred to the P & EE Shoeburyness. We had several considerations to take care of before we moved. I have to say that in those days it was automatic that you should be transferred when taking up promotion. It was considered that this afforded the person being promoted to make a fresh start and be able to make his, or her, stamp at a reasonable time rather than to be tangled up with officers who had become their "mates." I had no problems with this way of thinking and in a way I entirely agreed with it. On reflection though, I often wonder whether striving for promotion was worth all of the stress and heartache that this caused. In today's circumstances it is not something that I would recommend to anyone, nor the actions that I would want to take myself. I can not really put my finger on what was so different in those days and why I would want to put my family through this turmoil. The only comfort that I can take from all of this is that none of us would be where we are in our lives today had we not taken those decisions that we took at the time. I take comfort from the fact that all of my family are where they want to be today. They are all financially stable and settled with their own families and hopefully will have a wide outlook on life, much as I did whilst growing up.

Chapter Forty Six

Shoeburyness

We moved to the Proof & Experimental Establishment at Shoeburyness sometime during 1984. In order to give us more time to find a suitable house to live in, we took up temporary accommodation in a Married Quarter. The quarters were located outside the wire of the establishment and so this did not restrict us having visitors and the like. We must have taken a while finding a suitable house to live in as for some reason we moved to a further temporary Married Quarter just around the corner from where we were living. We were certainly getting used to moving houses.

We eventually moved to a really nice house in Rochford on a road called Weir Pond Road. This was very near to Southend Airport. It was only a few miles from my place of work and was in a good location. On a Sunday morning you could hear engines being tested on some of the jets which was quite noisy at times. The village shops in Rochford were well represented and there is a plaque in the market square which states that a John Simson was burned at the stake there in 1555 because of his protestant beliefs.

I actually liked Rochford and we had some good friendly neighbours but for some reason that I do not recall now, we moved house again to an estate called the Bird Estate and we lived on Eagle Way which was almost opposite a very good Catholic school which had a high reputation for teaching and the discipline of the kids. Unfortunately we couldn't get any of the children in to that one and had to make do with other local schools, which were still good schools anyway.

Back at work, I really enjoyed my job. The area that we were responsible for was quite large and included two villages, Courtsend and Churchend, and a couple of pubs. The villages were located on an Island called Foulness and could only be accessed by way of a bridge over an inlet from the North Sea. The area was all on MOD Land which was sensitive as an Atomic Weapons Research Establishment, a subsidiary of AWE Aldermaston, was located on it. This meant that anyone entering the Island, including residents and their visitors had to pass through a MOD Police Checkpoint. Obviously the Police Officers who were on duty there got to know the residents and a good atmosphere was always present. It was a bit strange though as only people who had been invited to the island by residents, and then notified to the MOD Police could enter the Island and therefore the pubs.

During this time, Pauline's mum, Joan, had visited us on a regular basis. She and her long time partner, Norman had split up before we had left Gosport. She used to like coming with us to the Police Club at Shoeburyness. It was while she was visiting the club one time that she started talking to one of the policemen on my section. He had recently become single after his wife had died. I was his welfare officer as he was from my section and so I got to know a lot about his private life. Joan announced one day that she and John had become an item. I was a bit dubious at first but they were both grown ups and could do what they like. John's second name was Jones and so it became comical to refer to them as John and Joan Jones, it just rolled off the tongue. They went on to become married and Joan moved into John's house that he had previously shared with his wife.

One night after having visited the police club, Me, John and Barry, Barry is Pauline's brother, were walking back to John's house as the women had managed to get a lift from someone. As we were walking from the club a group of young people were just behind us and had obviously been drinking in one of the other clubs which were also within the establishment. As they approached some cones in the road they started to pick them up and thought it was fun to throw them across a field or put them on top of their heads and walk around with them on. John turned around to them and told them to behave themselves and to put the cones back where they had been. Of course we had not declared ourselves as police officers and so this little crowd had no idea who we were. There were three girls and five boys all about late teens or early twenties.

The little crowd did not take kindly to being told off by John and started to give him a bit of lip and so we just carried on walking towards home. As we got a bit further ahead of them they shouted something at us and one of us, I can't remember who, retaliated with another verbal message. I have to say that the girls were a lot louder than the boys and they encouraged the boys to attack us. When we looked back at them they were running towards us at full pelt and shouting what they were going to do to us. We had gotten outside the establishment by this time and passed through a MOD Police entry point. As they reached us I tried to talk my way out by trying to reason with them. Unfortunately this did not satisfy their present intentions and they began to punch and kick out at us, goaded by the nice young ladies that were with them. I remember hitting the floor and then a shoe being kicked into my face but not much more as it became very confusing and busy.

The MOD Policemen who had been on duty had heard the kerfuffle going on along the road and had sent some officers out to see what was going on. They were aware that someone was being assaulted but had no idea that it was two of their own colleagues, me and John. Barry by this time had disappeared back to John's house and so me and John were on our own. The MOD Policemen arrested the five men and had taken them back inside the establishment to the police offices and had commenced taking statements from them. I had walked into the building to see what was going on and I heard one of the policemen say to one of the lads, "You have made a big mistake mate, that is our Inspector". Anyway they were all taken to Southend police station and only one of the lads was charged with the assault and later found guilty and ended up with a fine. I ended up with a couple of hundred quid from the Criminal Injury Compensation Board and so all was well in the end. No one ended up with any permanent injuries. I had been off work for about a week which resulted in a Superintendent from my Divisional Headquarters coming to give me a welfare check. My injuries were not serious but my pride was badly shaken. I had always been capable of looking after myself and then all of a sudden I was a victim of violence. That was the worst feeling of all.

The difficulties in my marriage had not gone away. Pauline and me had already had rows before we had left Gosport regarding my suspicions between her and my best friend. An allegation she strongly denied. She kept telling me how I was spoiling our marriage with my suspicions. They had kept in touch after we had moved and even though the chap concerned was my so called friend I kept getting bad vibes. Pauline managed to convince me that it was all in my head and that I was damaging a good friendship whilst at the same time showing that I did not trust her. My instinct was that my marriage was in trouble but my heart was in denial. This all sounds very stupid now as I write these words but at that rime I was very confused and I was beginning to think that there was something wrong in my own head. I couldn't sleep and every waking moment was filled with my suspicions, even whilst I was at work.

Back in my working mode, I had been detailed off to manage the rosters for the 160 officers who were employed at Shoeburyness. This was an additional duty alongside being a shift commander in charge of my own section of officers. I was responsible for allocating Annual Leave, Special Leave, Courses and also for ensuring that all shifts were kept up to strength during periods of detached duties or sickness etc. I was never so pleased to be doing this task when a big operation took place as what was secretly called "Station X'. I had to deploy a load of our officers within 24 hours to attend a mass demonstration and all officers had to be suitably qualified in Public Safety training. The station turned out to be the American Air base at RAF Molesworth. The weather was one of the coldest on record and officers were very inadequately supplied with suitable clothing. We even had a couple of officers who were hospitalised with hypothermia. I never ended up being deployed there, after all, I was in charge of the rostering!! Molesworth in effect was similar to our times of policing Greenham Common. A lot of the demonstrators were the same people and were all demonstrating for the same reason the storage of American arsenal on UK land.

Even though I managed the rosters I had to attend a few other courses as well whilst I was employed at Shoeburyness. I had attended a few public order training courses and as the Inspector I had to be trained to command a group of officers who were carrying what was called long shields. I would be at the back of them barking out orders whilst carrying out a short shield. I loved this training as we were bombarded with bricks and eventually bottles of paraffin which had been set on fire. We learned all of the techniques involved in this kind of duty and I thoroughly loved and enjoyed them. My kids will remember me coming home and not being able to speak for a week or so where I had lost my voice. These were the days before any suitable communication method had been introduced and so I had to make sure that my team could hear the instructions that I was giving them. I was given lots of advice from former military personnel, such as, gargle with vinegar and honey which apparently was supposed to lubricate the voice box. I never really had chance to try this method out, especially as I was always living away from home when carrying out these duties.

I was always looking for something different to do during my career. I think that this is what drove me on to get promotion. I am easily bored and need stimulation by trying out different activities. It was during my time at Shoeburyness that I toyed with the idea of becoming a Training School Instructor. Before I could carry out any Instructors Courses I had to attend a a two-week assessment course at our Training School in Medmenham. I was given a date for the course and also one of my sergeants accompanied me as he had also shown an interest in training.

The course was very disappointing for me as the main emphasis was discipline, having to have shiny shoes, being able to run three miles in a given time etc. There had recently been a few scandals within the training department where one or two of the instructors had, shall we say, taken advantage of their positions over recruits. We also had to present two subjects each, such as Theft or Criminal Damage but we were not allowed to used any modern technology. We had to do the Blue Peter thing and make our own slides and props in order to put the subject matter across. This ended up not being my forte. At my end of course interview the superintendent and me agreed with each other that I was not cut out to be an instructor. My sergeant ended up with a similar end of course interview. In the end, I was more than happy not to be involved in that side of my Force.

Chapter Forty Seven

Adoption

By 1985/6 We had lost all contact with Kelly's biological Mum and Dad. Since we had moved away from Gosport her mum had even had another child, not with the same father. Kelly's Mum and Dad had at last agreed that it would be fairer on Kelly if me and Pauline should adopt her instead of continuing to Foster her. So we attended the courts at Southend on one very special day and it was made official that Kelly was no longer a fostered child, but was now a bona fide member of our own family. I have to say that during this whole process the boys were marvellous and never once showed any resentment with us taking on another member of our family.

Pauline had never settled around Southend and was constantly complaining that she wanted to get back to Gosport or around that area. I could never understand why Pauline felt that Southend was such a bad place to live. We had the sea, the beaches, it was a lot closer for her to go and see her Dad in North London (Enfield), her Mum was now living there as well. There was no logical reason for us not to enjoy the life that we had there. The stress that came with work, quite often twelve hour shifts, and then coming home to an unhappy household was beginning to have its effect on me also.

I was still working as a shift Commander when an opportunity arose for us to move back to Gosport. Back to my old station at RNAD Bedenham. I would be the Deputy Senior Police Officer with a Chief Inspector in overall charge. I would also be on a Monday to Friday 9 - 5 shift with every weekend off. I saw this as a good opportunity to keep Pauline happy by moving back to an area that she was happy in and also it would be a good advancement move for my career as well as gaining experience in a different role within my Force. I was desperately hoping that our marriage might start to heal itself even though we going going back to an area where "my mate" still lived. I guess this was getting to a "make or break" stage of our marriage.

We can never forget the time that we moved back to Gosport. Again we were lucky enough to get some temporary accommodation over in Portsmouth whilst our purchase was finalised on a house that we had bought in Fareham. We were housed in some Royal Marines flats on a Naval Estate in Portsmouth. We were there on the night of the 15th October 1987. This date is very relevant as we had been watching the weather forecast given by a presenter called Michael Fish who had predicted very blowy wind but he assured us that it was not going to be a hurricane. That particular broadcast of his would haunt him for the rest of his life.

On that particular night we had been sat watching the television in our flat and we could hear the wind outside start to get louder. Eventually we could see the glass in the windows start to bend and I closed all of the curtains in case the glass should smash. The wind had started to howl and we could see that some trees outside had been blown down and the loft hatch inside the flat kept rising and crashing back down. It was very noisy and it was obvious that this was no normal storm.

There was a knock on our front door and when I opened it, there was a whole family asking if they could seek refuge with us because the roof of their flat had been blown off. Apparently the loft covers had been literally sucked through the roof. We didn't know this family but we were happy to share our flat with them. Shortly after they had come into our flat there was another knock on the door and another family were also seeking refuge. We were becoming very crowded now and we all listened to the storm raging outside. Our own loft covering was rattling and we were getting a little scared for our safety. We couldn't leave the flats as outside there were bits of trees and all sorts of other materials being blown around like missiles and if any of them were to hit you, you would have been seriously injured. There was literally nowhere to seek refuge other than to take our chances inside our own flat.

During the early hours of the 16th October the wind had dissipated and this was the day that our contract on our house in Fareham had been exchanged. The scenes all over Portsmouth was one of complete devastation everywhere. There were small boats way up on the land smashed to bits. A lot of roads were impassable because of trees and debris everywhere. None the less, this was our day for moving to our new house and we needed to get over to the other side of the water from Portsmouth to Gosport.

We travelled over to Fareham via the M27 and then on to Templemere Close which was the address of our newly acquired house. What we were presented with made our hearts sink. As we approached our new house, we noticed that the high brick wall that had surrounded one side of the garden was missing. Not so much missing as actually laying on top of four cars that had parked along the side of it. The cars were in a legitimate parking area unfortunately my wall had been almost completely demolished in the storm the day before. My first reaction was to check the rest of the house out and I noticed one ridge tile was missing but other than that we had gotten away lightly. This was going to be a very awkward meeting of new neighbours.

Fortunately for us, the damage caused by the storm was deemed to be "An act of God" and we were not liable to the repair of the damaged cars, nor of the damage caused to the wall. All car owners had to claim from their own insurance, which was alright provided that they were fully comprehensive. Had they been only Third Party, they would not have been able to claim from their own insurance. Anyway, our wall was eventually repaired with no cost to ourselves. I think that we still managed to be friends with our new found neighbours despite the circumstances of our arrival.

It is always a little bit unsettling when having to start a new job for the first time. It was possibly even stranger going back to Gosport as an Inspector instead of a sergeant which had been my rank the last time I had worked there. I started my new job and found it to be very challenging and I really enjoyed it. I should have had a Chief Inspector as my boss but the incumbent had retired and his replacement had not yet been found and so for three months I ended up carrying out an Acting role as the Chief Inspector. The Chief Inspectors role also included the responsibility of what was called the Group Headquarters and we were responsible for loads of other satellite stations around Hampshire. This threw me straight into the Lions Den.

The Royal Naval Air Station at Fleetlands just up the road from me also had an Inspector in charge of it. I had known this Inspector from my previous service at Bedenham and he was indeed senior in length of service to me. Because I was now carrying out the role of a Chief Inspector, this then put me in charge of him because of my acting rank. I have to say that this never caused us any problems at all as we were both too long in the tooth by now. Anyway, the way he ran his station never gave me any cause for concern and I never had to intervene in any way. In fact it was a good location for me to go and grab a nice cup of coffee and a chat with a fellow officer.

I was detailed off to attend the second part of my Inspectors Promotion course back up in Ripley in Derbyshire. This one was going to last for six weeks but I would complete the course hopefully, with a Diploma in Supervisory Studies. The course was really interesting but intense. Much studying and research was required in order to merit receiving the Diploma. I made life interesting for myself and conducted a study in to pornography and to whether it caused harm, or not. That is a different story.

As part of the course I and a few others from my course had opted to visit a local mine. We had to be careful which mine we chose as there was still bad feeling against the police after the coal miners strikes. However, Nottingham coal mines were agreeable to us as the majority of coal mines in Nottingham had refused to strike and did not agree with Arthur Scargill. In the event, we attended the Bentink coal mine in Nottingham. The experience was wonderful. We travelled in the cage to the bottom of the pit and then had to walk along the mine to visit the coal face. It was extremely hot I can tell you. I don't know how the miners managed to work in these conditions. We were all knackered just walking through the mine. The miners were very kind and helpful to us and we had a great experience with them.

One of my fellow Inspectors on the course with me was an officer named Dave Coleman who eventually made the dizzy heights of becoming the Chief Constable of the Derby Constabulary. I really should have accepted my invitation to work at my Force Headquarters all them years ago!!!

One of the most innovative ideas that we had for the boys christmas present this year was to buy them all skate boarding equipment. This included all of the safety gear including wrist pads, shin guards, safety helmets etc. Who would have believed that after

211

over forty years later that they were still skating and meeting up with their skater friends that they had made during all these years.

The problems within my marriage raised its ugly head again. During the six weeks course, I would travel home on a Friday evening at the end of our lessons but would need to travel back to Ripley on the Sunday afternoon. Because some of us had so far to travel home, (I think I had the furthest to travel) we did finish a bit earlier on the Fridays. Every Sunday afternoon without fail, Pauline and me would have an argument, more often than not over my suspicions of her infidelity. We had gotten in touch with my "old friend" and his wife. I remember the horrible feeling in my stomach travelling up the M1 with the feeling that I was helpless to do much about saving my marriage. Again Pauline had convinced me that my suspicions were in my mind and that my Best Friend was indeed my "Best Friend" and that I should try to get this jealousy feeling out of my head. I tried really hard for this to happen for the sake of my marriage, but I was struggling.

A dramatic moment came one day when a hand written letter had been posted through the front door of our house. When I read it it was from the mother of the wife of my Best Friend. It would appear that my mate and his wife were also having marriage difficulties and that the blame was being placed squarely at Pauline's feet. The mother was accusing Pauline of ruining her daughters marriage by having an affair with her son-in-law. I didn't know what to do but Pauline soon had the solution for us. Together we went to see the mother of my Best Friends wife to explain to her how silly she was being. I stated my absolute trust for Pauline and the fact that if I thought that something undesirable was going on, "Would I still be here?" This seems to calm things down for the time being. It was only a few weeks after that that my Best Friend left his wife to live with another married police woman from my station. I think this may have put doubts in my mind that perhaps I had been imagining my own problems as obviously now, my Mate was with a completely different woman altogether.

Work-wise I was probably never so happy. I had two female police officers who were looking after my administration and eventually I also recruited a male to join the team. One of the women was engaged to a police officer in the Hampshire Constabulary and they had a date to get married.

My reason for mentioning this is, that in order for a police officer to get Police Rent Allowance, the Senior Police Officer of that Station had to declare that they knew the location of the house and that the accommodation was suitable for a police officer to live in. After submitting her application to me, I stated these facts and then forwarded the application for favourable consideration by the Assistant Chief Constable, who was the overriding authority for approval. I made the recommendation and forwarded the application to my Area Headquarters which was located on Aldershot.

Meanwhile, before the application was returned to me, a substantive Chief Inspector was posted in to the station. This meant that I then reverted back to being an Inspector. I had not met this Chief Inspector before and it was all very embarrassing when one of his first tasks was to take me aside and give me suitable advice, in a very strong way. It appeared that the mistake that I had made was to recommend that a Policewoman should be allowed to live immorally with another police officer. This was because they were not legally married. The letter from the Assistant Chief Constable stated that how dare Inspector Tonks forward such an application to him for approval for such immoral practice of living together without being married. I was flabbergasted but had to take the dressing down and get on with it. The couple in questioned did soon get married and were successful in their subsequent application.

The Royal Naval Air Station at Lee-on-the-Solent was holding an Open day and an Air Display. There was an officer of Sergeant rank who was the Senior Police Officer at that station and he did all of the arrangements necessary for this day. I was detailed off to overlook the proceedings and be in overall command for the day of this event. The event was very well organised between the Navy and the Sergeant who was responsible for all policing and security arrangements. The day was well attended and my kids also rocked up to see what was going on. They still remember it to this day. One of the highlights was when Concord flew overhead and then took a track along the runway without touching down. She was on her way to America and was fully laden with passengers who were waving from their windows as they flew along the runway. I do not think that this would have gotten past Health and Safety regulations today. I think this would have been summer of 1988.

My marriage was still strained but running along in its own way. The house we were in was great and we had put a conservatory on the back to get a little more living space. The concrete floor had been laid and we were looking forward to going to choose the flooring and furniture to kit it out with.

Before the concrete floor could dry I received notice that I was to be transferred to RAF Wethersfield as the a Senior Police Officer in charge of my own station. We had only been living in our house for nine months. This news was broken to me whilst I was at work and now I was dreading going back home to break the news to my family. I had no choice in this matter. Apparently there was another Inspector over at the Portsmouth Naval Base who was having health problems and they needed him to take my place at Bedenham. I obviously knew RAF Wethersfield a little bit as I had been there on a detached Duty previously to police the mass demonstrations against the American Air Bases in this country.

When I broke the news after arriving home I was expecting fireworks but instead Pauline seemed to take it all in her stride. She didn't seem to mind the prospect of moving which was a bit of a shock to me, but also made life a bit easier as well. The problem was that my eldest son Albert did not want to move with us. He was 16 years of age and wanted to stay in this area to complete his education. I was not going to force him to move with us as I felt that he was now old enough to make his own decisions. After all, he always had a home to come to wherever we lived. The choice had to be his.

Our biggest problem before we could move was finding Albert somewhere to live. He actually did this himself and had a friend whose parents were in agreement to give Albert his accommodation for a fee. We obviously met with the parents and talked things through with them. This is how we left Gosport with a heavy heart, we were leaving our eldest child behind and that was not a good feeling.

Chapter Forty Eight

Problems with Bertie

My new role at Wethersfield required me to work nine to five, Monday to Friday, and to be on call at all other times that I was not on duty. I had a sergeant who was classed as my deputy and between us we managed the running of the policing arrangements at Wethersfield for the British personnel on base. The Americans had their own Police Service whom we worked alongside, but would often come into conflict with one another.

I was on duty one day when I received a telephone call from an Inspector in the Hampshire Constabulary back down in Gosport. I had worked with him on something when I had been working down in Gosport and so he knew me personally. He was phoning to inform me that one of his officers had had to arrest Albert who had been found to be drunk and disorderly in Fareham Town. Apparently Albert had not been so disorderly, but more drunk and incapable. The officer had had to arrest him for his own safety as Albert was unconscious in the middle of the town with no one else around to look after him. The Inspector told me that he just wanted to tell me not to worry and that they were just looking after him overnight and that when he had sobered up the next morning they were going to release him with a police caution. I was grateful for the phone call but became very concerned over Albert's behaviour. I didn't like the fact that his so called friends that he had apparently been drinking with were not helping to look after him, but mostly upset that I could not be there with him there and then.

During Christmas of 1988, Albert came home to spend the Christmas with the rest of the family at Great Yeldham in Essex, which is where we were now living. We had a lovely Christmas but Albert was due to travel back to Gosport before the New Year. In fact he caught a train from Braintree on the 30th December 1988. I remember taking photos of him in the railway carriage and I can still see the sadness in his eyes whilst we were all saying goodbye to each other. It reminded of me leaving home around that age when I joined the Merchant Navy. I had a very heavy heart even though Albert could always stay with us any time he wanted to. What I did not know until very recently was that my eldest son was going through a black period in his life and that I was completely inadequate in realising this and therefore incompetent in being of any help to him.

Unbeknown to me, Albert had fallen out with the household he was living with. Neither Albert or any of the family had informed me that anything was wrong. It now transpires after all of these years that Albert had been living rough on the streets. I take this as a total failure on my part for not knowing this. Why did I not know what was going on? I can not remember now but I was certainly paying for Albert's board and lodgings, whether that was directly to Albert, or to the family who were meant to be looking after his accommodation for me. I was getting a monthly allowance from my work for him and so there was no reason why he should have been living on the streets. It was not as if I couldn't afford it because I was not actually paying for him, my work was. I was not expecting anyone else to actually look after Albert, but a word in my ear that things were not working out would have been useful. Whatever went wrong, I guess I will never know with certainty. Only Albert can be my judge.

Chapter Forty Nine

Trouble Brewing

It was during the late 80's that the mortgage interest rate soared to 17% or more. I had really stretched myself to get a really nice house but that meant that my mortgage was very high. I remember struggling so much financially. I had a garden that I couldn't even afford to look after and make nice. It was also around this time that my marriage started to really unfold. I had strong suspicions regards Pauline and my best friend from Gosport. There had been a few other occasions during our marriage where the Green Eyed Monster had poked his head out.

There was also another friend of ours where we were now living in Great Yeldham in Essex, who Pauline had grown an attachment to. On one occasion when I had to work away from home my sons had followed her up to this so called friends house and actually observed them. They have never told me exactly what they had observed. The boys were devastated and confronted Pauline themselves. This resulted in Pauline phoning me and telling me that the boys were being over protective and could I put them right that everything was ok and that they should stop following her wherever she went. Of course being the fool that I was, I took my wife's side and had a word with the boys not to keep annoying their mother and that they were out of order. I don't know what they must have thought of me, but I know now what I think of myself. At that time I would have done anything to keep my marriage and my family together. I know that the boys gave up on me because in their eyes, I would not take any notice of them. At the end of the day I was trying to trust and believe in my wife.

I had to go through the humiliation at one stage when the landlord of our local pub asked to speak to me and Pauline in private. He informed us that there were rumours going around the village that Pauline was having an affair with this so called friend of ours. This was based on how many times Pauline's car was observed outside his house when I was at work. This friend had a live in girl friend at the time who also worked away from home during the week. This gave the two of them ample opportunity to carry on their liaisons, if that was what was happening.

During 1989/90 I was transferred to Chilwell Station as the Senior Police Officer. The Americans were moving out of Wethersfield and the rank of Inspector would no longer be required at that location. I was also hoping that this might be a new start for me and Pauline as a close female friend of hers who we had know very well when we lived in Gosport, ran a pub nearby to where we were going to live. Sadly she was now divorced from her original husband who I got on really well with and she had remarried to another nice chap. We lived in Married Quarters within the Chilwell Camp in Nottingham. Life was moving along at its normal pace but I was having to spend some time away from home again with work commitments. By this time, all of the kids were living back at home, Albert included and I was overjoyed with this. We were back to being a complete family again.

During 1990 we had somehow managed to purchase a narrow boat. The boat was named "Samantha" and she was moored at the Castle Marina in Nottingham. I was inexperienced in boat handling at this time and so the whole prospect of taking the boat out on the water was really quite exciting. I was sure that I had lot to learn, but with my family background regarding my fathers side of the family, I was sure that this would not take me too long.

I was not wrong in feeling that I had a lot to learn and this was demonstrated one fine day during the winter of 1990. It was a lovely sunny but cool day and we had decided to take the boat out from Nottingham up to Shardlow for the weekend. Shardlow is only a few miles. We must have started out some time in the afternoon.

The River Trent was fairly fast flowing but not in flood, and at this time of year, the evenings were closing in pretty early. We had just passed a place called Beeston Marina with then not far to go to get to Shardlow. However it was now becoming a little bit dark and so we decided that perhaps we should just turn about and and moor in the Beeston marina overnight.

I turned the boat around and all of a sudden we were going with the flow of the river at a fair old pace. Quicker than I had anticipated. As we reached near the Beeston Marina I commenced to turn the boat in order to moor up outside the Marina Club House. Unfortunately, as I commenced to turn, the flow of the river caught us broadside and pushed the boat sideways, not allowing me to completely turn. We were then pushed very close to the weir at Beeston. The noise from the weir was like thunder and there was a real possibility of us being swept over the top.

I struggled with the rudder and tried to "swim" the rudder by pushing it from Port to Starboard in rapid succession whilst keeping the revs on the engine at full pace. Eventually Bertie managed to jump ashore and tied the bow of the boat on to the shore side which then allowed me to get the boat turned in the right direction and eventually to be able to moor up where I had originally intended. The whole scenario was frightening and we were very lucky that none of us had come to any harm.

When we did manage to get ashore and into the Club House, we could feel everyone looking at us. We spoke to several people who told us that they had seen our predicament and were on the verge of calling for emergency assistance. Over the years, Beeston weir has seen many bad incidents occur and there have even been people killed there for one reason or another. We were very lucky to escape unharmed.

Albert, Tony, Kelly and Alan in the bar of the Victoria Inn, Hucclecote.

Mum playing with Alan and Kelly in the sandpit of the pub garden.

Albert, Tony, Kelly and Alan in a garden at Rochford, Essex

Shopping at Southend with my four children.

Kelly's adoption.

Receiving my diploma from the Acting Chief Constable at Portsmouth Dockyard.

At my desk as an Inspector..

My Dad dockside at HMS Dolphin, Gosport. The naval museum which now houses HM Submerine Alliance. He was stationed on this sub when I was born.

Me, Tony, Albert, Alan and Dad while on our famous boating trip in 1991..

The four generations of Albert Tonks. Taken at my Grandfather's 80th birthday.

My Mum has just fed my four kids.

Aileen and Dawn sing Karaoke with Mum and Kelly watching.

Chapter Fifty

The Boat Trip

During May 1991, arrangements had been made for me and my three sons, as well as my Dad, Uncle, and poor old Poppy, the dog, to take a two week tour on the boat and we were going to travel around the Cheshire Ring. Pauline was insistent that we should all do this as it would be bonding for all of the "Lads" to get away together on a one off opportunity. However there was a caveat from Pauline in order for "the lads" to take this opportunity".

The trip away with my Dad and my sons and uncle was very memorable. We had such a great time together. We had such a laugh. Unfortunately the boat broke down at Harecastle Tunnel and I had to call on the assistance of "Pete, the Boat Doctor" to come and rescue us. It didn't take long for him to get us up and running again although we lost our timed slot on that day to actually go through the tunnel. The tunnel is only open at certain times of the day as it is a "One Way" stretch of water and is under the control of a "Tunnel Keeper".

During the trip my Dad had managed to phone my Mum to let her know how we all were. It transpired that she was not very well herself at this time and it was touch and go whether my Dad should leave our voyage and go back home to look after Mum. However, my Mum would not hear of it and insisted that my Dad should finish our boat trip together to the end. I think Mum had been suffering with a bad cold at the time.

We had worked out a great routine for getting ourselves through the locks. For a start, the Admiral, my Dad, would always made sure that we were underway really early in the morning, between 7am and 8am. This was in order to beat "holiday makers" who were out and messing about on the water. When approaching the locks a couple of the boys would jump ashore and run up to the locks to make sure that they were ready for our arrival. Quite often Poppy also used to jump ashore and run alongside them. Our unobstructed travel in the mornings meant that by the early afternoon we were ready to tie up for the rest of the day and usually visit a pub for the afternoon. We had borrowed a "movie camera" from someone we knew and this required the batteries to be regularly charged up. As we never had any mains electricity on board the boat, we would ask the pub landlords to charge the batteries for us. We were lucky and never encountered any refusals.

The boys, Bertie, Tony and Alan, also found a game that they loved to play. As we approached a bridge they would stand on the top of the boat. When we reached the bridge they would hang on to the side and then climb on to the top of the bridge before running across and jumping back on the boat as we emerged from the other side. This created a lot of hilarity.

We always ate really well. As my Uncle Cyril had been a chef in the army many years ago, we made him "Head Chef" which was a role he did not mind filling. We had a full size cooker and Uncle Cyril's cooking was exceptional and we never went hungry. Poor old Uncle Cyril used to get really emotional whenever the song "Sacrifice" by Elton John was played. Apparently this song always reminded him of his daughter Carol who he loved so much. Of course because he used to get emotional and start to tear up, my boys thought that this was hilarious and would continually play the song just to see him crying. Have I mentioned that my boys were outrageous and were always game for a good wind up?

We were only on the trip for two weeks but the memories have lasted a life time.I eventually sold the boat to Uncle Cyril's daughter, Carol who used it much more than I ever did with her husband, Paul. When I had the boat she was called "Samantha" but Carol changed the name to "Rebekah" after her daughter.

I remember that our penultimate night on the boat was the 30th May 1991 as it was Bertie's birthday. By this time we had run out of food and were hoping to get a pub lunch in Shardlow. Unfortunately the pub was not doing any food on this particular night and there was only one cob left under their food covering. Bertie managed to grab this for himself and the rest of us had to watch him eat it whilst we all had a packet of crisps each.

After making all of the arrangements for the boat trip, Pauline announced that she wanted to take Kelly on a holiday with her while we were away. She wanted to go abroad to Mykonos in Greece. I was not happy about this and again we had our usual arguments. However Pauline had obviously confided in her friend who had the pub. Between the two of them, they convinced me that there was nothing untoward and there was no harm in it. After all, Pauline would have Kelly with her and Kelly was only eleven years old at the time and so how could she get into any trouble?

I was constantly thinking about how Pauline and Kelly were doing. My own trip on the boat was an experience that will live with me till my dying days. The trip was a magical experience and I loved being with those guys every minute. Our experiences could almost make up another book!! Whatever happened after this trip, I will never regret having spent such quality time with my boys and my Dad.

At the end of our trip we all went back home. The boys and the dog obviously coming back with me to Chilwell. Pauline and Kelly arrived back home a few days later and I collected them from East Midlands Airport. Pauline was very quiet for a couple of weeks and told me that she had a tummy upset, probably from something she had eaten she told me. The atmosphere in the house was very subdued and I was not quite sure why. My concerns were being met with the answer that Pauline was just feeling a bit under the weather.

Chapter Fifty One

End of a Marriage

One night as Pauline was preparing dinner after I had got home from work she just said that we needed to talk, which we did as the kids were not in the room with us at this point. She told me that she had had enough of our marriage and that she did not love me any more and was going to leave. She explained that the kids were all old enough now to not need her. Albert was 19, Tony 17, Alan 15 and Kelly 11 years of age. Within a couple of days she had moved into the pub with her friend. I was devastated.

Within a day or so whilst I was at work Pauline had cleared all of her clothes out of our wardrobes and gone to stay with her mother in Shoeburyness in Essex. I was still distraught at this time and sent the biggest bunch of flowers that I could afford to her. I was practically pleading with her to come back home so that we could sort our marriage out. She never did see the flowers because by then she had arranged to leave the country altogether.

Pauline disappeared off the face of the earth for about three months. Nobody knew where she had gone, not even her own mother. Apart from wondering what was going on, there was also concern for her welfare. We knew that she had gone abroad somewhere but nobody knew where - as far as I know.

It later transpired that Pauline had met a Doctor of some sorts (I don't think he was GP, but I do not know) while she was away and had proceeded to have a holiday romance. She had now gone to see him (I can't remember where he lived, but it was something like Luxembourg - I may be wrong about the country). Whatever, she had gone to be with him. I was devastated and it felt like she had died. Only someone who has lived through this type of experience could possibly know how it feels. I carried on working and looking after the house on a daily basis. I only had Alan and Kelly at home with me because Tony had moved to Shoeburyness to be near his girlfriend and to set up a window cleaning business. Albert had moved off somewhere else again but that did not last very long and before too long they all returned back home to me again.

Initially, I think that at the time if Pauline had come back home saying that she had made a big mistake and had now realised how much she really loved me and so on, I would have considered taking her back. The problem was that after three months of not knowing where she was, and then realising how selfish she had been by not telling anyone where she was and that she was OK, my own feelings had changed. I realised that if you really loved someone then you would not have put them through everything that I was going through. I came to accept that my marriage was ended and to be honest once I had done that, a great weight was lifted off my shoulders. The Green Eyed Monster no longer existed and he had been sent away for good.

Pauline came back to this country at some point, I do not know much about it. She did also write me a letter saying that she had made a mistake and that she would like to come back. Unfortunately by that time, too much anger, tears, self pity and all of those other emotions that are raised in these circumstances had ceased to exist. I had accepted that it was not possible for us to be together again and that life had now moved on. I was also able to look back at myself and I realise how indecisive and stupid I had been in the past. In all honesty our marriage had stopped working for many years before now. The marriage was well and truly over. I can now look back clearly and realise that as difficult and hurtful it was for me at the time when Pauline left us all, in the long run, particularly for myself, she did me a big favour. It just never felt like that at the time.

Having accepted the demise of my marriage I got on with life as best as I could. Looking back I realise that I was in a bad place in my life. I was attempting to carry on with a normal life but of course my life was not normal at this time.

I was really touched one day when I was at work in my office. Some of the police officers who work with me had become concerned for me and had contacted the local Civil Service Welfare officer who paid me an unexpected visit. I convinced the welfare officer that I was doing just fine and that I had my life under control. I actually felt that this was the case, but looking back now, I do realise that I needed some help somewhere, I just would not admit it, or I did not realise that I needed help. I still appreciate the fact that some of my staff were actually concerned for my welfare. I have to say that I was never once contacted by any of my own senior officers to see if I was coping, in fact, they were utterly useless in all respects as far as my welfare was concerned.

After not too long, and for reasons that escape me now, both Tony and Bertie ended up living back at home with me. They will never realise just how much this meant to me and how much I wanted this to happen. Tony had tried to become a window cleaner down in Essex and this had not worked out for him.

One of the worst times for me was when I was required to be away from home on a Special Duty (I will explain later). We did not have mobile phones in those days and so communications with home were difficult. I had tried to get out some of my duties requiring me to be away from home but I met with no assistance from my senior officers and in fact I was made to feel that the circumstances I was now in were entirely my own fault. I would like to think that I was a better boss to my staff than they ever were to me.

The kids were beginning to get used to my cooking as well. It had been a steep learning curve as I had not been used to having to prepare meals before. Pauline had not worked (apart from an occasional part time job) and so was a full time house person which included organising meals. My Sunday dinners were notorious. The roast potatoes were rock hard and squirted fat into your face when you cut into them. My trifles were massive, made from swiss rolls, two tins of fruit salad and then covered in custard with a sprinkle of one thousand and ones on top of the squirty cream. Come on now, who wouldn't love all of that?

On one particular occasion when I had to be away from home overnight, I managed to phone home and spoke to Tony who explained how Kelly had started her periods whilst I was away and he didn't know what to do. I knew that a few doors away from where we lived, an Army Welfare Officer (Female) lived and so I told Tony to take Kelly around to her. I knew the welfare officer and she was fully aware of the my circumstances. Thankfully she took care of Kelly for me. Life was really not easy at this time.

I had still been visiting the friends who owned the pub in Toton.

The name of the pub was *The Other Side Of The Moon*. A strange name isn't it? I do not know of any other pub by that name. We didn't discuss Pauline and we almost carried on in a normal manner. My friends names who ran the pub were Lisa and Paul. One night during a lock down when the pub was shut, a conversation took place about me finding another lady in my life. I was only 39 years of age at this time although I must admit, I felt that I was at the end of my courting days. How mad is that idea now?

When Pauline had made her decision that she had wanted to leave our marriage we were heavily in debt. I had never really taken an active role in our household accounts and generally left this side of things up to Pauline. Of course we had the loan for our narrowboat as well as catalogues that Pauline had which were all still outstanding. Unbeknown to me at the time we had also accumulated large electric and gas bills that had not been paid for a long period of time. Even our paper bill was outstanding for a large amount. There was no such thing as on line banking in those days and therefore it was much more difficult to keep an eye on our finances. It is easy to look back now and understand that both partners in a marriage should be fully aware of how they are managing their household accounts but throughout our marriage, Pauline had always taken care of this side of things and I was happy to let her do so.

Chapter Fifty Two

Please Turn Back The Clock

Anyway, we were in the company of Lisa's Mum and Dad in the pub one evening when Lisa said that they should introduce me to her aunty, Amanda (not her real name) who was a cheerful happy go lucky sort of person. Apparently Amanda was divorced or going through a divorce. I forget which now. I think Amanda was about my age or slightly younger and so I agreed to meet her at the pub one evening in company with everyone else of course.

The meeting went well and Amanda was a bubbly, happy and cheerful person and we clicked, just the sort of person I needed to be around right now. My life was certainly almost as low as it could get and I was feeling totally inadequate in all areas of my life. Amanda had two daughters, one eleven years of age and the other was nine years of age. We saw each other a few times and it was kind of a whirlwind relationship. Amanda was looking to sell her family house and I suppose she must have needed to give some money to her husband. To be honest the finer details escape me now.

Somewhere along the line we discussed Amanda and her two girls moving in to my Married Quarters. This was going to solve my problem regarding Kelly in particular when I had to be away from home, but would also be very convenient for Amanda under her circumstances. As I lived in a Military Married Quarter, I needed permission for them all to move in with me. The idea of just "living in sin" at that time was not feasible and would not have been approved by the Military Authority who own the Married Quarters. They were still very old fashioned and "proper" in their attitude towards these sort of things.

I came up with the idea that Amanda could move in officially as a housekeeper/child minder. At this time I was qualified as an Augmentation Commander and was required to be away from home and my home station on various occasions. I have to say that I tried to get out of these duties but my Force were not that sympathetic to my circumstances. There were only two Inspectors trained up for this role at the time and I was one of them. I can not comment too much about this role that I was trained in, but it involved nuclear material being transferred around the country and needed to be protected with an Armed Capability. My team had been specially trained in field craft and dealing with demonstrators with the possibility of encountering terrorist activity. We were a very efficient team and worked and trained together regularly in order to get to know each other.

For quite a while after Amanda moved in with me life seemed to be great. I introduced Amanda to my Mum and Dad and the rest of my family and they all approved of our relationship. I did not notice the gradual deterioration of not necessarily our own relationship, but the way in which my own children were gradually being sidelined . Amanda had stopped working and decided that she would be a full time house person. She had a small pool of money from her house sale and we were living on my salary which I had budgeted for us to survive.

Amanda was not a dog lover and I still had Poppy living at home with us. She was a lovely mongrel dog with a really kind and affectionate manner. Poppy had been a brilliant dog when I had gone on the "Boys" boating holiday with my Dad and my Sons. Amanda and her children had moved in to my Married Quarter and Amanda was home all day, having given up her work to move in with me. Anyway, whilst I was at work, on several occasions, I was embarrassed to get a phone call from the Military Authorities to tell me that Poppy was running wild throughout the Military Estate and barking at people. As much as I tried to remedy this with Amanda who was at home at the time, the situation was becoming impossible. It was beginning to dawn on me that she was probably letting the dog out on purpose just to demonstrate to me how inconvenient the dog was. I decided that the best course of action was to let Poppy have the chance of a loving home where she would be cared for properly. This sounds very callous but I still believe that this was the best course of action for the benefit of poor old Poppy.

I took some time off work and one day I took Poppy to a Dog Rescue establishment. I remember that day so well. I was in tears as I handed Poppy over to the Dogs Home. People were looking at me as if I was a really uncaring person, or at least that is what I was feeling. Poor Poppy looked back at me as she was taken to her new kennels. I hope and pray that she would have been found a good home to see the rest of her life through. I am sure that she would have done because she was such a beautiful dog. I think that this was the beginning of the end of my relationship with Amanda. This whole episode still haunts my memories to this very day.

As life continued I began to sense a feeling of unrest and unhappiness amongst my children with regards to Amanda. Several little things had happened that had made me stop and think about how our lives were developing. For instance, my friends from the Merchant Navy had got together and came to visit me, this was a rare occasions but they wanted to see how I was getting on following my split from Pauline. We were going out for the evening somewhere but before we left the house, Amanda had decided to drink a cider I believe was called *White Lightning*. This was a very strong cider, which as I remember. This meant that she was well under the influence of alcohol even before we left the house. I also think that she also had a bit of jealousy over my friends, for some reason, I don't know why. It really is hard for me to imagine what was going on at this time. All I knew was that I was not liking the whole atmosphere and was a little embarrassed with introducing Amanda to my friends and I knew that I should not be feeling this way. I was also feeling very much trapped as Amanda had given up her own family home and so she, and her two daughters, didn't have anywhere else to live.

At this time Pauline was living in Spain and arrangements had been made for Alan and Kelly to fly out to visit her. Kelly was probably only 12 years of age and Alan maybe 16 years of age. I remember so well going to the airport and handing them over to the airport personnel and seeing them disappear into departures on the back of one of those gulf buggies airport vehicles that you see. I was devastated seeing them disappear and my heart was in my mouth. I can not explain how miserable I was at this time. My life was a real mess and I had no one else to blame except myself as I hadn't taken enough time to think things through properly before making all of the big decisions. No one else could have made these decisions for me.

Over a period of time me and Amanda had not met eye to eye

on several issues. The last straw was when she had taken to hiding biscuits and cakes and such things from my kids when we were not at home for whatever reason. At first I was completely unaware as to what was going on around me and then it became all so clear to me that Amanda's children were getting preferential treatment over my own. This was not going to continue.

Whilst Alan and Kelly were visiting their mum in Spain, Amanda had arranged for us and her own children to visit Florida and Disney world. Amanda was using the payout from her divorce and so had come into a lump some of money. You can imagine my feelings at this time. My kids were going to Spain to visit their mum whilst I was off with Amanda and her children to Florida. I know that Amanda was paying for the Florida trip but this was an obvious action to ensure that my own kids were separate to our so called relationship, and that her own kids were not going to miss out.

On top of all this Amanda had bought an engagement ring from the proceeds of her divorce and actually informed me that we were now officially engaged. She chose the ring and paid for it herself. I never had any spare money as I was still trying to pay all of my debts. I found the whole situation to be getting to be really uncomfortable and also embarrassing. It was now obvious to me that this relationship was not destined to last, however, I wasn't sure how it was all going to pan out. Time was running out very fast for this whole situation

On our return home from Florida, Alan and Kelly were still Spain. Once we were home we settled back into our, what I now understood to be, our uncomfortable routine. Amanda had again started hiding some food from Bertie when we were going out somewhere. I just could not put my own kids on the back burner whilst her own kids were treated "normally". This routine turned out to be the proverbial straw that broke the camels back. All of a sudden, everything became clear to me. My own children were being treated so differently to Amanda's. I had had enough and told Amanda we could not continue in this manner and that I no longer wished to associate myself with her. We had of course discussed the problem but that never resolved any of the issues. I was no longer happy being in our relationship.

On the very day that I told Amanda that our relationship was finished, I then drove to Gloucester to see my own Mum and Dad.

I just needed someone to talk to really. Alan and Kelly were still in Spain with their Mum. Dad had given me his old car after Pauline had taken the family car. That was fair enough as her Dad had bought it for her. I spent a day or two with my Mum and Dad. Before I had left my Married Quarter, I had told Amanda that I wanted her to be gone by the time that I returned. On reflection, I should have supervised her departure. It was a very strange feeling going through this process and one which I would not ever want to or have to go through again.

On my return from Gloucester to my own home, I was relieved to see that Amanda had cleared her belongings and there was no sign of her left. My relief was unimaginable. It was as if a whole weight had lifted from my shoulders and it was a lovely feeling. Amanda had gone back home to her mother as I understand it. Her mother was living on her own at the time. It was not until later that I realised that she had also taken my crucifix that my Mum and Dad had given me when I joined the Merchant Navy. She had also taken a 'Sailors Grave" (another type of crucifix) that one of my old ship mates had bought me which was also of great sentimental value. Amanda certainly knew how to hurt me. But at the end of the day, the fact that she was no longer in my life (or so I thought) made it all worth while.

I will never forget the day when I had to collect Alan and Kelly from the Airport when they returned from Spain. My final departure from Amanda had all taken place whilst they were in Spain. Alan in particular was not looking happy on his return as he emerged through the Customs area. I said to him, "Something really great has happened since you went away". He said, "Are you getting married to Amanda? I said, "No, something much better than that".He said, "What?" I then told him that Amanda was no longer in our lives and that from now on, it was just the three of us. I can't remember if Bertie and Tony were back home by then because they were kind of nomadic at this time. I don't think that it sank into Alan straight away as he was neither jubilant or down hearted, at least not that it showed. All I knew was that we were going to have the house back to ourselves and that life was going to be much more easy going than they had been for a while.

I have to say that throughout the whole episode of Pauline leaving us, and then the mess that I made with Amanda, Alan was the one that suffered the most. Kelly was the type where she had never shown any of her true emotions and on this occasion, she could take it or leave it. Alan on the other hand had shamefully seen me upset on both occasions. I am sure that it is very hard for a young child to see your own father crying and not be able to do anything about it.

Chapter Fifty Three

Tony

Life took on some semblance of normality now, although my work was still a pain and required me to spend the odd night or two away from home. Tony had returned home and was out of work. Bertie was flitting between living at home and not. I had a vacancy occur at my Police Dog Section for a Kennel Person. I had six dogs and handlers within my compliment of officers. I asked Tony if he was at all interested in the vacancy, which he was.

I could not become involved in the selection process of the kennel person as this was to be carried out by the Area Dog Advisor. Of course he knew that Tony was my son and I am sure that this would have some influence on Tony eventually being awarded the position. I genuinely never interfered with the recruiting process but this never stopped my Area Commander from investigating me for any corrupt practices. I was able to show that the selection had nothing to do with me and that I never interfered in any way. The Area Dog Advisor in fact stated that Tony was still the best person for the job. Everywhere I turned there seemed to be someone trying to stuff my life about.

I was not immediately aware how much difficulty this was going to cause me as well as everything else that was going on in my life at this time. Right from the beginning, I was aware that I should not show Tony any favouritism. I deliberately ensured that I did not frequent visiting the kennels any more than I should in my official role as the Senior Police Officer. Because of my concerns about showing undue attention to Tony, I think that I paid him less attention than I should have. Had my Kennel Person been someone different I would have visited them more regularly as a matter of routine.

Tony did an excellent job after receiving his Kennel Training at the Royal Army Veterinary Corp in Melton Mowbray in Leicestershire. At that time, the Army were responsible for acquiring and training our police dogs. Tony passed his course with flying colours and I was really proud of him. I was obviously also very happy that I could be a small part in letting him have this experience. I reminisced how I had attended the RAVC at Melton Mowbray twenty years earlier in order to be trained as a dog handler for my Force.

However, on a rare visit from my Divisional Commander, who held the rank of Chief Superintendent, he questioned me about Tony's employment. I must admit that I had been naive to let Tony apply for the job, but I could see no real reason why he should be barred from applying like anybody else. Needless to say that I was not popular with any of my senior officers, seemingly getting jobs for my family through the back door. Life was being so unfair to me at that time. Tony in particular was also feeling that I was not interested in how well that he was caring for the dogs and kennels and that I was ignoring all of his efforts.

I must admit that I felt very vulnerable at this time. Whilst I did not want to put too much worry on Alan and Kelly in particular, I also had no one to talk to. Bertie and Tony were older but they were living their own lives. Tony had recently split up with his long term girlfriend, Heather and Bertie was just the freelancer that he was. Bertie and me had also had a big fall out at one point where he had left home and ended up living with some "dodgy" characters. But now he was back home again. This was really my saving grace because having all of the kids back home gave me something else to think about other than myself and my predicament.

I also remember going shopping one day with Alan and Kelly in the local supermarket. We had two trolleys of food filled to the brim. Most of it was tins of something or other, especially them Fray Bentos pies in a tin. We all loved them with potatoes and some vegetables. However when we had loaded our shopping on to the conveyor belt, the load was too heavy and the belt did not move. We had to take some tins off to allow the belt to start rolling.

Back at work I had support from some of my own staff, in particular one constable who sat down in my office and said something like, " Are you OK Boss? The rest of the 'lads' are worried for you and want you to know that we are all behind you". He then went on to say, "If my wife ever left me, I don't know what I would do, let alone having everything else going on around you".

Chapter Fifty Four

The Accusations

I was still in the process of trying to sort my finances out. I had a lot of debt when Pauline left such as a narrowboat on HP, a vast gas bill for about £400 which I was not aware of, newspaper bills that had not been paid for months as well as catalogue debts. I became very adapt at using an Excel Spreadsheet to help me budget my salary each month.

Whilst I was at work one day, out of the blue and unannounced, the Area Chief Inspector made a visit to me at my station. This was quite unusual as nobody hardly paid visits to me, mainly because I kept a fairly steady ship without too much hassle to my senior officers. I made him the obligatory cup of coffee when he said to me, "I guess you know why I am here?" At this time I just thought that he was paying me some sort of a supervisory visit, but I was soon to be proved wrong when things took on a more sinister turn. At this very moment I had absolutely no idea why all of a sudden a supervisor should have any interest in me at all. Perhaps he was here to check on my welfare after everything that had been happening to me. No chance.

The Chief Inspector was very polite but oh so official when he handed over some papers to me which I was soon to realise were commonly called "Regulation 7" papers. These are the papers that were handed to the recipient to inform them that they were formally being investigated for an offence or offences, against the Disciplinary Code of Conduct. After over twenty years in the Force and being promoted to the Rank of Inspector, this was the first time that I had ever found myself in serious trouble. The Chief Inspector also "cautioned" me as if I was a criminal and had acted in a criminal fashion. At this point I was totally confused as to what was going on and I definitely did not have anything to say at this time. I am afraid that "No Comment" had to be used by me as I had no idea as to why I should be being investigated.

I was informed that I was being investigated for the following breaches of Disciplinary Regulations:

Being employed in a Public House
Using a Police vehicle for non-police purposes
Making a false statement regarding a live in child minder

These allegations had been made by Amanda who was determined to cause me as much damage as she could. I guess the phrase about a woman being scorned is true. These allegations were presented to me in 1992 and normally when a Senior Police Officer (which I was) is under investigation, they would be suspended from duty pending the outcome of the Disciplinary Investigation. My present Chief Constable did not agree with the latter and he believed that if an officer is getting paid, he should continue with his duties. In actual fact, I was grateful for this as it took my mind off what was actually happening to me.

I was to spend two years with the weight of this investigation hanging over me. I was informed that the Disciplinary proceedings would be heard by the Chief Constable himself. This only occurs so that any punishment could be the maximum proscribed, such as dismissal from the Force entirely. In other words, my whole career and the rest of my life was at stake. In all this time, other than a visit from a local welfare officer that my own officers had informed, I never once received any help or assistance from within my Force. I still feel bitter resentment about this, even to this present day when I think too hard about it. My Senior Officers had heard the allegations and immediately distanced themselves from me, even worse than that, they had already judged me guilty of all charges. The last 21 years years of my time in the Force stood for nothing. I still had my four children at home as well, even though the two eldest were twenty and eighteen years of age at the time. Kelly and Alan were thirteen and sixteen years of age respectively.

On top of all this, the following year I was due to receive my Long Service and Good Conduct Medal (having then served twenty two years in the Force). I was informed that I would not be entitled to this at this time because of the allegations being made against me. I became very bitter with my Force and still am after having now been retired for many years. I was well and truly left out to dry.

The allegations that I faced were ridiculous. I had never been employed by anyone other than my Force once I had become a police officer. This allegation came about apparently when someone had seen me collecting glasses after time, in my friends pub. I do not disagree that this took place. The investigating officer approached my friends to ask them if they had employed me or if I was on the books of the brewery to receive any payment. Of course I was not, but the Force still pursued this particular allegation. It was all very frustrating for me as nobody was taking my side of the allegations.

Use of a police vehicle for non police duties was an allegation that I could not deny. One day when I had been shopping with Amanda my car had broken down and I had reason to take it directly to a Halfords which was less than a mile away from my Married Quarter. I knew that my officers carried mobile patrols around this area and so I called my on duty sergeant and asked if there was a patrol car in the area that could give me a lift back in to the station. Bearing in mind that I was still living on station. The sergeant replied that a car was in the area and would pick me, Amanda and the shopping up, which they did. Unfortunately at a later date I had reason to have to a disagreement with that particular sergeant and he was the one who subsequently brought forward this allegation against me. As if I never had enough to deal with. I guess he more than managed to stab me in the back as soon as the right opportunity arose.

Regarding a live-in Child Minder, my application was not untrue. Because of the role that I was in at work, there were only two Inspectors in the area who were trained and qualified to carry some particular duties. This meant that we had to be away from home on occasions. I did tell the Divisional Commander that I was finding it difficult to meet my commitments but was informed by him that that was not his problem and that it was up to me to sort my personal life out and to carry out the duties that I was expected to carry out. I really should have been stronger and told him to get stuffed. The problem was that I had been informed that there was a strong possibility that I could be dismissed from the Force. This would not only have left me out of work, but also homeless as I would obviously have had to move out of my Married Quarter. I was trying so hard to try and not rock the boat, get people to understand my situation, and to run a family home all at the same time.

This whole investigation and subsequent hearing lasted for two years. During this time life continued and I carried on with my duties as the Senior Police Officer at my station. My life was on hold with the prospect that at the end of it all, I could be homeless and without a job. It was a living nightmare. I had no-one to turn to for help. I didn't even live anywhere near any of my family to be able to talk it all through with someone. There was no such thing as mobile phones or any of that technical stuff that allow us to communicate with each other today.

My life during this period was in a real turmoil. The disciplinary proceedings against me were serious enough on their own, in fact the end result one way or another was going to be life changing. On the other hand I was also going through divorce proceedings which were definitely life changing. I did my best to not involve my children in any of my worries and to this very day I have never sat down with any of them and discussed the situation that I was in.

Had I lived near my Mum and Dad I think that I would have found some solace in being able to talk with them. They were always supportive and I loved them so much.

Chapter Fifty Five

Blind Date

During the course of all that was going on around me both at work and in my private life, the constable who had voiced his concern to my welfare asked if he could have a word with me in my office. He told me that his wife was working at East Midlands Airport and that she worked with a very nice girl who would be open to a 'blind date' if I was interested. To be honest, me and women were not exactly on good terms right now. Anyway I needed a night out and I agreed to go on this blind date with a couple of my staff who I would now call my "friends". We had agreed to meet up in a pub called "Eaton Farm" in Derbyshire.

On the night of the blind date, my friends had collected me from home as I was not familiar with the location of the pub. The blind date did not arrive until quite late in the evening. Her name was Wendy and she eventually showed up as she had her own car. I was attracted to her from the start but I was also not that bothered whether we hit it off or not. Anyway at the end of the evening, Wendy was taking me back home, I think that this was engineered by my friends. When we pulled up out side my Married Quarter I asked Wendy if she wanted to come in for a coffee. The lights were on inside the house and so I knew that the kids were up watching the TV. I was trying to reassure Wendy by telling her that it was OK because the kids were all still up, but she declined to come into the house. We pecked each other politely on the cheek and she bade me farewell with a promise to get in touch with each other at some other time.

Wendy later told me that had I not informed her that my children were waiting up for me, then she might have accepted my invitation for a coffee. Apparently when she had told her mother that she had had a date with a man who had four children she had laughed at her because Wendy had always stated that she could not stand children!! When her sister, Sally, had asked her what she thought of me, she had replied, "He is OK but he will not be the love of my life."

Anyway, several weeks passed and neither of us had been in touch with each other. I am not sure whether that I had thought too much about our date as I was getting used to being on my own and also getting quite used to rejection from the women in my life. One day, my friend (one of my police officers that worked under me) who had actually arranged the blind date in the first place, informed me that Wendy had been asking after me and had been wondering if we might meet up again sometime. I did not particularly have a hectic social life at this stage and so I agreed to another meet up with Wendy on our own. I had insisted on picking her up in my car which I now had. It was given to me by my Dad. It was an old car but it was better than nothing.

Wendy had drawn me a picture of where she lived and I had arranged to pick her up and we were going to another pub that she knew. I was still not familiar with many places around other than the pub that my friends run. As I was going through the disciplinary proceedings because of the allegations made by the landlady's aunty (Amanda) it no longer felt appropriate to frequent that particular establishment.

Wendy lived on a street called Booth St. in Derby. She had lived there with her sister Sally and their mother. Their mother had since left the house and was now married and lived in Mapperley Village in Derbyshire with her husband, Jim. The house was probably described as not being the tidiest of houses. There were two girls living there, both single and with the age of 30 years and 28 years. Although an effort had been made to tidy the place up for my arrival, there were signs of what the house might normally be like. To their defence, being single girls, both Wendy nor Sally didn't really spent a lot of time in the house. They used to hop from one relatives house to another whenever food was offered to them.

I don't know why I had reason to look inside the cooker, but look inside the cooker I did. Inside was all the washing up that had accumulated over quite a long time. One or two of the plates had even started to form a penicillin substance around the edges.

We arrived at this particular pub that Wendy had nominated and I was driving the car. Of course this meant that I could not drink alcohol. At one point of the evening I had sat down next to Wendy in the bar when all of a sudden there was the sound of loads of coins falling to the floor and then rolling across the length of the room. It transpired that the pockets in my trousers were not really suitable for holding coins and when I had sat down, all of my loose change had fallen out. I immediately started to laugh (It is the Irish trait in me to be able to laugh at myself) and Wendy tells me that this was the point where she had thought, "He's not bad after all." Apparently if I had become flustered, that would have put her off me. Women's logic I suppose.

We continued to see each other regularly after this and our feelings for each other had grown. Both of us will admit that there was no "instant attraction" when we first met, but now we were beginning to get to know each other better, a real relationship was forming. After a while, I had met all of Wendy's family and Wendy had met mine, including my Mum and Dad.

Before we knew it, Wendy was spending more and more time with me and my children in my Married Quarter inside the Chilwell Barracks. We now had mutual friends, Wendy got on well with my kids, and all was well. We got to the point where my finances were getting back on track, Wendy worked as a cargo and freight agent at East Midlands Airport, and we had progressed our relationship to where we were now looking to buy our own house somewhere around our immediate area. It was becoming cumbersome living in a married quarter to what is called "behind the wire". This meant that Wendy could only have a temporary pass to visit me as obviously, living together without being married is a sin. Wendy got to know the guards on the gates very well.

The Constable who had been responsible for introducing me and Wendy together came in to my office one day and asked to speak to me. As I told you earlier he had told me that if he was in my position then he would not know what to do. Well he sat in my office and broke down in tears as he told me that his wife had left him for another man who she was working with. I felt so sorry for him and I felt that there was some kind of bond between us. If his wife had left him a week or two before, me and Wendy would never have been introduced to each other.

There was also an officer who was employed as a Military Guard Service officer on station who I had recruited some time before. It transpired that his long term relationship had also just broken down and he was also devastated. The three of us joined up together and called ourselves the Three Amigos. Isn't it funny that even when times are a bit tough, we can still rustle up a sense of humour.

We three sat in a pub one night having ordered ourselves a pint of beer each. We were all totally depressed and feeling sorry for ourselves. Then we happened to look up at each other at the same time and just burst out laughing at ourselves. We must have looked a right old sorry threesome.

Chapter Fifty Six

The Discipline

This calmness did not last very long as I received a date for my disciplinary hearing which was to be held at RAF Stafford and would be presided over by the Chief Constable. I can not begin to tell you how worrying this was for me. A Chief Constable only chairs a disciplinary hearing for one reason, and that is because they can inflict the ultimate punishment, which would be dismissal from the Force. By this time I was forty three years of age with no qualifications or interest in anything other than the job I had been doing for the past 22 years.

Through the Police Federation I was afforded the luxury of having a barrister to represent me. His solicitor had carried out all of the groundwork for him, getting my side of the saga etc. I don't know if you have ever tried talking to a barrister but they could be quite aloof. I had not had a great deal of contact with him which is probably just as well because they charge a fortune for even looking at them let alone talking to them.

Because I had waited nearly two years for my case to be brought to a hearing, I had become less confident that I would receive a satisfactory outcome. My own supervisors from my Divisional Headquarters were still conspicuous by their absence and there was not one sprinkling of support for me. I knew that I was completely innocent of one charge which was that I had been employed by any persons to be working in a public house. That charge was completely ridiculous. That would have meant that anyone returning their own empty glass to the bar was in essence, working for the brewery. I was aware that serving police officers were barred from any other employment without specific permission and therefore this would not have been a risk that I would have dared to take, especially as the public house was so close to my place of work and even one or two of my own officers frequented it.

The second charge of making a false statement to allow someone else to live in a Married Quarter with me was a little bit messier. The statement itself was not untrue and indeed a great weight was lifted off my shoulders when Amanda had moved in to "keep house" for me, particularly so when my job required me to be away from home on a fairly regular basis at that time. It was Alan and Kelly who I could not leave alone as I considered them to still be too young to be on their own. The complication of course was that Amanda was not just a "Housekeeper" as per my request for her to live in my MQ. I have to remind you that at this time, the Military, as well as The Ministry of Defence Police, did not condone cohabitation outside of wedlock and so this was quite a big deal.

The last charge of using a police vehicle for non-police purposes was completely justified and I was bang to rights on that particular charge. I should not have requested my officers to collect me from a garage where I had had to drop my own car off for whatever was wrong with it. My mitigation was that I had several bags of shopping with me that I needed to get home and that I was merely about one mile away from my MQ which was obviously also the base for the patrol car that would be picking me up. The patrol cars had to pass by these points several times a shift and so they did not have to divert from any other duties. However, I accept that I was unwise to request this assistance. I must say that I had not considered this accusation very serious. I had heard that our previous Chief Constable had used a police car and driver to take his daughter's mortar board to her when she was having her graduation ceremony many miles away. Nothing was ever said about this so my less than a mile use of a police car faded in comparison. But you know that old adage - "Do as I say, not as I do".

The day of my hearing arrived and it was to be held at RAF Stafford which was where my Divisional Headquarters was based. I arrived in plenty of time and was met by my solicitor and barrister. We had a brief discussion before I was ushered into the room allocated for the hearing. I saw my barrister talking to the Chief Constable as if they were old friends. I was not too impressed with my barrister who seemed to be quite indifferent to the proceedings. It certainly felt that he preferred to mix with my senior officers than with myself. It was almost as if they belonged to the same club or something.

The hearing commenced and I was embarrassed to have to sit in a room with lots of people around who were discussing what, as far as I was concerned, was my Private Life. Amanda was called to attend the hearing and gave evidence against me stating that she was never my "Housekeeper or Child Minder" and that it was always understood that she would just be my Live in Lover. There were also discussions about the state of my finances which of course were not too good at the time. My whole life was being dragged through the dirt for everyone to be able to just look at me and think the worst. I have never been so humiliated in my entire life. Well done Amanda! You partly achieved your aim.

I was eventually called for questioning by the barrister representing the Chief Constable. Apparently because I was entitled to a barrister, the Chief Constable was compelled to use one on behalf of the Force. Again the questioning was intimate and certainly nothing that I would want to discuss with complete strangers. This whole hearing had taken two years to put together and during that time, no one had ever bothered to ask me how I was coping or how I was feeling. I was completely alone and now here I was for all intents and purposes, likely to lose my job, my home, and what I believe to have been a good reputation within the Force over the last 21 or so years. There was every possibility that I would return home today a completely broken man.

I had heard many stories about our Professional Standards Department. Their original name was the "Complaints and Discipline Department". I know that when they put a big case together, which mine was, otherwise the Chief Constable would not be presiding, if they were to get a guilty verdict they would all cheer and celebrate for a job well done on their behalf. I had no reason to believe that they weren't preparing to celebrate my dismissal from the Force. Worst of all, I actually knew and worked with some of the officers in that department. I don't believe for one instant that this was a personal vendetta against me, it was just another Long Running case that they would have "won", and be vilified for bringing the accusations against me in the first place.

Just before the Discipline Hearing, I had heard from a good friend of mine who was a Detective Inspector and had been tasked with trying to pin a case of "Allowing Underage Sex" to have taken place in my Married Quarters with my knowledge. This related to one of my son's girlfriends who occasionally stayed with us. The girl and her parents were subsequently interviewed and of course there was no evidence to support such a case. I would never have consented to such a thing. This whole situation regarding the discipline and now these further serious allegations were very upsetting for me. My immediate bosses had already distanced themselves from me and that was even more upsetting. I knew that if one of my team was in a situation where they could possibly lose their marriage, career, the house that they were living in, I would damn well at least talk to them to see if there was anything that I could do for them. This was a hard lesson on how the people in my Force were actually serious about staff welfare. I will never forgive any of them for that, even though some of them have since passed on.

The whole investigation was proving to me that it did not matter how well you had done in your career, if there is any doubt that you may have fallen at some point, everyone will stand back and you will be completely on your own. Of course I had a few closer colleagues who were trying to support me but for two years there was a total feeling of isolation.

The hearing took place and was concluded in one day. It came to the time when the Chief Constable asked me to stand so that he could read out his conclusion and any punishment he felt fit. At this moment my heart was beating so fast I could swear that everyone could hear it. I felt weak at the knees and it was almost as if I was being sentenced to death. I was thinking of where I was going to live once I was thrown out of my Married Quarters. How was I going to be able to care properly for my own kids. How was I going to be able to get a job to pay for it all never mind the debts that I still had. To the Complaints and Discipline Department, this was a nice juicy case where they could investigate and get rid of a bad egg. To me, my whole life lay in ruins in front of me. I was totally downbeat and had no choice but to surrender myself to the judgement of the Chief Constable.

The Chief Constable commenced by saying that before the hearing, when he had first read the charges as put forward by the professional Standards Department, he was in no doubt that I was the type of officer who did not belong in the Ministry of Defence

Police. The allegations made against me were appalling (I agree). However, after listening to all of the evidence as submitted to him today he awarded me the following punishment.

Using a Police vehicle for non Police purposes – I was given a reprimand
Making a false statement to allow someone to live in a Married Quarter with me – I was awarded a Caution
Being employed by a Brewery without permission – I was fined £100

The relief that came over me when this judgement was read out is indescribable. Apart from not losing my job, including the Married Quarter that I was living in, I also was not demoted to a lower rank which was also another option open to the Chief Constable. I had three months in order to appeal against the verdict if I wished to. Of course I was really annoyed about the fine for something that was not correct, but after two years of this hanging over me, I just wanted to put it all to bed and then move on with my life. I never pushed for an appeal, I just wanted it to all be over with and then to try to get my life back on track. I am not a bad person. I did not want any of this to happen. I can't deny that I made some bad judgement calls but in my defence, my mind was not in a good place during this period.

I came back home that day and everything felt surreal. The whole situation had gone on for so long it was hard for me to understand that it was now all over (or so I thought). Of course it was not really all over because later on the Force would find another way of punishing me further.

Chapter Fifty Seven

We Haven't Finished With You Yet

I was still seeing Wendy at this time and at least I had someone to talk to now who I could explain my feelings to. I wanted to feel like celebrating but I couldn't. I think that I was numb that all of this could be happening to me. I had now been a Senior Police Officer running my own stations for over seven years. I like to think that I had looked after my staff and tended to any welfare issues with a lot more compassion than the Force had given me. I was now set to continue with the rest of my life and for that I was truly grateful.

I did say that I had a three month period in which to appeal the findings of my hearing. Well these months came and went. I was carrying out my duties without any further upsets and I was happy with my lot. I had all of my kids living at home at the time and life was getting back to some normality. Wendy and I were hitting it off and after the past two years of hell, everything was rosy in the garden. We had even considered buying a house together.

The kids had been winding me up during this whole period as well. I was having difficulty trying to keep the house clean and tidy as well as getting dinners for everyone, doing the shopping etc. I had not had a car for some time at one point and so even the shopping had to be done on foot carrying a load of shopping bags. I often roped Alan and Kelly in to helping me with this task.

I had gotten home from work one day and I guess my patience at this stage was running low. The kids bedrooms were overflowing with dirty clothes and all sorts of other rubbish that teenagers collect. I gathered all of the rubbish and clothing into black bin bags and just threw them out side the back bedroom windows. When Alan arrived home from school he asked where all of his clothing and belongings were and I told him that I had thrown everything in the rubbish bin and explained why. Alan just looked at me and said that he did not care because I would just have to buy him some new stuff. I can not explain what it is like to have four kids living at home with you, especially when there was only one parent at home, but those who have children can maybe imagine what it was like. Don't get me wrong, there was nothing wrong with my kids and I love them all, but they were just what I consider normal.

After the three month period allowed for me to appeal against my hearing, I received notification that I should attend Empress State Building in London which is where my Police Headquarters was. I was to attend an audience with the Assistant Chief Constable.

I knew the Assistant Chief Constable (ACC) personally many years ago when I had first joined the Force at RAF Quedgeley. He was a Detective Constable whilst I was just a newly recruited Constable. He, along with some other officers from my Station, would often meet at my Dad's Pub in Gloucester and end up having drinks after time. Whilst I did not expect any favours from him, I did expect some consideration, which of course was foolish of me.

I did not know London at all to get around and so Wendy said that she would come with me as one of her friend's husband was in the army and was stationed in Mill Hill, around London. We could then get the underground to Albert Hall which was just around the corner from Empress State Building, which is what we ended up doing. Having left Wendy to hang around outside the building I then proceeded to my appointment with the ACC.

When I arrived in his office, he had a Chief Superintendent sat in the corner of the room. I was beginning to fear that something untoward was going to happen. The ACC said to me "I guess that you know why you are here?" I said, "How would I? Nobody had had any conversations with me about anything." He seemed surprised at this. He then told me that I was being relieved of my command as a Senior Police Officer and was being put back as a Shift Commander at a larger station. This did not mean that I was losing my rank or seniority, merely that I would not be in charge of my own station.

The problem with this decision meant that I would have to move away from Nottingham where I was presently based and would mean me having to transfer completely to a new area. I said to the ACC that I hoped that this was not another form of punishment being thrown on me because that would be illegal as double jeopardy even though this was not a criminal procedure that I had been put through. Of course he assured me that this was not the case and to be honest,

I was exhausted with the whole affair. I had no trust or confidence in any of my Senior Officers. I like to think that I would have been far more inquisitive as to what had gone on and from that, probably would have been a lot more supportive to one of my own officers. It was clear that none of the aforementioned was coming my way. I could not get my head around who it was exactly who was trying to make life as difficult as possible for me. whoever it was had failed miserably to get me thrown out of the Force and had also failed to get me demoted. I seriously think that a little bit of welfare concern for my circumstances would have prevented any of this happening. As I have said before, no one had any concern for welfare, whether they knew me or not. There was absolutely no support for someone in my circumstances because people above me were all on their high horses and judgemental as if this sort of thing could never happen to them. All I can say to them is that I thought that nothing like this would ever happen to me either.

I accepted my fate in having to move location yet again. The Assistant Chief Constable, then asked me if I had a preference of any stations that I would like to be transferred to. I did not want to go up to Scotland for a starters and also I did not want to go to the Atomic Weapons Establishment at Aldermaston. Out of the top of my head I just said that if I was having to be transferred then I would rather go to somewhere that I have not been before and so I opted for the Royal Naval Base in Devonport in Plymouth. There really was no point trying to make any argument at this point. Decisions had been made and my personal circumstances did not concern anyone within my Force.

Chapter Fifty Eight

First Visit to Cornwall

It took about another three months for my transfer date to come through. In the mean time I was temporarily transferred to RAF Stafford which was my Divisional Headquarters. I could commute there daily from my Married Quarter. By this time, Wendy had more or less moved in with me only this time I did not request permission and could deny that she actually lived with me.

My Divisional Commander and his Deputy treated me appallingly. They hardly ever spoke to me and ignored me whenever they could. To this day I can not reason why except for the possibility that the Chief Constable may have expressed his own concerns over my treatment for the last two years, bearing in mind the result of my Disciplinary Hearing. Anyway, that is how I console myself with the treatment I was given. It is beyond my comprehension that neither of them asked to speak to me, even at this stage.

I used to work a 8am to 4pm shift as this allowed me to miss a lot of the heavy traffic from Nottingham to Stafford. One day my Division Commander asked what shift I was working and I told him, and my reason for doing so. He just said that he didn't care about the traffic and that I was to work 9am to 5pm because that was the hours that he worked, bearing in mind that he lived local to RAF Stafford. Again there was no point in making argument and so I had to comply with his instructions. I disliked him and his deputy so much after this as it was clear that there was a real vendetta going on to make life uncomfortable for me rather than to assist me in any way possible. What is going on with these people!!

After telling the kids that I would be moving lock stock and barrel down to Devonport, I gave them all the option to move down with me. Bertie and Tony were a definite no, but Alan was uncertain at this time. Kelly by now was 15 years of age and had no choice. Alan was still taking exams at college.

I arranged for a preliminary visit down to Devon to look at my new station and to try to find some suitable accommodation. By this time there were no available Married Quarters for Police Officers and so I would have to find my own accommodation. This suited me fine as I think that by this time, me and Married Quarters needed to part company.

Wendy came with Alan and Kelly and we stayed for about a week in a mobile home over in Cornwall at a place called Notter Bridge. This was a great location for us allowing us to search for housing both in Devon and in Cornwall. Alan fell in love with a meal served in the nearest pub call the Notter Bridge Inn which was run by a mother and her daughter and specialised in homemade curries. However the meal that Alan fell in love with was not a curry but Gammon, Egg and Chips. I think it is still one of his favourite meals to this day. At the end of our visit we had still not found anywhere suitable for us to live and so back home we went to Nottingham.

By this time the relationship between Wendy and I had grown and we had decided that we would stay together, no matter what. This meant that when I moved down to Devon, she would come down with me. Alan though had decided that he would rather stay in Nottingham with Bertie and Tony and finish his college off where he was. I had no objection to this, especially as I would be given an allowance for him to stay in Nottingham because my transfer was on compulsory terms rather than Voluntary. If I had known then what I know now on how Bertie coped when I left him in Gosport all those years back, I would never have allowed this to happen. Hindsight and all that.

I told you earlier about "The Three Amigos". Well my mate Andy, who worked for the Military Guard Service, had also embarked on a new relationship to a very nice lady. It just happened that they had a couple of Jack Russell dogs, well a dog and a bitch really who had become too friendly with each other and had had puppies. The problem was that Andy and his new lady, Kim, were going away on holiday and needed to find someone to look after their dogs and one of the puppies. They asked us if we would consider helping them out. Wendy jumped at the chance as she is crazy over dogs and in particular, puppies.

They brought the two adult dogs and their little puppy over to us. The puppy was eight weeks old at the time. They had named the puppy "Nipper". Wendy had a great time looking after him. The time came when Andy and Kim were back off holiday and needed to collect Nipper from us. They could see that Wendy had great trouble letting go of the puppy and although I had made sure that Andy & Kim knew she would have loved to have kept him they departed with all three of the dogs and thanked us for looking after them. Wendy was left feeling really sad and miserable.

Within a couple of minutes we had a knock on our front door and there was Andy and Kim again, with Nipper in their arms. They said that they could see how much it meant to Wendy to have to let the puppy go, that they had had a discussion and had decided to let Wendy have Nipper permanently if that was what she wanted. They already had the puppies parents, as well as one other of the litter to keep for themselves. This is how we had our first dog and how Nipper ended up travelling down to Cornwall with us to live and to spend the rest of his days as a beach bum.

Chapter Fifty Nine

Departure Day

The problem then was to find Alan some suitable accommodation that both he and I were happy with. By this time Bertie was 22, Tony was 20 and Alan was nearly 18 years of age. They had all expressed a wish to live together and therefore look after each other. With that in mind I managed to find a house where the landlord was willing to accept them with the appropriate deposit which I paid up. I also agreed to send an amount of money to Bertie each month to pay for Alan's Board and Lodgings also, with a sum of spending money.

On Friday 29th July 1994 Wendy, Kelly and myself set off from Nottingham to live in Cornwall or Devon. We had rented some temporary accommodation in Saltash, Cornwall to give us time to find more permanent accommodation. I was driving down in my Ford Granada with Kelly while Wendy followed behind in her Fiat Uno. We had planned an overnight stop with my parents in Gloucester leaving Kelly for a short holiday with them while we got settled in. I left Nottingham with a very heavy heart and admit to crying several times en route for having to leave my boys behind. I felt so miserable but could not apprehend an alternative to what I was doing. I was 42 years of age with no other skills other than my work within the Ministry of Defence Police. On reflection, maybe I could have promoted my skills as a manager and all that that entails as well as my Diploma for Supervisory Studies. However, at that time my head was all over the place and I did what I did. I was just hoping that my boys would all be okay. They were always more than welcome to come back home to me. I had been 17 years of age when I first left home and I firmly believed that my boys were now old enough to make their own decisions.

As I crossed the Tamar Bridge from Devon in to Cornwall, my whole life was flashing in front of me. I thought about all of the events in my life that had brought me here. Was I happy now? Not entirely. I had split my family up and left my boys a long way away. I was less than happy, in fact I was feeling quite miserable again. My heart was thumping as apart from leaving my boys, I was having to effectively start a new job again and find a house to live in. This was the end of a long and horrible period in my life and now I was about to start a new chapter. Who knows what will be in store for me and my family in the future?

Only time will tell.

I do wear my heart on my sleeve and I have opened up my life for all to see, but to be honest, this is *Only The Half of It*.

Myself and Wendy

Acknowledgements

The first person to thank for the writing of this account of this period of my life is my son Bertie. Let's face it, who would think of doing such a thing under normal circumstances. However it has been quite an experience remembering so many facts which I have been assisted with by Edward Foote and his mum, Hertha Foote. Thank you both so much for your kind contribution and I hope you enjoy reading your accounts.

I would also like to thank Mick Shaw, my old friend who put me in touch with Bryan from Magic Flute Publishing who gave me so much confidence to go ahead and publish this book. Thank you both.

My Daughter-in-Law, Lorraine, has also kindly given up some of her precious time to assist me in making this book a better read and I thank her from the bottom of my heart.

Most importantly I have to thank my wife Wendy. She has given to me her time, her patience in proof reading my text for me and also helped me out considerably with some of the technical issues that I have encountered. Without her help, I would still be at the writing stage. Last and not least I suppose is that I should show my appreciation to all of my kids, as well as Bertie there is Tony, Alan and Kelly and the rest of my family, Dawn, Aileen and Terry and in particular my Mum and Dad. Lets face it, without any of you, there would be nothing to write about. So thank you all and I sincerely hope that this book has raised some memories with you all.

9 781915 166128